———— GENDER AND MODERNITY IN ANDEAN BOLIVIA ————

GENDER AND MODERNITY IN ANDEAN BOLIVIA

BY MARCIA STEPHENSON

 UNIVERSITY OF TEXAS PRESS
AUSTIN

Copyright © 1999 by the University of Texas Press
All rights reserved
Printed in the United States of America
First edition, 1999

Requests for permission to reproduce material from this work should
be sent to Permissions, University of Texas Press, P.O. Box 7819, Austin,
TX 78713-7819.

♾ The paper used in this publication meets the minimum requirements of
American National Standard for Information Sciences—Permanence of
Paper for Printed Library Materials, ANSI Z39.48-1984.

Library of Congress Cataloging-in-Publication Data

Stephenson, Marcia, 1955–
  Gender and modernity in Andean Bolivia / Marcia Stephenson.
    p.   cm.
  Includes bibliographical references and index.
  ISBN 0-292-77742-6 (cl.). — ISBN 0-292-77743-4 (pbk.)
    1. Indian women—Bolivia—Ethnic identity.   2. Indian women—
Bolivia—Social conditions.   3. Indian women—Government policy—
Bolivia.   4. Sex role—Bolivia.   5. Bolivia—Race relations.
6. Bolivia—Social conditions.   7. Bolivia—Politics and government.
F3320.1.W65S74   1999
305.48′898084—dc21   98-42658

This book is dedicated to my parents, to Tom, and to the memory of Marion P. Love, Theda Herz, and Roberto Santos Escóbar.

CONTENTS

~

ACKNOWLEDGMENTS

~

Many people have participated in this project, from its beginning and throughout the different points along the way. Without their intelligent engagement, critical insight, and encouragement it would have been difficult to finish. My greatest debt of thanks is to the Taller de Historia Oral Andina (THOA), especially María Eugenia Choque Quispe and Carlos Mamani Condori, for their generous support, patience, and guidance. Their writings and conversations challenged me intellectually at every turn and helped me to rethink many of the project's fundamental assumptions. Ramón Conde, Félix Callisaya, Cristóbal Condorena, Bárbara Centeno, Rosendo Jaillita, Nicanor Huanca, Roberto Santos Escóbar, and Ema López also took precious time away from their own work to discuss and debate numerous issues that have made their way into the fabric of this book.

The work never would have been possible without the intellectual collaboration, goodwill, and friendship of fellow draft group members Nancy Peterson and Aparajita Sagar, who read the entire manuscript from beginning to end and then some. Their insightful assessment and detailed feedback directly influenced the shape of the book, and their companionship has provided both motivation and great pleasure.

I want to extend my deepest gratitude to Josefa Salmón, who contributed to the project from its inception. She read many sections of the manuscript, often on short notice, offered her critical expertise and advice with wisdom and good humor, and has sustained me through her friendship. Special thanks go to Norma Alarcón, a dear friend and intellectual trailblazer, whose conversations and writings have impacted this study in immeasurable ways.

My friends and colleagues at Grinnell College generously supported the project in its initial stages. The Grinnell College Grant Board and Wayne Moyer, chair of the Rosenfield Program in Public Affairs, International Relations and Human Rights, generously funded preliminary research trips to Buenos Aires, the University of Pittsburgh, and the Library of Congress. I also want to grant particular acknowledgement to Dennis Perri and Theda Herz, mentors and friends, who helped me to define the scope of the endeavor. My friends and co-conspirators Alan and Jill Schrift, Paula Smith, Caroline Gebhard, and Roberta Atwell read preliminary drafts and offered much-appreciated suggestions and commentary.

Purdue University has also provided generous institutional support for my project. Two Dean's Faculty Incentive Grants and a Purdue University Research Foundation Summer Research Grant enabled me to travel to Bolivia as well as to purchase videos and collect photographs. Professor Christiane Keck, head of the Department of Foreign Languages and Literatures, has kindly offered supportive guidance over the years, while Berenice Carroll, chair of Women's Studies, fostered a welcoming space for an exciting intellectual community of women. I owe special thanks to Becky Brown for her unflagging encouragement and to Cindy Weber for her wise counsel on the stages of the publication process. Ana Gómez Bravo and Mariselle Meléndez both offered many valuable suggestions on the manuscript; their friendship and collaboration continue to be a source of strength.

Javier Sanjinés has kindly encouraged me over the years, providing straightforward feedback and criticism for which I am very grateful. In addition, several people read specific chapters and offered much-appreciated commentary and sound advice; to each I am beholden: Doris Sommer, Reed Benhamou, Debra Castillo, Jean Franco, Leonardo García Pabón, Jill Kuhnheim, Ximena Medinaceli, Darlene Sadlier, and Fernando Unzueta. Other friends and colleagues have offered their support and encouragement of this project from the beginning: Marjorie Agosin, Danny Anderson, John Beverley, Margy Eastmond, Earl Fitz, Geri Friedman, Patty Hart, the Latin American Subaltern Studies Group, Kathy Lehman, Joy Logan, Ani McCune, Monica Macaulay, Paz Macías Fernández, Pat Morris, Willy Muñoz, José Rabasa, Oscar Rivera Rodas, Russell Salmon, Verónica Saunero-Ward, Sally Staley, and Akiko Tsuchiya.

Many good friends in La Paz generously opened up their homes to me on numerous occasions. In particular, I want to express my gratitude to Fidelia Barrientos and Teresa Salinas, longtime sisters and friends, as well as to Clara and Jaime Revollo and Chichi Salmón. Special thanks are also due Blanca Wiethüchter, Alberto Villalpando, and Yolanda Bedregal for their wisdom and their hospitality. Gonzalo Leonardini of the *Fundación*

San Gabriel kindly introduced me to the leaders and participants of women's grassroots organizations from La Paz's Eastern zone.

My heartfelt thanks go to Theresa May, editor extraordinaire of the University of Texas Press, for her interest in this book and for her expertise and professionalism. Readers Ileana Rodríguez and Guillermo Delgado generously gave a strong endorsement of the project and provided helpful suggestions. Leslie Tingle and Teri Sperry provided valuable help in creating a clean final manuscript.

I gratefully acknowledge Carlos Mamani Condori for granting me permission to include photographs from the THOA archive; Eusebio Choque Quispe for allowing me to use his magnificent drawings and photographs; Jorge Saravia Valle for the use of his architectural drawings; *Mujer y Sociedad* for permission to reproduce the comic illustration by "Alfredo"; the *Revista de Estudios Hispánicos* for permission to include in Chapter Two material that appeared in volume 28, number 3 (1994), and *Dispositio* for permission to include in Chapter Five material that appeared in volume 19, number 46 (1994). In addition, I thank Ali Broach, Cheryl Kelly, and Shannon Snyder for their skills as photographers.

All translations are my own unless otherwise noted; as such, I accept full responsibility for any misreadings or errors. This notwithstanding, several people generously gave of their time to assist in the best rendition of difficult passages. In particular I want to recognize the work of Iván Krsul Andrade, who spent long hours improving the translations, and that of Yolanda Gamboa, Ana Gómez Bravo, Mariselle Meléndez, Blanca Rardin, and Josefa Salmón, who helped on many sections.

Finally, I would like to express my love and deep admiration for my family, both the Stephensons and the Brodens, and, most of all, for Tom Broden. Accompanying me every step of the way, he graciously read drafts and steadfastly maintained a sense of humor and adventure; his life and work are a continual source of inspiration and joy.

RACE, GENDER, AND MODERNITY
IN THE BOLIVIAN ANDES

"*¡Unidos para el cambio!*" [United for Change!]. In the June 1993 Bolivian elections, this slogan galvanized popular support for the slate pairing reformist presidential candidate Gonzalo Sánchez de Lozada (Movimiento Nacionalista Revolucionario [Revolutionary Nationalist Movement]) and the Aymara Indian vice presidential candidate, Víctor Hugo Cárdenas (Movimiento Revolucionario Tupaj Katari de Liberación [Tupaj Katari Revolutionary Movement for Liberation]). The conventional reading of the phrase suggests a commonality of purpose among diverse ethnic and social groups in support of state and economic reform. At the same time, the slogan and the poster images of the two politicians together position the running mates in such a way as to enable a reading of them as marriage partners in a union that paradigmatically correlates modernization with miscegenation. Indeed, the prevailing historical tradition has consistently aligned rural indigenous peoples with the feminine insofar as they are perceived by the (white) metropolitan criollo elites as being outside the dominant socio-symbolic order. The seemingly egalitarian guise of pluralism represented in the presidential ticket effectively negates the legitimacy of those demands put forth by urban and rural indigenous social movements because the new government's policies privilege a racially neutral modernity of private property and individual rights over and against "underdeveloped" indigenous peoples and their communal identities (see Rivera Cusicanqui 1993).[1] To gain full understanding of this impetus to create a coherent, totalizing identity, one needs to appreciate how modernity tries to relocate subjects in terms of their cultural, racial, gendered, and spatial identities.

Hegemonic appeals to modernize attempt to legitimize political, social, and economic practices that endorse racial homogenization. By promoting racial acculturation, modernization seeks to "reform" communal indigenous socioeconomic practices based upon exchange and reciprocity in favor of a liberal economic enterprise that endorses participation in market systems as individual producers and consumers. In Bolivia, therefore, hegemonic discourses have anxiously reiterated a desire for the selfsame throughout the twentieth century. Such desire can guarantee its own reproduction only through the repression of both internal and external contradictions. Hegemonic criollo notions of modernity consistently emphasize the dividing line, or threshold, that distinguishes between the familiar (civilized) interior and the unfamiliar or unrecognizable (barbaric) exterior. This prevailing imaginary depends on the deployment of multiple boundaries that necessarily reinforce differences between the inside and the outside.

These boundaries differentiating the space of the modern selfsame from the premodern other, however, are neither fixed nor stable. A brief consideration of the terminology used to delineate the territories of identity in Andean Bolivia reveals their ambiguous contours. For example, during the twentieth century, the words "criollo," "mestizo," "*cholo,*" and "Indian" have conveyed spatial, economic, political, and racial implications. If Indians tend to be associated predominantly with a rural, agrarian, collective identity, criollos, mestizos, and *cholos* are more apt to live in urban centers. Although the term "criollo" originally designated people of Spanish descent born in the Americas, in the Andean region, it has come to mean a member of the oligarchy, someone who holds sway over economic, legislative, and judicial power. Often referred to by Indians as "*los blancos*" [whites], criollos speak Spanish and identify generally with western notions of civilization, progress, (neo)liberal market relations, and citizens' rights.[2]

On the changing meaning of the term "Indian," Olivia Harris contends that during the colonial period, Indians were a "fiscal category," thereby being defined and situated in relationship to the colonial state according to their economic obligations (Harris 1995: 354). This positioning underwent change during the mid-nineteenth century as increasing distinctions between Indians and mestizos became more significant: "The contrast between tribute-paying Indians and those who enjoyed access to their labor and resources as intermediaries of the state was thus increasingly inscribed as an ethnic difference" (361). In accordance with Harris, Brooke Larson notes how, during the period between 1880 and 1930, the designation "Indian" underwent social, economic, and ethnic transformation when liberal and positivist discourses recast the Indian as "an impoverished, hapless, illiterate, and uncivilized subject . . . who remained on the margins of the market economy, neither interested in nor capable of mercantile initiative or productive enterprise" (Larson 1995:

29; see also Harris 1995: 364–367). Larson and Harris identify this period of the fin de siècle, with its shift in economic and ideological discourses, as the historical era when criollos defined the Indian as a being situated politically and economically at the periphery of the incipient culture of modernity (Larson 1995: 29–30).

Mestizo identity similarly underwent redefinition during the nineteenth century to take on increasing importance as an economic and political category. Moreover, new racist ideologies facilitated the notion of a homogeneous indigenous people, distinct from the mestizos: "In fact, it is plausible to argue that it was precisely because the relationship between mestizos and Indians was not securely a class one that ethnic difference became so important a means for mestizos to legitimate their domination over the Indians. This would help explain the paradoxical nature of mestizo 'identity,' which in some cases seems to reside in nothing more secure than *not being Indian*" (Harris 1995: 366–367; emphasis in the original). In the twentieth century, the phrase "acculturated mestizo" refers to someone who can pass as white. Passing, in this context, similarly carries racial, cultural, and economic meaning. An acculturated or westernized mestizo speaks Spanish (even though the person may be bilingual), wears western clothing, and emulates western values and market relations.

In contrast, the *cholo* is an urban mestizo whose cultural and ethnic ties associate him more closely with communal, indigenous practices than with western traditions and values. Some contend that, in particular, the working-class *chola* constitutes a third term in the white–indigenous binary. For example, historian Rossana Barragán has observed that *cholas* consciously distinguish themselves through their clothing from criollas as well as from indigenous women (Barragán 1992).[3] It can be argued, therefore, that Andean tradition and western modernity collide in the figure of the *chola*: "Así, la emergencia de la figura de las cholas [18th c.] representa no sólo la ruptura de la dualidad indios versus españoles-criollos relacionada a la emergencia de nuevas actividades económico-sociales, sino también la interferencia de los valores entre ambos mundos y la creación de una identidad conflictiva que lleva en su seno, simultáneamente la 'tradición' y la 'modernidad'" (Barragán 1992: 61) [In this way, the emergence of the figure of the *cholas* (18th c.) represents not only the rupture of the duality Indians versus Spanish-criollos caused by the emergence of new economic and social activities, but also the interference of the values of both worlds and the creation of a conflicting identity that carries in its core, simultaneously, "tradition" and "modernity"].

Due to the reformulation of the terms "Indian" and "mestizo" at the turn of the twentieth century, the country's complex matrix of race relations came under increasing scrutiny, generating consternation and alarm among many upper-class intellectuals. Because racial difference was cast by criollos in positivist terms as a pathological illness, many feared that Bolivia's strides toward modernity would be cut short by its own festering disorder. Modernity, in other words, was understood as being guided by the logic of the criollo selfsame.

A central claim of *Gender and Modernity in Andean Bolivia* is that hegemonic desire for the selfsame unfolds not only in and through the racialized body but in and through the *gendered,* racialized body. In Andean Bolivia, racial and cultural differences are most visibly marked on women, notably through their clothing and hair styles as well as their language choices (Aymara, Quechua, Spanish), and occupation of public and private spaces. Reading modernization through psychoanalytic and feminist theories reveals that criollo desire for the selfsame represents a *modern* desire. What's more, this modern desire is cathected and deployed through images of womanhood that reinforce the notion of rupture or turning away from a premodern (indigenous) ontology.[4] The modern imperative requires a process of loss and replacement, specifically the loss of the indigenous mother and her replacement with the westernized mestiza through disciplinary practices that project the virtues of an idealized, acculturated body.[5] The maternal body thus claims symbolic currency in repressive and resistant practices.

Gender and Modernity in Andean Bolivia engages a variety of texts, including critical essays, novels, testimonials, education manuals, self-help pamphlets, and position papers of diverse women's organizations, to analyze a series of interlocking tropes present throughout the twentieth century. It contends that in order to facilitate this fetishizing process of loss and substitution, hegemonic discourses of desire deploy a succession of associated metaphorical images of domestication, incorporation, consumption, and hunger (appetite). Each metaphorical cluster, in turn, is both racialized and gendered as it is strategically rendered through dominant ideologies of womanhood. By investigating specific themes rather than following a strictly chronological approach, this book makes visible ongoing patterns of countervailing movements to oppression as disparate groups position themselves and are positioned differently with respect to dominant cultural symbols.[6] For example, images of womanhood (motherhood) and therefore of related features such as domesticity, fashion, hygiene, and hunger are seized and shaped by nationalist discourses to serve upper-class interests of political, economic, and racial unification.

The closer a woman comes to the indigenous pole of what sociologist

4

Silvia Rivera Cusicanqui terms the horizontal axis of identities (1993), the more she is perceived as a bodily presence and, consequently, the more she is linked emblematically to racialized images of pollution and disease. Mary Douglas has argued that cultural constructions of pollution essentially define order and disorder. The multilayered *pollera*[7] worn by the Indian woman or the urban *chola* consequently emerges as a hegemonic symbol of a disorderly, polluted body that can only be cleaned up once the traditional garb has been exchanged for a (modern) skirt. Nevertheless, *cholas* resist being conscripted by certain kinds of gendering, particularly notions of motherhood that would relegate them to the private confines of the domestic sphere. The testimonials and other texts examined show that *cholas,* because they work in the public realm of the marketplace and as domestic employees of the middle and upper classes, have traditionally been able to resist the seduction of ahistorical, nationalist discourses. Thus the *pollera* becomes a visible symbol of resistance that exemplifies the many struggles lived out each day for indigenous and *chola* women who deliberately refuse to be "refashioned."

Drawing from dominant ideologies of womanhood, nationalist discourses similarly interpellate Woman through hegemonic depictions of the home. The idealized, acculturated mestiza is represented as a woman readily taking up her assigned place inside the home as a housewife with the primary responsibility of reproducing the equally idealized nation. This modern housewife inhabits a normative home that architecturally emphasizes the privatization of space and clear-cut distinctions between inside and outside. In contrast, actual rural indigenous houses are characterized by communal living spaces and by more permeable interior-exterior boundaries—women work outside the house in the fields, for example. Thus modernization's discourse emphasizing privatization/individualism and racial acculturation cannot be separated from the architectural layout of the house nor from dominant representations of woman as housewife. This relationship can be taken one step further to suggest that hegemonic depictions of modernity are structured through a rhetoric of the house insofar as the individual dwelling functions as a spatial metaphor through which representation can be controlled or domesticated precisely because it distinguishes between modern interiors and uncivilized exteriors.

By juxtaposing discourses on fashion and hygiene, *Gender and Modernity in Andean Bolivia* turns to the question of how the modern transforms gendered and racialized bodies into sites of conflict. This analysis elucidates some of the ways in which both fashion and the disciplinary practices of bodily hygiene can be seen as primary metaphors of the cultural incorporation of the dominant socio-symbolic contract. Most obviously, of course, as individual bodies become increasingly regulated, so, too, does the larger social body. As already suggested above, the clothing worn by Indians and *cholas* is considered to be, by definition, unclean. The pathology of the premodern body is thereby transferred onto the clothing itself. Indian women in particular become identified with disease and contagion because customarily they are the ones who produce and wear native Andean clothing. Similarly, in urban areas, *cholas* who don the *pollera* and *manta* [shawl] visibly depict racial and cultural difference and therefore are perceived as the embodiment of disorder.

The investigation of pedagogical manuals for rural coed and urban girls' schools from the 1920s and 1930s brings to light early links between hygiene, fashion, and modernization through models of consumption. Indian schoolchildren were introduced to the values of the liberal market economy as they rehearsed make-believe trips to the store to buy their own bar of soap and toothbrush. In contrast, the upper-class schoolgirl was warned against the seduction of fashion that would lure her away from the protected domestic sphere of the home. Perceived as eroding the boundary between public and private worlds, the fashion industry epitomized the negative side of modernity because it appealed to woman's "irrational" nature to consume voraciously. Girls were encouraged to focus their energies on personal hygiene instead, because it instilled dominant, patriarchal values emphasizing bodily and household management.

Of final consideration is hunger and the related phenomena of eating and appetite as they intersect with racial and economic questions of incorporation and consumption. These issues, in turn, are linked to cultural constructions of desire (appetite). If, indeed, we are what we eat, the distribution and allocation of food resources become central micro-practices in the regulation of ontological, political, and economic relations. Recent studies of women's relation to eating and hunger suggest that a specifically "feminine" appetite is perceived as threatening a "masculine" self (Bordo 1993; MacSween 1993), and thus it can be argued that the "racialized" (indigenous-*chola*) female appetitive body in Bolivia looms as an eruptive hunger and dangerous desire that threatens the dominant criollo order. Moreover, hunger (desire) calls attention to a permeable sense of self and to the appetitive relations that throw into question boundaries between the self and the other. For example, the hunger strikes initiated by the miners' housewives during the late 1970s generally resulted in political concessions from the military government because the collective manifestation of hungering mothers and children in the public arena provoked an outpouring of support throughout the nation. Ultimately, the strikes were important catalysts in bringing about the downfall of General Hugo Bánzer Suárez's military dictatorship.

In contrast to the previous two decades, the 1980s saw draconian economic and political reform resulting in enormous social cost for the working and popular classes. The New Economic Policy (NEP) effectively dismantled labor's formidable political power through the massive layoff and relocation of miners, factory workers, and public employees, definitively reshaping urban class structures. The NEP promotes citizens' rights over and against communal indigenous identities, in part through an even more aggressive emphasis on individual consumerism (Rivera Cusicanqui 1993: 90–96). Prioritizing consumerism in the face of widespread unemployment, homelessness, and hunger suggests, ironically, that the same "unifying" processes of consumption and incorporation are driving an even larger wedge between culturally and economically diverse subjectivities. In the same way, the growing pervasiveness of a discourse of consumption appears to have forestalled the ability of hunger to estrange onlookers.

These tropes—motherhood, desire, the home, fashion, hygiene, and hunger—when read together define a complex paradox. On the one hand, each culturally coded thematic locus is deployed by hegemonic discourses as a vehicle for enjoining the racialized others to cross the threshold of the dominant symbolic and become modern (civilized). However, the ability to cross over points to the instability of the same boundary. Neither unbreachable nor impermeable, the boundary is instead precarious and subject to reconfiguration or even erasure. This fluidity creates anxiety in the criollo imaginary because it suggests that the other can transgress the boundary after all and cease being identifiable as other. Hegemonic desire is therefore split between the desire to incorporate the other and the desire to maintain the self inviolate.

The ambiguous racialized and gendered underpinnings of Andean modernity are foregrounded in the spatial ordering of the city of La Paz and its immediate environs, the primary geographic area on which this study focuses. From its founding in 1548, Nuestra Señora de La Paz [Our Lady of La Paz], referred to in Aymara as Chukiyawu, Chuquiago, or Chuquiabo, has been encircled by communities of indigenous peoples; indeed, one might say that the racial and geographical boundedness of the city reflects the boundedness of the criollo imaginary haunted by a self-other oppositional logic.[8] The racial divide that indigenous peoples were enjoined to cross in order to become modern had an actual physical manifestation in the wall that enclosed La Paz up through the nineteenth century. This wall separated whites who lived inside the city gates from the Indians who lived outside them. The outlying areas, or *"extra-muros,"* encompassed peripheral neighborhoods that had once been communally held indigenous lands which, after the 1874 Law of Expropriation, were gradually incorporated into the limits of the city (Barragán 1990: 224–228).

The increase of *comuneros* [Indians] living in La Paz gave rise to new social classes, particularly as indigenous migrants developed artisan trades or became small-scale merchants. This process of transformation and adaptation often created a rupture between the incipient artisan class and the rural, communal way of life (Barragán 1990: 228). Rossana Barragán has argued that the rise in numbers of the mestizo population noted in the 1877 census was due not to an increase in white-indigenous unions, but instead to the gradual loss of ties with the indigenous community structure known as the *ayllu*[9] and the subsequent donning of western dress by men and the *pollera* and *manta* of the *chola* by women (Barragán 1990: 232–236). By the twentieth century, the growth of the urban upper-class population created the need for more domestics and providers of labor services such as sewing, tailoring, and laundering. Not surprisingly, then, the number of *cholas* working in the central, predominantly white neighborhoods of La Paz also began to increase. Although the growing presence of indigenous women and *cholas* reflected, in part, a response to the expanding demand for their services, their presence also reproduced the upper-class oligarchy's anxieties that the (white) social body was being invaded by an alien other.

This image of the outskirts breaking into the center becomes a metaphor of subaltern movement and resistance found throughout this book. In spite of the often violent means adopted by the state to force indigenous peoples to conform to the strictures of western modernity, native opposition has proved to be long lasting. The large-scale mobilization of indigenous peoples, witnessed particularly since the 1970s, has enforced their ideological stance that they will negotiate the terms of modernity but always *"as Indians."*[10]

∽

ONE

SKIRTS AND *POLLERAS*

Ideologies of Womanhood and the Politics of Resistance in La Paz, 1900–1952

∽

I n 1990, the journal *Mujer/Fem-press* published a special issue on women and humor that included comic strips highlighting feminist issues from all over the world. One of the cartoon drawings, reprinted from the Peruvian journal *Mujer y Sociedad,* depicts a woman who is in the midst of a conversation with a man (see Fig. 1.1). With her fist raised high, the woman sternly declares: "Women have the right to demand equality and justice." At that moment, a maid who has been listening behind the door bursts in, crying out: "Bravo!" Surprised, the first woman turns to the maid to admonish her: "I said women, I did not say domestic employees."[1]

This comic strip ironically underscores the complex and often contradictory dynamics that have historically grounded gender interests in Latin American countries, suggesting that these interests cannot be easily reduced to an oppositional male-female identity politics. Nevertheless, while the cartoon shows pointedly how women position themselves according to class differences, it does not address the articulations of race and ethnicity that also shape feminist debates; secondly, it does not tell us how maids have organized nor does it describe the nature of their resistance. In this comic strip the maid is effectively silenced after her eruption from the margins into the center scene.

This chapter analyzes the trajectories of feminism and practices of resistance in Bolivia, focusing primarily on the first half of the twentieth century. It argues that the dominant ideology of womanhood in Bolivia during the 1920s, 1930s, and 1940s played a key role in the ongoing negotiation among urban criollo sectors for hegemonic control. In order to understand its function within these hegemonic struggles, the chapter examines how nationalist discourses of the time—prior to the Revolution

FIGURE I.I.

Drawing by "Alfredo." Courtesy of the journal Mujer y Sociedad *(Peru).*

of 1952 and the subsequent formation of the modern state—posited a homogeneous cultural identity, one that depended upon the primacy of certain specific representations of woman and the maternal body. Because nationalist discourses predicated on binary oppositions, including the gendered division of public and private spaces, served the interests primarily of men of the oligarchy, both upper-class and working-class women began to organize themselves, negotiating spaces for maneuver in spite of the enormous restrictions placed on them. As a result, the early decades of this century constituted a vital conjuncture in the history of women's organizations in Bolivia. Forging alliances between women of diverse backgrounds was virtually impossible, however, and few groups worked collaboratively across race and class lines. In fact, Bolivia shows that feminist analyses must engage cultural and material realities. For example, if the dominant ideology of womanhood constituted the primary matrix of relations whereby white women or criollas of the upper classes negotiated their own position with respect to the patriarchy, at the same time the dominant ideology of womanhood also constituted the framework whereby these women consolidated their socially privileged position over mestizas, *cholas,* and indigenous women.[2] Thus, the prevailing ideology of womanhood reconstructed hierarchies based not only on gender but also on economic and racial differences, thereby establishing the parameters that determined who were "women" and who were "not women" (see Carby 1987: 23). Indigenous women and working-class *cholas* continually resisted dominant notions of womanhood that defined them as nonwomen, refusing to be circumscribed by hegemonic discourses and practices.

The historical circumstances of the period immediately preceding and following the Chaco War (1932–1935) brought about important changes in gender interests that ultimately affected the roles of women across class and race lines. The late twenties, thirties, and forties witnessed the emergence of a number of women's organizations and societies formed by upper-class criollas, as well as all-women anarchist labor unions comprised primarily of artisans, market vendors, cooks, and domestic workers. Women from the upper classes limited their interests chiefly to winning the right to study, work, and vote. The forums in which they debated the struggles for these rights included women's cultural societies such as the Ateneo Femenino and journals like *Feminiflor, Eco Femenino,* and the Ateneo's *Indice.* In contrast, the militant labor unions of working-class *cholas* came together under the umbrella organization Federación Obrera Femenina [FOF], an organization which, in turn, was part of the anarchist Federación Obrera Local [FOL]. The principal arena in which *cholas* sought work-related reforms was through their participation in the FOF, which organized large-scale street demonstrations the likes and magnitude of which have not been seen again in La Paz since 1952, when political and labor reforms closed down these critical spaces of resistance and contestation for women. During the 1920s and 1930s, however, the women of the FOF were perceived to be crucial allies of the FOL because of their combativeness and unity. Nevertheless, even as the women supported the anarchist ideology, they introduced into the FOL demands formulated according to their specific needs as working-class Aymara women and mothers. The members of the FOF organized child care, literacy courses, numerous cultural events, and a library, all of which were designed to meet the needs of working *cholas*. Thus, what Sonia Alvarez has noted in the instance of Brazil, I contend can be extended to La Paz, Bolivia: both upper-class women's organizations *and* working-class *cholas'* labor unions "constitute[d] deliberate attempts to push, re-define, or reconstitute the boundary between the public and the private, the political and the personal, the 'natural' and the 'artificial'" (Alvarez 1990: 23), a boundary which was vital to the development of elite interests and the consolidation of the new tin oligarchy.[3]

In spite of what might first appear to be a shared goal of confronting female oppression, the enormous gulf between women of different economic, racial, and cultural backgrounds—a gulf endemic to the existing socioeconomic structures as a whole—made it impossible for any sort of commonality of purpose between various women's organizations of different classes. Furthermore, these differences marked the site of often oppressive relations of power between women as well as between women and oligarchic structures. The symbol donned by many women of the FOF and which visibly manifested the convergence of these gendered, racial, and class demands in the urban public realm was the *pollera*. The ubiquitous presence of women wearing the *pollera* in the streets of La Paz foregrounded the resistant position many *cholas* occupied with regard to prevailing debates on nationalism and modernity as they refused to be domesticated by hegemonic discourses. The *pollera* remains a resonant trope that ties together the gendered and racialized practices of resistance in La Paz throughout the twentieth century.

IDEOLOGIES OF WOMANHOOD
AND RESISTANT PRACTICES

The dominant ideology of womanhood in Bolivia during the first fifty years of this century was a major structuring force that facilitated the reproduction of already existing social and political structures. This ideological construction depended upon the primacy of specific representations of women and the maternal body. For example, the upper-class girl became a woman within a complex matrix of cultural practices that were perceived as "natural" because their source was understood to be the body; thus different bodies "naturalized" social differences. These differences, in turn, legitimized the "logical" and "rational" exclusion of woman from certain sectors of society, such as the public realm, because of her "natural" condition as mother. Consequently, there evolved a "commonsense" boundary between the public world, which was the domain of the upper-class male, the bearer of civilization and reason, and the private, domestic realm of the woman, who was defined as the summation of her bodily functions, such as nurturing sentiment.

These "natural" categories of the body were also tied to economic and racial-cultural differences such that certain groups of people were privileged "naturally" over others. To cite one example, in her examination of Bolivian legal documents from the first two decades of the century, Ximena Medinaceli calls attention to the way in which women were designated by the law. According to her findings, an upper-class *criolla* was consistently addressed as "*señora*"; the woman dressed in a *pollera* was referred to as "*la mujer*" [woman], and the indigenous woman from the rural countryside was "*la indígena*" [the Indian woman]. The last two terms, and especially the third, affirmed the woman's inferiority before the law (X. Medinaceli 1989: 72–73). This nomenclature illustrates ways in which female subjects were interpellated by the legal system according to a particular relationship to the body. For example, the word *señora* distanced the body to emphasize, instead, civil and social relationships; *la mujer* accentuated a gendered body but one that was without visible ties to any particular social or ethnic category, the word "*mujer*" rendering the *pollera* invisible. *La indígena,* in contrast, both gendered and racialized the body. These hierarchical representations of women introduced the body as an increasing presence endowed first with corporeal and second with racial significance. This illustration calls attention to how women as women were interpellated by virtue of their embodied relationship to the racially and economically bounded category *señora*. As a result, only certain women were legitimated as women within the oligarchic state.

The many contradictions of the prevailing ideology of womanhood forcefully emerge in Carlos Medinaceli's consequential novel on nationalism, *La Chaskañawi* (1947). Of particular interest is the way in which the seemingly irreconcilable categories "*señorita*" and "servant" are capable of being disrupted. In the novel, Julia, the upper-class *señorita,* is raped by the protagonist Adolfo. The violent event shocks Julia with the unexpected realization that her own position of privilege within the four walls of the home cannot ultimately protect her from the male's unconditional right to assert his power. Bewildered, she asks him: "¿Por qué abusaste de mí como de una sirviente . . . ?" (C. Medinaceli 1955: 135) [Why did you take advantage of me as if I were a servant?].

The violation of the rape and resulting pregnancy ultimately transform Julia. No longer able to claim for herself the sacred place she once held as *señorita,* Julia acknowledges that she has become the female grotesque of her former self: the servant. From this position alone can she plead with Adolfo to marry her so that her honor might be salvaged at least in the public eye: "he de ser siempre buena contigo, como lo he sido siempre; no te he de faltar nunca ni con el pensamiento; te he de atender en todo, como tu sirviente, resignada a todo; he de ser tu esclava, tu trapo viejo, y, en cambio, no he de exigir nada de ti, nada, ni un poco de cariño siquiera" (136) [I will always be good to you, just as I always have been; I will never be unfaithful to you, not even with my thoughts; I will look after all your needs, resigned to anything just like your servant; I will be your slave, your dirty rag, and, in exchange, I will not ask you for anything, nothing, not even a little affection]. Conversely, Claudina, the beautiful *chola,* gains unexpected legitimacy at the end of the novel when her white bloodlines are revealed to all. As I propose in Chapter 2, the disruption of the categories "*señorita,*" "servant," and "*chola*" can be linked to the reconfiguration of upper-class masculine desire during the 1940s. This transformation of desire enabled the ideological shift to *mestizaje* that would eventually become the cornerstone of the emergent modern state.[4] By recovering Claudina's white bloodlines, the narrative suggests that the social dislocations that occur and shock so many of the novel's characters when Adolfo abandons Julia and moves in with the *chola* are not so far-reaching after all.

In contrast, the testimonies of working-class *cholas* bear witness to how these women profoundly unsettled the dominant ideology of womanhood by powerfully disrupting gendered categories of the "natural." As the cooks, laundresses, and domestic employees of the upper class, they demystified the supposed sanctity of the privileged sector's domestic sphere by formulating specific demands for changes in their workplace when they called for better working conditions, a raise in their wages, and an eight-hour work day. Until the rise of anarchist women's labor unions during the 1920s–1940s, the presumed inviolability of the domestic realm had protected it from public discussion and debate.

The circumstances of these confrontations as well as the history of the *cholas'* resistant practices recently came to the attention of contemporary audiences with the publication of two important volumes, *Polleras libertarias* (1986) and *Agitadoras de buen gusto* (Wadsworth and Dibbits 1989).[5] These hybrid texts are comprised of personal life stories, *testimonios,* interviews, newspaper clippings, and historical commentary of the anarchist women's labor movement (1927–1958). As the titles of these publications suggest, working-class *cholas* seized images generally used to suppress them, such as the *pollera,* and transformed them into symbols of resistance; hence the unionized cooks self-identified as "agitators of good taste." The *cholas'* demands clearly demonstrate their opposition to the ways by which hegemonic ideologies of womanhood attempted to de-politicize economic relations between the working and upper classes. The *cholas'* reconstruction of the domestic sphere in economic terms thus re-futed the notion of an essentialized (female) domestic realm and reintro-duced its historical and material foundations.[6] As a consequence, activist working-class women problematized the "natural," biological link that dominant discourses claimed existed between Woman and the Home.[7] Moreover, as these texts indicate, the women were well aware that their claims ultimately called for radical political and social transformations (see *Polleras* 1986: 15).

A pattern of resistance that emerges in these *testimonios* of working-class women is that of one subaltern group speaking for another. Clearly this dynamic of mediation can also be filled with contradictions because the ability to speak for someone else only arises where there are differen-tial experiences of privilege. Among urban household workers, for ex-ample, cooks generally had more prestige than other employees. As a group they also tended to live elsewhere, away from their place of work (*cama afuera*), and therefore could exercise more independence from their employers than other female domestic workers. Otherwise, regular household or domestic workers generally lived in servants' quarters at their place of employment (*cama adentro*), where they had few privileges.

Nonetheless, urban *cholas,* be they servants or cooks, had more free-dom of movement and suffered less discrimination than *mitanis,* indige-nous women from rural areas forced to serve a *señora* under the system of *pongueaje*.[8] Many *cholas* narrating their histories call attention to the fact that as part of the urban working class they enjoyed certain privileges that were denied bonded indigenous women. For example, as late as 1950, the newspaper *La Tribuna* published the story of one Indian ser-vant brought from the altiplano who, while working, accidently dropped an expensive object made of crystal. To teach the servant a lesson, the *señora* of the house first whipped her and then cut the palms of the bonded woman's hands with the crystal shards: "Cuando las autoridades conminaron a la señora Machicado para que explicara su actitud habría dicho que 'se trata de una costumbre generalizada para que las sirvientas no destrocen los objetos delicados'" (*La Tribuna,* 5 de enero, 1950; cited in Wadsworth and Dibbits 1989: 79) [When the authorities coerced Mrs. Machicado into explaining her actions, she would have said that "it's a common way of treating servants so that they do not destroy fragile objects."]. The *señoras* domesticated the majority of the *mitanis* with a vengeance, often keeping them isolated within the house and allowing them few opportunities to leave the premises; participation in the unions for this group was unthinkable. One cook, doña Tomasita remembers: "Las mitanis no podían venir al Sindicato porque la patrona⁹ si la veía ahí, la podía ahorcar, la podía matar. No les gustaba" (78) [The *mitanis* could not go to the union gatherings because if the mistress of the house saw her there, she could throttle her, she could kill her. The mistresses didn't like it at all].

Describing the abuses that indigenous men and women from the rural countryside endured at the hands of upper-class criollos, many of the unionized *cholas* explain that they felt paralyzed, unsure of how to intervene. The cook doña Exaltación laments: "Yo decía: 'cómo es, ni a quién quejarse, ni a quién decir: ésto es lo que ha pasado.' Nosotros bien calladitos teníamos que quedarnos. Así hemos vivido en esos tiempos" (54) [I used to say: "that's how it is, no one we can complain to, nor to whom we can say: this is what has happened." We had to keep our mouths shut. That's how we lived in those times].

On some occasions, cooks directly confronted their employers to speak out in protest of the treatment that the Indians received. For example, unionized cook and activist leader doña Petronila would defend the indigenous workers against the abuses of the *patrón*. Her daughter, Alicia, remembers: "A los pongos, mi mamá no permitía que los trataran mal. Al igual comían en la cocina, igual se les daba la comida; en la casa del Coronel del Carpio también. Ella decía que el Coronel era loco, que cuando bebía les pegaba a los pongos; pero cuando mi mamá entró a trabajar ahí, ya no ha permitido. Se enfrentó al Coronel: le dijo que ellos eran seres humanos y que él no podía maltratarlos porque no eran sus esclavos" (55) [My mother did not allow the *pongos* to be poorly treated. Just like anyone else, they ate in the kitchen, the same as anyone they got their food; even in the house of Colonel del Carpio. She used to say that the Colonel was crazy, that when he drank he would beat the *pongos;* but when my mom began to work there, she did not permit that. She stood up to the Colonel: she told him that they were human beings and that he could not mistreat them because they were not his slaves].

As this testimonial demonstrates, cooks, at times, had more freedom to confront the *patrón* and serve as mediator during a situation of conflict between the boss and the *pongos*. Nevertheless, the unionized women were conscious of the fact that interventions on an individual basis were insufficient to change the devastating situation in which the *mitanis* and *pongos* lived. During the 1920s urban male and female anarchists committed themselves to uphold the struggle for political and economic autonomy carried out by Aymara Indians. The workers established important links with indigenous leaders and offered diverse forms of assistance, including legal advice (Lehm and Rivera Cusicanqui 1988: 40–41).

Given the differences in treatment that the *mitanis* and urban working-class *cholas* received, the designation *polleras libertarias* underlines the unionized women's desire to emphasize the common struggle against colonialism they shared with the *campesinos*. By placing emphasis on the reproduction of communal Aymara values, these histories problematize the homogenization of the dominant symbolic space and the concomitant exclusion of the majority of Bolivians from every element of the state's decision-making process. Addressing oppositional concerns led to the creation of new subaltern spaces, or sites where popular subjects were formed.[10] The *cholas* organized a library for themselves (Wadsworth and Dibbits 1989: 91–92) and a variety of cultural events where the women gave speeches and participated in dramatic presentations and poetry readings. As one woman explains, "Eran poemas de libertad, poemas de que hemos sufrido, de cómo somos; era muy lindo" (148) [They were poems about freedom, poems telling about what we have suffered, what we are like; it was very beautiful]. Similarly, Doña Petronila Infantes analogizes her experience with that of religious devotees:

Hay que vivir para recordar. Yo era pues así, como una beata que dice: "no voy a ir a la iglesia" y siempre es su costumbre ir a la iglesia; así es pues la organización. Yo cuantas veces decía: "ay, ya no voy a ir, dejo a los hijos, hay que atender, hay que lavar, hay que cocinar." Pero pasaba la hora, cambiaba de idea y decía: "iré nomás [*sic*] un rato siquiera, a ver qué dicen." (179)

[One must live to remember. Well, I was like that, just like a puritanical and devout woman who says: "I'm not going to church" and yet she routinely goes to church; that's the way it is with the labor organization. How many times I would say "oh, I'm not going, I leave the kids, I have to look after the chores, I have to do the wash, I have to cook." But the time would pass, I would change my mind and say: "I'll just go for a little bit, just to see what they're saying."]

Schools became an increasingly prominent factor in the preparation of girls for their differing social and national roles. Throughout the 1920s in Bolivia, newly published pedagogical manuals included a vision of education that focused specifically on working-class girls to ready them for their future employment; at the same time young girls from the privileged classes were also to be prepared for their "natural" station in life. The upper-class woman's role was generally defined in relationship to the domestic realm of the home, where she gained status through motherhood. The image of the mother constructed in education manuals disembodied the upper-class woman by representing her with a religious and horticultural vocabulary that distanced her from the impurities of the flesh. Thus, for example, in 1927, educator Raquel Ichaso Vásquez described the ideal woman and her assigned position within modern, civilized society in the following way:

> Bien sabido es el rol que juega la mujer dentro de la vida de los pueblos civilizados; ella no es sólo un componente pasivo, sino también un factor social activo de vital importancia; ella, nacida para amar y hacer del amor la fuerza suma de su propia debilidad; ella que por corazón tiene un cáliz rebosante de ternuras y arrullos, de suspiros y de lágrimas; ella, flor preciada de la familia como hija, encanto como hermana, ángel como esposa, apóstol como maestra, en el hogar se transforma en sacerdotiza [*sic*] como madre, en cuyo cálido regazo, aprenden las generaciones, como en un santasantorum, el culto de los cultos, el culto a la Humanidad o sea la religión de Cristo. (Ichaso Vásquez 1927: 51)

> [The role that woman plays in the life of civilized nations is well known; she is not just a passive component, but also an active social factor of vital importance; she, born to love and through that love overcome her natural weakness; she, who for a heart has a chalice overflowing with loving tenderness and cooings, sighs and tears; she, precious flower of the family as a daughter, the delight as a sister, the angel as a wife, the apostle as a teacher, she is transformed into a loving guide at home as a mother, in whose lap, a holy shrine, generations learn the worship of the cults and the veneration of Humanity, in other words, the religion of Christ.]

The virtuous woman idealized here was really not "of the flesh" because female desire (or presence of the flesh) was eliminated in an ideology of womanhood that exalted the mother who practiced unconditional love, self-sacrifice, and abnegation. Her "missing" body would be "recuperated" through the birth of sons, or healthy white citizens. Thus through the metaphor of the warm "lap," the criolla woman's maternal body was transformed into the embodiment of national space that lovingly embraced all its citizens.

In contrast to this image, Adela Zamudio's epistolary novel *Intimas* (1913) offers one isolated instance that briefly alludes to the ambiguous manifestations of this fetishizing of motherhood. In Zamudio's novel, Juan, the writer of the first letter, describes how his brother and sister-in-law forced their Indian servant to abandon her own starving and sickly baby to come and serve as a wet nurse to their own. Reflecting on this situation, Juan writes: "Recuerdo que cuando niño oí afirmar muchas veces que sólo las madres saben amar y compadecer a todos los niños. Hoy creo lo contrario: la maternidad, en ciertos casos, hace a la mujer egoísta hasta la ferocidad" (6) [I remember that when I was a boy I heard it affirmed many times that only mothers know how to love and to pity all children. Now I believe the opposite is true: motherhood, in some instances, makes a woman selfish to the point of ferocity.]. The incident is dropped after this aside and never picked up again. Nevertheless, the moment is striking for its revelation of a fundamental contradiction: if motherhood ruled, it did so perversely. In other words, the mother described by Ichaso Vásquez as a woman who inhabits "civilized nations" and is "born to love" takes on another dimension in Zamudio's novel. That unconditional love manifested in the metaphorical space of the criolla mother's warm lap apparently defines the nation's boundaries in such a way as to exclude indigenous peoples from its confines.

Notwithstanding the exception that Zamudio's novel *Intimas* represented, the figure of the woman-mother described by Ichaso Vásquez became a vital symbol of economic development and the accomplishments of modernity in Bolivia. This idealized image of the feminine took on critical significance in the years prior to the Chaco War (1932–1935), when dominant nationalist discourses began to attribute Bolivia's backwardness to its racial impurity. Bolivia would continue to be a "sick" or disordered nation until its population had become homogeneous (read: white). As writer and essayist Alcides Arguedas explained in his famous study *Pueblo enfermo* (1936; first published in 1909), "Los elementos étnicos que en el país vegetan, son absolutamente heterogéneos y hasta antagónicos. No hay entre ellos esa estabilidad y armonía que exige todo progreso, pudiendo decirse que aun está en germen el carácter nacional propiamente dicho . . ." (Arguedas 1936: 26) [The ethnic elements which lie latent in the nation are absolutely heterogeneous and even antagonistic. There isn't among them the stability or the harmony demanded by progress; thus we might say that the national character strictly speaking is still evolving . . .]. He added, "De no haber predominio de sangre indígena, desde el comienzo habría dado el país orientación consciente a su vida, adoptando toda clase de perfecciones en el orden material y mora y, estaría hoy en el mismo nivel que muchos pueblos más favorecidos por corrientes inmigratorias venidas del viejo continente" (32) [If there had not existed the predominance of Indian blood, from the beginning the country would have provided a conscious orientation to its life, adopting all kinds of perfections in the material and moral order, and today it would be at the same level as those nations more favored by waves of immigrants coming from the old world].

Given the obstacle to progress and modernity that the country's racial heterogeneity represented according to criollo intellectuals of the period, nationalist discourses invested the maternal body of the upper-class woman with a sense of national, public duty; the healthy future of the nation depended on her. In other words, the criolla mother's body represented the "somatic literalization" of the imagined nation (see Heng and Devan 1992: 344). According to Geraldine Heng and Janadas Devan's study of Singapore, the new feminine duty to serve the nation "with their bodies—that they take on themselves, and submit themselves to, the public reproduction of nationalism in the most private medium possible, forcefully reveals the anxious relationship, in the fantasies obsessing state patriarchy, between reproducing power and the power to reproduce: the efficacy of the one being expressly contingent on the containment and subsumption of the other" (349). In her influential 1989 study Ximena Medinaceli notes how, during the 1920s, new scientific and medical discourses reaffirmed motherhood as a model of Bolivian nationalism. For example, in 1926 the journal *Arte y Trabajo* published an article that decried prevailing attitudes that projected motherhood as an illness: "La mujer que cría no es un ser enfermo, esta verdad conviene no olvidar, pues en la mayoría de las poblaciones bolivianas se tiene la pésima costumbre de mortificar a la madre con una serie considerable de prejuicios" (cited in Medinaceli 1989: 27) [The woman who raises a child is not unsound, and it would be wise not to forget this truth, because among the majority of the Bolivian populations there exists the dreadful custom of mortifying the mother with a considerable number of prejudices]. Throughout the first decades of this century then, the anxious relationship between the reproduction of power and the power of reproduction converged in the maternal body of the criolla woman, understood as both the instrument and emblem of the healthy, modern nation.

The criolla mother was, almost by definition, a teacher, because the destiny of future generations of men rested on her shoulders. She was to fulfill the charge of educating her children by setting a rigorous example in her own actions and behavior. In 1925, *Vida Pedagógica,* the journal of the Cuerpo Docente de la Escuela Municipal Modelo de Sucre, published an article that emphasized a maternal responsibility that was not only "natural" but also "social" (cited in Medinaceli 1989: 38). The first upper-class women's organizations appropriated nationalist discourses that exalted the "mother-teacher" to justify a woman's right to an education. These activists began to defend the right to work as teachers, appropriating this aspect of nationalism that called for both a natural and social maternity to insist on the moral propriety of women who sought to fulfill their natural mission in the professional arena. They argued that a female teacher knew best how to educate and prepare a young girl for her fundamental role as mother in society. Indeed, magazines and pedagogical manuals of the time repeatedly described the role of the female teacher in maternal terms. For example, in 1927 Ichaso Vásquez characterized the school as the extension of the home (178) and the ideal female teacher as a woman who, like a second mother, enveloped young pupils with "la ternura y los cuidados maternales" (133) [tenderness and motherly care].

Because self-sacrifice and abnegation were the two basic characteristics of motherhood and the teaching profession, some maintained that a woman could not be both a mother and a teacher. For example, in 1924 government officials attempted to pass a decree that would prohibit a teacher from marrying: "El Ministro dijo que el decreto no prohibía el matrimonio, sino solamente establecía una disyuntiva entre el casarse y atender el hogar o no casarse y atender la escuela" (*La República* 1, no. 1, 1924; cited in Medinaceli 1989: 38) [The Minister said that the decree did not prohibit marriage; rather it merely established the separation between getting married and taking care of the home, or not getting married and taking care of the school.]. The fact that this decree never passed suggests that most people considered motherhood and teaching as complementary rather than exclusionary roles. Therefore, throughout the twenties there was an ever-increasing number of young women who entered the teaching profession, and in 1927 the Belgian educator Ademar Gehaín directed the complete reorganization of the Normal School for Young Ladies [Escuela Normal de Señoritas] in Sucre.

The desire to have access to both an education and a profession gave rise to increasing efforts on the part of upper-class women to obtain full civil and political rights. Even when these women were careful not to disrupt hegemonic images of their "natural" domesticity, their debates underscored the inability of nationalist discourses to bring about social equality. Women had to keep searching for forums where they could articulate their stance as "separate but equal." Thus, groups such as the Ateneo Femenino argued that Woman was equal to Man, even though she was of a different "nature." One member maintained that the acquisition of political and civil rights for women would not endanger their "femininity": "no creemos que por tener los derechos que le corresponden, la mujer pierda su feminidad, pues ella reside en el corazón, en el alma" (*Eco Femenino* no. 9, 1924; cited in Medinaceli 1989: 157) [we do not believe that by obtaining the rights that are legitimately hers, a woman will lose her femininity because it resides in her heart, in her soul]. For these new organizers, their identity as women was based on their "essential" difference from men as mothers and, therefore, they never questioned the primacy of the home for themselves. As one woman observed, "el hogar, que es todo para nosotras porque allí está nuestro reinado, en él esperamos a nuestro compañero" (*Atlántida* no. 10, 1920; cited in Medinaceli 1989: 55) [home is everything to us because there is our kingdom; in it we await our partner].

Some men, many of whom were backed by conservative religious sectors, railed against these newly founded women's organizations, claiming that their influence would adversely affect the *señoritas* of the upper class. In 1936, the newspaper *El Lábaro* (Sucre) carried an editorial which cautioned men against these "masculine" activists, reminding them that, if their needs were no longer being satisfied by the women of their own class, they should turn to the *cholas:*

[S]i la mujer de su clase, si la señorita de su medio, ya no es mujer con las virtudes que atraen, con las gracias candorosas que impresionan, qué sucede sino otro masculino, más corrompido que él, tiene que buscar en la clase baja, a nuestras mujercitas, a nuestras cholitas, que junto con la pollera, conservarán el feminismo natural y necesario para inspirar el amor, que los masculinos no inspiran." (Sept. 10, 1936; cited in Villanueva y Saavedra 1970: 54)

[If the woman of your class, if the young lady of your social circle no longer is a woman with the virtues that attract, nor with the innocent charm that makes an impression, what follows is another "man," more corrupt than the first. You will have to look to the lower class, to our very womanly women, to our cholitas, who, together with the pollera, will retain the femininity that is natural and necessary in order to inspire the love that the masculine ones do not.]

This passage suggests some of the ways in which nationalist discourses served the interests of the men of the oligarchy because they facilitated the divisive manipulation of different cultural and racial groups of women.

Unexpectedly, the men praised the *cholas* for their femininity, linking their continued use of the *pollera* to essentialist notions of native authenticity (i.e., the natural) which could then be utilized to subdue the upper-class women's feminist "rebellion."

In April 1929, the Ateneo Femenino organized a National Women's Convention the intention of which was to initiate a formal discussion of the issues affecting the Bolivian woman. This occasion provided one of the first opportunities for women from diverse organizations and economic and cultural backgrounds to come together. According to one commentator from the newspaper *La Razón,* representatives from women's organizations throughout the country were planning to attend (*Polleras* 1986: 33). Nevertheless, this unprecedented gathering excluded the unionized working-class *cholas.* Therefore, on May 1, when one delegation from the Federación Obrera Femenina (FOF) arrived at the convention anyway with a paper titled "La ignorancia es madre de la esclavitud" [Ignorance is the Mother of Slavery] to denounce the social and economic situation of the working-class *chola,* upper-class women reacted in horror at what they perceived to be a crude eruption of the Other into their midst (Lehm and Rivera Cusicanqui 1988: 37–38).

The *cholas'* presentation apparently "causó gran revuelo en el recinto y la delegación de la FOF fue obligada a retirarse, pero no antes 'de dejar expresadas verdades tan grandes que algún día han de germinar en las mentes de las mujeres de Bolivia'" (*El Hombre;* cited in *Polleras* 1986: 34) [caused a great commotion in the meeting room, and the FOF delegation was compelled to withdraw, but not before "having expressed truths so remarkable that one day they will take seed in the minds of Bolivian women"]. One anarchist leader, doña Petronila Infantes, explained that the women organizers of the convention disapproved "lo que las cholas han venido en medio de las señoras" (Lehm and Rivera Cusicanqui 1988: 38) [of the *cholas* coming among the *señoras*]. Other women surmised that the delegates of the FOF were expelled from the convention and their paper rejected "para guardar una apariencia de armonía y unidad, ya que toda la opinión pública tenía los ojos puestos en este evento" (*Polleras* 1986: 35) [in order to maintain the appearance of harmony and unity because all public opinion had their eyes fixed on this event].[11]

From the information available on the opening ceremony, it is clear that the traditional elites maintained a firm hold on the convention, ultimately reproducing existing social hierarchies in the organization of the assembly.[12] These "disencounters" that took place at the convention suggest that a "logic of identification" constructed on the basis of gender where woman was defined in opposition to man was not enough to explore the complex relations of class and ethnicity that existed among Bo-livian women.[13] For this reason, an authentic dialogue between the different women's organizations was impossible on this occasion because the boundaries separating them appeared to be insuperable.

WOMEN'S ORGANIZATION AND AGENCY FOLLOWING THE CHACO WAR: CONTESTING THE PUBLIC-PRIVATE DIVIDE

The documents from upper-class women's organizations and testimonials from the working-class women of the Federación Obrera Femenina demonstrate that, following the terrible devastation of the Chaco War, these very different groups shared hopes of initiating a series of national reforms. For each group there was an increasingly urgent struggle to obtain a public voice and visibility and, with these, to put into action social reform. Nevertheless, the similarities between the groups ended there as the primary goals of each took very separate routes.

In the case of the *cholas,* the postwar period represented a new phase of organization that was strategically articulated through unprecedented references to themselves as Bolivians and through claims that as Bolivians they deserved the rights and privileges guaranteed to the upper classes. Nationalism, however, was claimed differently by the *cholas* than by upper-class women. These working-class women, many of whom were economically destitute, justified their demands on the basis of their sacrifice to the nation as widows, mothers, daughters, or sisters of men killed in the frontline trenches of the Chaco War. For example, in 1938 two thousand of the poorest vendors, all women, came together to call for the construction of more markets since the authorities were in the process of having them dislodged from the streets where they sold their products. The newspaper *La Calle* described the demonstration as "un parlamento proletario de la más extrema trascendencia" [a proletarian parliament of the greatest transcendence]:

> Las oradoras hablaron en Aymara, Quechua y Castellano, diciendo: "Qué somos nosotras, chinas o turcas? No somos bolivianas? Nuestros hijos y maridos no han reventado como sapos en el Chaco, que ahora nos quieren quitar el pan de la boca? Abajo los privilegiados pudientes! Queremos la Calle, necesitamos la conquista de la calle [. . .] es una vergüenza para la ciudad que se venden [sic] en las calles las pobres?" (La Calle, Aug. 10, 1938; cited in Polleras 1986: 12)

[The female orators spoke in Aymara, Quechua, and Spanish, saying: "What are we, Chinese or Turks? Aren't we Bolivians? Didn't our sons and husbands burst like toads in the Chaco War, and now they want to take the bread from our mouths? Down with the wealthy privileged! We want the Street, we need to take over the street (. . .) is it so shameful for the city that poor women sell their wares in the streets?"]

Supported by other women's unions of the FOF and by men of the FOL, the vendors demanded access to public spaces such as the street and the marketplace on the basis of the rights they deserved as *Bolivians* (*Polleras* 1986: 12). The appeal to nationalism ultimately was successful for the *cholas* when city officials granted most of their demands.

For the women of the privileged classes as well, the years immediately following the Chaco War would constitute an important conjuncture in gender politics that enabled them to make claims based on their participatory role in the reconstruction of the nation. In 1935, during the early stages of the war, Laura Graciela de la Rosa Torres, president of the Liga Filial de Oruro [Affiliated League of Oruro], published her firsthand testimony of the conflict, *La Guerra del Chaco: Mi visita a las trincheras y zanjas del "Velo"*. Although the Liga Filial had been established several years before the war as a women's cultural organization interested in promoting social programs for the poor, during the conflict it was the first women's group to visit the front lines (de la Rosa Torres 1935: 3–4). Together with the women of Sucre's Red Cross, the members of the Liga Filial distributed blankets, sweaters, mail, cigarettes, coca, candy, and magazines to the soldiers. Upon their return, the women delivered long-awaited news and letters they had been given by the soldiers to their families. According to one official, the Liga Filial was meritorious because, in his words: "es que esa institución hubo señalado a sus hermanas de la República, el camino del Chaco" (de la Rosa Torres 1935: 5) [that institution showed their sisters of the Republic the road to the Chaco War].

The horrors of the Chaco War, witnessed firsthand by women like de la Rosa, inspired a pacifism which prompted a call to action for the woman of the upper classes: "Envuelta en el dolor de esta tragedia humana no conoció el desmayo moral y, alzando su alma fortalecida por la serenidad, comprendió que las dolencias no se curan con vulgares sollozos o lamentos: enfrenta su corazón en la acción de servicio que la llama como a madre en las míseras angustias y la precisa en la reconstrucción social" (Villanueva y Saavedra 1970: 21) [Consumed by the pain of this human tragedy, she did not experience flagging spirits and, raising her soul fortified by serenity, she understood that sorrow is not cured by com-

FIGURE I.2.

Market vendors. *Photograph courtesy of Taller de Historia Oral Andina.*

monplace tears or lamentations: her heart meets this challenge in the action of service that calls her like a mother from amidst the wretched
agonies, requiring her for social reconstruction]. These women organized because, as mothers, they were committed to the reconstruction of
the nation and to those efforts that would ward off future conflicts. Thus,
even as they continued to invoke motherhood they sought to open up

new spaces that would legitimate their presence and participation in the public arena.

One of the most important of these organizations was the national branch of the Legión Femenina de Educación Popular América, through which Bolivian women also entered international feminist debates. Bolivia's president of the league, Etelvina Villanueva y Saavedra, described the women's call to action in the first pages of her history of the organization, *Acción socialista de la mujer en Bolivia* (1970), as one grounded in their common interest as mothers:

> Al extinguirse la hoguera chaqueña, quedó una legión de juventud que buscaba ansiosa nuevos horizontes de paz, de rehabilitación en su integridad espiritual y material. Respondimos las madres a este llamado con una obra social y cultural modesta y sincera que idealizaba la defensa y capacitación civil y jurídica de la mujer, anhelando elevar su jerarquía ciudadana para dejar escuchar su voz y voto cuando la vida del hijo estuviese en peligro . . . (17).

> [When the fires of the Chaco War subsided, a legion of youth was left anxiously searching for new horizons of peace and for rehabilitation of their spiritual and material integrity. We mothers responded to this call with modest and sincere social and cultural works that idealized the defense of women as well as their civil and legal training, with the desire to raise the woman's citizen hierarchy so that she might make her voice and vote felt when the life of a son is endangered . . .]

Making frequent reference to their "natural" condition as mothers and their new duty as guardians of national peace, the women of the Legión articulated an unprecedented connection between politics and the domestic sphere. This linkage, in turn, gave them the authority to speak about politics and demand the right to vote. This strategy was especially important given the widespread devastation caused by the Chaco War; the women of the upper classes found it imperative to legitimize their connection as mothers to national and international peace efforts. As such, however, this discourse was still haunted by the specter of biological naturalism.

The women of the Legión justified this role, or social action, on the basis of their "natural" role as mothers, with the difference that now motherhood was extended beyond the realm of the home to embrace a new ideal of "social motherhood." Motherhood, both "natural" and "social," became a vehicle that enabled these women to gain more access to public spaces. Under this new rubric, the women developed programs that would provide assistance to the poor and needy, as well as a social defense of children and unwed mothers; other innovations included the establishment of a "Maid's Day" (Villanueva y Saavedra 1970: 24–27). Through these social assistance programs, women who normally were confined to the domestic realm began to organize outside the home, assuming public responsibility for the moral direction of the nation. Gloria Ardaya explains: "La Legión planteaba una sociedad ideal basada en la profundización de las tendencias de la coyuntura política. Rescataba la democracia como espacio eficaz para alcanzar la liberación femenina, entendida dentro de la liberación social" (Ardaya 1992: 27) [The Legión proposed an ideal society based upon the deepening of the trends of the political arena. It rescued democracy as an efficacious space for obtaining woman's liberation, comprehended within social liberation].

Nevertheless, this maternalist discourse in its double articulation as "natural" and "social" consolidated a notion of the feminine based on racist and classist values because it recreated existing social relations at the same time as it authorized the reproduction of dominant values and the hegemonic moral code within the family and society. For example, the conceptualization of the home as woman's natural realm established a kind of hierarchy headed by the father in whose absence governed the mother; after her came the children and, finally, the domestic help. As a kingdom [*reino*], the home was defined as a private, autonomous space, protected from external eyes. In a parallel fashion, the extension of natural motherhood to include social motherhood legitimized a social hierarchy headed by the upper-class woman who functioned as a symbolic mother; under her were the women of the working-class sectors, designated as "daughters" or "children" who needed moral guidance. This maternalist discourse structured the parameters of femininity within already established social hierarchies. The discursive representation of domestic workers, for example, as "girls" or "young children" manipulated familial and familiar vocabulary to fix them in a position of dependence and subordination, essentializing them as "minors"; as such, they did not merit the same rights and privileges as other citizens. Instead, they were depicted as being dependent on the protection of an upper-class *señora* (or symbolic mother).[14] As late as 1988, Ana María Condori, in her testimonial *Nayan Uñatatawi: Mi despertar*, described her own experience as a domestic worker, demonstrating an acute awareness of the ambivalent position she occupied in the households where she worked: "Yo me acuerdo que para mí era terrible que me digan 'hija.' Era como un insulto porque después igual estaban hablando mal de mí diciendo:

'Esta india . . .'" (Condori 1988: 112) [I remember that for me it was terrible when they called me "daughter." It was like an insult because afterwards they still spoke disparagingly of me, saying: "This Indian girl . . ."]. The *señora*'s use of the word "*hija*" created a fictitious kinship that occluded the operations of the economic and racial hierarchy and from which the domestic space was not exempt. As Condori's *testimonio* confirms, this simulated relationship, based on an inclusion that excluded, could be revoked at any time, thereby generating a paradox in the very foundations of this maternalist discourse (cf. Balibar 1991a).

The testimonies included in *Polleras libertarias* and *Agitadoras de buen gusto* insist on the destabilization of the public-private opposition when, throughout their pages, they continually problematize the equation of Woman and Home as structured by the dominant ideology of womanhood. For example, working-class *cholas* did not find the "separate but equal" affirmation of the upper-class women's organizations compelling because they had never been confined to the domestic sphere in the first place. Moreover, the struggle over the right to work was not relevant because *cholas* were already part of the labor force. In the same vein, the testimonies from *Polleras libertarias* demonstrate that the *cholas* displayed little interest in the struggle for women's suffrage. For them, "su reclamo de ciudadanía cubría aspectos más vitales y cotidianos que el puro derecho a acudir a las urnas cada cuatro años" (*Polleras* 1986: 24) [the claims of citizenship had more to do with the exigencies of daily life than the right to go to the polls every four years].

Even though the *cholas*, for the most part, paid negligible attention to the suffrage movement, the testimonials indicate that following the Chaco War they did claim the right to define themselves as Bolivians and, on the basis of this identity, they argued publicly for improved working conditions. As for their private lives, however, many *cholas* rejected institutions such as marriage, perceiving them to be yet another form of colonialism. Due to their material positioning, these women could not be conscripted by certain kinds of gendering and, as a result, they were not readily seduced by nationalist discourses.

In general *cholas* lived much more independently than women of the upper classes. Often they earned higher wages than their husbands or partners because there tended to be more work available for cooks and domestic workers. It was not uncommon for a woman to maintain economically her household. One woman commented proudly: "No, yo no conozco su plata del hombre, ni un centavo. Esa suerte he tenido" (cited in *Polleras* 1986: 25) [No, I have never seen the man's money, not even a cent. That luck I've had]. Division of labor by gender was less clear for the working class, because both women and men worked as bakers, shoemakers, tailors and/or seamstresses, hat makers, and in similar trades (X. Medinaceli 1989: 83). During and after the Chaco War women took on even more traditionally "masculine" jobs as a consequence of the high numbers of mestizo and indigenous men killed in the war. Many women from working-class sectors did not marry but practiced instead the Andean tradition of cohabitation with their partner. Doña Catalina Mendoza explains: "Nunca he tenido marido, no me gustaba, porque eso de atención al marido, ay, se necesita paciencia, por eso he sido enemiga de tener marido" (*Polleras* 1986: 28) [I never had a husband, I didn't like the idea, because this business of giving attention to the husband, oh, you have to be patient. That's why I have been an enemy of having a husband]. Doña Petronila Infantes tells how she only married in a civil ceremony, "por 'el qué dirán,' no por la Iglesia. Es que no estaba de acuerdo, porque se veía tanta cosa en la capilla, agarraban un plato y recogían fondos y esos fondos ¿a dónde iban?" (Wadsworth and Dibbits 1989: 19) [because of "what people might think," but not by the Church. It's just that I wasn't in agreement, because you always saw so many things in the chapel. They would take up a plate and collect offerings, and this money, where did it go?]. Thus, as Ximena Medinaceli has observed, the traditional indigenous practice of living with a companion but not marrying took on a new context: "Es ya una forma de rebeldía explícita contra la sociedad y contra el Estado" (X. Medinaceli 1989: 81; see also Lehm and Rivera Cusicanqui 1988: 176–178) [It's now an explicit form of rebellion against society and against the state]. In summary, if recourse to a new nationalism was deemed necessary by working-class women in order to achieve specific work-related reforms, this same discourse did not extend to their private lives, where the women rejected the practices that fundamentally structured the state, such as marriage, as these practices were perceived to be the source of many (state-sponsored) abuses.

By problematizing the "natural" link between Woman and Home, the histories narrated in the various working-class women's testimonials deconstruct the dominant symbolic representation of the mother as a sacred and ahistorical figure. On the basis of their collective experience as working-class mothers, the majority of the women of the FOF were well aware that they did not share in any of the benefits or privileges that the mother of the upper classes enjoyed. Rather, motherhood was another source of oppression. The burdensome conditions of domestic work together with the long hours of the work day meant that often children had to help their mother, usually for no economic compensation. The daughter of doña Petronila Infantes remembers, "Yo en la casa de don Guillermo

Estrada, iba acompañando a mi mamá. Veía a las wawas o me decían: 'planchámelo.' Bueno, planchaba. No ganaba pero almorzaba bien, comía bien y a veces: 'para tu cine,' me decían" (Wadsworth and Dibbits 1989: 38) [In Don Guillermo Estrada's house I always accompanied my mom. I looked after the babies or they told me: "Iron this for me." Ok, so I would do the ironing. I didn't earn anything but I had good meals; I ate well and even sometimes: "take this for the movies," they told me]. On the occasions that she participated in public demonstrations, doña Petronila Infantes explained that when she was arrested her young daughter would also be put in the cell with her (*Polleras* 1986: 9–10).

According to the oral histories, the woman with children had greater difficulties finding work because *señoras* did not want domestic employees and cooks bringing their children along with them (Wadsworth and Dibbits 1989: 138). As doña Petronila remembers, the women of the FOF entered the Chamber of Deputies insisting on the need for day care centers: "Nos hemos llenado ahí en las Cámaras y hemos pedido que se resuelva, hemos pedido Casas-cunas para que en todas las zonas podamos dejar a nuestros hijos mientras estemos trabajando" (138) [We filled up the chambers and we asked that it be resolved, we asked for day care in each zone so that we can leave our children while we work].

Just as the *cholas'* daily experiences belied the sacrosanctity of motherhood, so, too, did their working conditions impel the women to debate publicly on different fronts the heretofore private matters of the upper-class domestic sphere. In November of 1936, the Worker's Congress met, and two representatives from the women's union, doña Petronila Infantes and doña Rosa de Calderón, also attended. In contrast with the National Women's Convention of 1927, the Worker's Congress gave ample opportunity to the two female delegates to take the floor and address their demands. These included Sunday afternoons off, an eight-hour workday, and the recognition of culinary work as a profession (Wadsworth and Dibbits 1989: 101–102). In addition, they asked for the incorporation of "domestic workers" into the social legislation, as well as for the replacement of the word "domestic" by *"empleada de labores de casa"* [housework employee] or *"trabajadoras del hogar"* [homeworkers] (*Polleras* 1986: 9). Their self-definition as *"trabajadoras del hogar"* together with the insistence that culinary work be recognized as a profession constituted a first attempt at obtaining greater recognition and wages for the labor that these women carried out in the homes of other women. The reformulation of the job name defied the commonly held notion that work arrangements agreed upon in the domestic sphere were private. The new emphasis on the rights of women workers served as an initial step in the efforts to open the private, domestic sphere of the upper classes to public debate.

All the workers present approved the women's demands. Nevertheless, one cook, doña Exaltación, remembers that the eight-hour workday was never respected by the *señoras:* "¡Huy!, pero las señoras que viven de la empleada decían: 'ay, ¿cómo eso van a hacer?, ¡ay hijas! ¡no, esas cosas no deben hacer!' Han correteado y no han dejado eso, las ocho horas de trabajo. No han dejado" (Wadsworth and Dibbits 1989: 105) [Oh! but those married ladies who live off the domestic worker would say: "oh, how can you do that? Oh, daughters![15] No, you shouldn't be doing those things!" They ran around and didn't permit an eight-hour workday. They did not permit that].

The organization of urban *cholas* into unions emphasized the collective nature of their struggle to achieve work-related reforms. In this context, the deliberate decision to continue using the *pollera* became an important signifier that linked these women not only to labor reform but also to their indigenous identity. The very title *"polleras libertarias"* manifests the use of the *pollera* by women within the anarchist movement as a symbol of what the Taller de Historia Oral Andina (THOA) identifies as "an ongoing activity of reproducing their own cultural values" [una constante actividad de reproducción de los valores culturales propios]. The majority of women who wore the *pollera* and the shawl were clearly very conscious of the meanings reproduced in the style and traditional weave of their clothing (THOA 1986: 42). Therefore, the seizing of such an image as the *pollera* required a rethinking of the body that attempted to remove it from the realm of the natural to reclaim it in specific historical and material contexts. The idea of the *pollera* as a symbol of resistance or refusal to wholly embrace western culture is further evidenced in the tenacity of *cholas* who continued to wear it in spite of tremendous pressures from their employers to exchange the *pollera* for a dress. As I will show in greater detail in Chapter 4, such symbols, when donned, were not taken up easily but instead were painful and had to be continually interrogated.

Indeed, it is important to call attention to the fact that not all urban indigenous women saw the *pollera* as a symbol of resistance. The testimony of doña Petronila illustrates one example where the *pollera* constituted an ambivalent symbol of identity that foregrounded conflicts and divisions within urban working-class sectors and racially mixed communities located on the outskirts of the city.[16] Doña Petronila tells how she decided to wear the *pollera* when she learned that her husband had been

killed in the Chaco War. Finding herself without any means of supporting herself or her children, she put on the *pollera* to go in search of work:

> Yo era de vestido siempre, así que la pollera me daba vueltas a un lado y a
> otro porque no sé si me sabía sujetar bien. No sabía caminar con la pollera,
> en vez de pisar adelante pisaba atrás. El sombrero también a un lado, al otro
> lado. Me cargaba la wawa aquí arriba y de repente se me salía. Después,
> tampoco me ha sido posible vender porque yo no sabía dónde se compraba
> las verduras, la fruta; ni cómo se agarraba el balay, la canasta y, a la vez,
> cargar a la wawa. (Wadsworth and Dibbits 1989: 21)

> [I had always worn a dress, so the *pollera* kept turning around on me from
> one side to the other because I don't know if I knew how to fasten it right.
> I didn't know how to walk with the *pollera*, instead of stepping forward
> I stepped backward. The hat, too, [moved] from one side to the other
> side. I carried the baby here, up high, and suddenly it would start to come
> out. Later, it was also impossible for me to sell because I didn't know where
> to buy vegetables or fruit; nor how to hold on to the baskets and, at the
> same time, carry the load of the baby.]

Because of her inability to adapt at the beginning, doña Petronila decided
to return home to stay with her family: "Resulta que cuando he ido
donde mis familiares, me han mirado de pie a cabeza, un desaire único
porque me he puesto pollera, porque ya parecía del campo: '¡ay!, nos vas
a poner en bajeza, ¡cómo pues!' Nunca más he ido. Sola he vivido en La
Paz" (Wadsworth and Dibbits 1989: 21) [It turns out that when I went
back to my family, they looked me up and down. They totally rebuffed
me because I had put on a *pollera*, because now I looked like I was from
the countryside: "oh, you're going to make us look bad, how can you do
this!" I never returned there. I lived alone in La Paz]. Within some contexts, then, the deliberate use of the *pollera* triggered a crisis of meaning
in which *cholas* consciously and often painfully constructed their identity.
The *pollera* thus exposed the raw edges of conformity and resistance
within the indigenous communities as well as outside them.

As a result of the newly unionized organizations of working-class
women throughout the 1930s and their participation in the many Workers' Congresses, most notably in 1936, the women formulated a
specifically urban political and cultural identity that was an outgrowth of
their collective experience as indigenous women or *cholas*, an identity
that would flourish until 1952. Doña Petronila explains, "Nosotros en el

FIGURE 1.3.

Assembly at Tiahuanacu. *Photograph courtesy of Taller de Historia Oral Andina.*

sindicato aportábamos, hacíamos veladas, matinées para recolectar fondos. . . . Eso quiere decir ser libres, tener control sobre la manera de vivir, tener esa libertad en la voz. Nos organizamos todas en virtud de que nadie nos dirija ni nos maneje. Por eso hemos organizado muchos sindicatos bajo el sindicalismo libertario" (Lehm and Rivera Cusicanqui 1988: 163) [All of us in the union contributed, we had afternoon and evening gatherings in order to raise money. That's what it means to be free, to have control over your way of life, to have that freedom in your voice. We women organized so that no one else could lead us or control us. For this reason we have organized many unions under the Libertarian labor organization]. As a crucial symbol of the unionized *chola*, then, the *pollera* defied the dominant sectors' nationalist projects of political legitimization that were reproduced within the structuring ideology of femininity. The *pollera* put into crisis the representation of a static, ahistorical Mother in favor of a symbol that represented the many struggles these women lived daily as oppressed, indigenous workers.

〜

TWO

MOTHERING THE NATION
Antonio Díaz Villamil's La niña de sus ojos

〜

$\mathbf{I}$f representations of motherhood fundamentally shaped both hegemonic and resistant discourses during the first thirty years of the twentieth century, the maternal body continued to hold symbolic currency for diverse groups during the decade immediately preceding the 1952 Revolution.[1] Throughout the 1940s, an emergent group of counterelites, identified by some scholars as an incipient bourgeoisie, actively promoted a discourse of *mestizaje* in order to abolish racially and economically the split between what many saw as two nations, one white, one Indian, and to advocate instead a third, mestizo nation. This chapter examines the paradigmatic novel *La niña de sus ojos,* by Antonio Díaz Villamil, to argue that *mestizaje,* with its emphasis on white, western values, rather than eradicating the polarization between the "two" nations, in fact reinscribed it. The ideological correlation between racial integration and economic integration was crucial, however, because it created an aperture for the counterelites that enabled them to break up the monopoly which the oligarchy had long maintained on economic and political structures and thereby claim a share in the power base.

Returning for a moment to the reference point of the 1993 presidential elections with which the book opened, I would like to draw attention once again to the undivided support for sweeping political and economic reform that the Sánchez de Lozada–Cárdenas slate supposedly represented. In his analysis of the MNR-MRTKL binomial, political theorist Fernando Mayorga emphasizes how the coalition's roots hark back to the unifying discourse of the Revolution of 1952, "*nacionalismo revolucionario*" [Revolutionary Nationalism]: "En suma, vivimos la vigencia de la *letra* del *nacionalismo revolucionario,* cuyos nuevos ejes (democracia representativa y modelo neoliberal) permiten articular los antiguos dos polos del modelo nacionalista-revolucionario (derecha e izquierda) en su versión post-nacionalista: lo *étnico* y lo *liberal,* que remplazan a *revolución* y *nación* . . ." (Mayorga 1993: 223; emphasis in the original) [In short, we are adhering to the extant letter of revolutionary nationalism, whose new axes (representative democracy and the neoliberal model) permit the joining together of the two old poles of the revolutionary-nationalist model (the left and the right) in their postnationalist version: ethnicity and liberalism which replace revolution and nation . . .]. Thus, what 1993 shares with 1952, evidenced in part by an analogous deployment of enabling words and phrases like "(inter)national integration," "pluralism" or "populism," and "modernization," is an expansion of hegemonic structures on the one hand, and a neutralization of alternate discourses on the other. In the case of 1952, Luis Antezana explains:

> Ideológicamente, el NR [nacionalismo revolucionario] habría logrado integrar los esfuerzos populares en la creciente constitución de una "burguesía nacional." En rigor, más que la ideología de la "burguesía nacional"—clase en busca de su conformación—, el NR es, más bien, un mecanismo ideológico que expande la hegemonía de los grupos dominantes al amplio espectro de la formación social boliviana, logrando desviar y/o anular los esfuerzos populares en beneficio de una "revolución burguesa" (anacrónica, dependiente, intermediaria), desarticulando permanentemente las condiciones ideológicas que podrían llevar hacia una posible "revolución proletaria." (Antezana 1987: 63)

> [Ideologically, Revolutionary Nationalism would have been able to achieve the integration of popular forces into the growing constitution of a "national bourgeoisie." Strictly speaking, more than an ideology of the "national bourgeoisie"—a class in search of its formation—Revolutionary Nationalism is an ideological mechanism that expands the hegemony of the dominant groups into the wide spectrum of the Bolivian social formation, succeeding in diverting and/or annulling popular efforts to the advantage of a "bourgeois revolution" (anachronistic, dependent, intermediary), permanently breaking up the ideological conditions that might lead to a possible "proletarian revolution."]

If "national integration" could not have been represented in 1952 Bolivia by the symbolic union of a white president and an Aymara vice president, it could be expressed more generally through the correlation of *mestizaje* with modernization. Indeed, throughout the 1940s this "narrative of progress" was constructed in political tracts, educational textbooks, and novels. A salient example of one such novel that has also been a basic component of Bolivian secondary school literature classes since its publication in 1948 is Antonio Díaz Villamil's *La niña de sus ojos*.[2]

According to critic Augusto Guzmán, *La niña de sus ojos* was the first novel in Bolivia to have as protagonist a mestiza, or in his words, "La 'Birlocha,' que así se llama a la señorita del pueblo, hija del matrimonio cholo que, por su belleza o por su educación, o por ambas cosas a la vez, pugna subir en la escala social, tropezando tanto con los prejuicios jactanciosos de los de arriba, como en el resentimiento de los de abajo" (Guzmán 1982: 191) [The *"Birlocha,"* the name given to the young lady of the common people, the daughter of a *cholo* marriage who, due to her beauty or her education, or to both at the same time, struggles to climb the social ladder, stumbling into the boastful prejudices of those up above, as well as the resentment held by those from below]. Although the novel introduces an unprecedented mestiza protagonist, to date critics have done little with the work except to praise its "realistic" depiction of Bolivian society.[3] This chapter argues that *La niña de sus ojos* constructs a discursive regime that confers legitimacy on the counterelites' efforts to seize political and economic power from the oligarchy on the one hand and to dominate indigenous peoples on the other.

As part of this counterelite discursive strategy, *La niña de sus ojos* negotiates such disparate spaces as the native and the foreign, the urban (white/mestizo) and the rural (Indian), through the mediating figure of a mestiza protagonist who functions as spokeswoman for those who want to integrate the Indian into the "new" nation as consumer and producer of modern goods and essentials (see Salmón 1986: 141).[4] The novel endorses the thesis that indigenous peoples can be modernized and peacefully integrated into the nation "bajo la ideología de 'civilización' que se llevará a cabo, según el manual de educación, por las escuelas rurales" (Salmón 1986: 141) [under the ideology of "civilization" which will be carried out, according to the education manual, by the rural schools]. Throughout the 1940s, counterelite intellectuals argued that once education's civilizing discourse had spread through the countryside, economic integration would gradually lead to racial integration in the form of *mestizaje*, a *mestizaje* neither tainted by the immoral and dehumanized behavior of the urban *cholo* nor by the deeply entrenched prejudice against the lower classes harbored by the white, upper-class, urban elite. However, as Josefa Salmón has pointed out, "el proyecto de homogeneización racial, a través de la educación, facilitaría el control político directo de las masas indígenas y disminuiría el control de los caciques campesinos" (43) [the project of racial homogenization, through education, would facilitate the direct political control of the Indian masses and diminish the control of the indigenous *caciques* or traditional leaders].[5]

This thesis promoting economic incorporation and national integration of indigenous peoples through education's "civilizing" curriculum had its origins in an earlier tract. Five years before the appearance of *La niña de sus ojos,* political essayist Carlos Montenegro published an influential work, *Nacionalismo y coloniaje* (1943), where he elaborated what later became designated as *"nacionalismo revolucionario,"* the unifying ideology of the political party Movimiento Nacionalista Revolucionario (MNR). This ideology joined all efforts of the left to dismantle the oligarchy's control over the land and mining industry into a single discourse: "nation versus anti-nation." Javier Sanjinés has aptly observed that the word "nation" functioned in this ideological discourse as an artificial accommodation between and among social classes that had never participated in any political decision making: "Hay, pues, en esta estructura significativa la búsqueda de la unidad nacional que abstrae los conflictos y las contradicciones de clase, subordinándolos a una armónica unidad que oscurece el sistema de dominación de las élites reformistas del MNR . . ." (Sanjinés 1992a: 58–59) [There is, in this significant structure, the search for national unity that sets aside class conflicts and contradictions, subordinating them to a harmonious unity that obscures the system of domination by the reformist elites of the MNR . . .].

Montenegro's discourse, "nation–anti-nation," provides the ideological ground for Díaz Villamil's narrative. At the same time, however, Montenegro's thought is inextricably linked to a second distinction between motherhood as nation and motherhood as anti-nation. To date, the critical nexus between motherhood and the construction of the modern nation in Bolivia has not been analyzed. The ideological emphasis on *mestizaje* that was gaining prominence among intellectuals of the incipient bourgeoisie demanded that there be a shift in upper-class male sexual choice from upper-class white women to educated mestizas. Thus *La niña de sus ojos* blazes the trail leading from the anti-nation (upper class oligarchy) to the nation (an educated, westernized *mestizaje*) by using the ambivalent figure of the mother who personifies both one thing and its opposite.[6] The compliant, desirable mother who symbolizes the "sexual order of patrilineage" (Levy 1991: 68) is no longer a criolla but a mestiza who has been educated and therefore completely acculturated to white western values, while the mother who represents sexual disorder and the fragmentation of the social body is all other women, Indian, white, upper class, foreign, and the urban *chola*. I suggest in this chapter that the privileging of a paradigm of motherhood that drew extensively from upper-class ideologies of womanhood and femininity was central to the reproduction of counterelite dominance within this "homogeneous" nation. Consequently, in the novel narrative desire converges on the fetishized, hence eroticized, figure of the acculturated mestiza who, ultimately, reproduces white, western values through the educational curriculum she brings to the rural indigenous school.

This convergence of desire necessarily depends upon a process of cultural and racial dismemberment whereby the mestiza mother metaphorically replaces all other mothers. In this way she literally embodies an "imagined" nation that is fully westernized and integrated, both racially and culturally as well as economically. At the same time, however, the "homogeneity" of the nation that is metaphorically represented by the mestiza mother is continually problematized when difference and separation resurface and reinscribe themselves. For example, throughout the 1940s, the project of national integration appeared to be threatened by what was perceived as increasing organization of and aggression from indigenous peoples. One event in particular alarmed criollo intellectuals. When the indigenous leader Francisco Chipana Ramos (*El Rumisonqo*) was photographed next to President Villarroel in 1946, hearsay alleged that Ramos had proclaimed himself president of the Indians, leaving Villarroel president of the whites. Soon after, the newspaper *El Diario* angrily denounced all rumors that suggested there might be two nations, one indigenous, one white. The MNR was of the same mind as *El Diario* and publicly reflected on the urgency of "la 'integración del indio a la Nación,' único modo de pacificar los espíritus y evitar una 'lucha de razas'" (cited in Rivera Cusicanqui 1984: 67) [the "integration of the Indian into the Nation," the only means of pacifying spirits and avoiding a "race war"]. Within this context the figure of the indigenous mother particularly threatens the modern nation imagined by the counterelites because historically she has represented and reproduced an Other Symbolic Order that resists domination and colonization.[7] Consequently, on the basis of this structural ambivalence emerging from a re-presentation of the mestiza/indigenous mother that alternates between desire and fear, reformist-elite dominance is marshalled and made legitimate. The overwhelming critical response to the novel, praising its realistic depiction of Bolivian society, is an instance of what Homi Bhabha calls the "regime

FIGURE 2.1.

Nosotros. *Original drawing by Eusebio Víctor Choque Quispe.*

of truth" (1983: 23), which has served nascent bourgeoisies everywhere to confirm their mission of power.

In this manner, the novel mediates racial and social inequalities through its deployment of the mestiza heroine, Domy Perales. The first half of *La niña de sus ojos* systematically develops a redefinition of what makes a woman desirable. This new definition of desire and its accompanying set of moral norms celebrates the virtues and beauty of the educated mestiza over the aristocratic *criolla* or European-born woman as well as over the working-class *chola*.[8] The importance of education cannot be overestimated as the narrative of femininity generated in *La niña de sus ojos* is one shaped by the educational curriculum and cannot exist independently of it. Education's ability to civilize and consequently acculturate an individual is incarnated in Díaz Villamil's Domy Perales. Twelve years spent at an exclusive boarding school metamorphose Domy from "*hija de recovera*" [market woman's daughter] into "*señorita.*" The success of this transformation can be measured against the racialized and class-based ideology of womanhood that was an integral part of the school curriculum.

THE HEGEMONIC ECONOMY OF DESIRE

Even before the turn of the century, Bolivian educators called for a curriculum that would prepare women to take up their proper sphere of influence in society. For the upper-class woman, this meant the home. Within the confines of the home, woman was to reign supreme as mother of the nation's future citizens, a gentle teacher who modeled a loving "curriculum" founded on the Christian tradition. Consequently, the education of upper-class women readied them for their proper role in life as "no sólo el ornamento social que triunfa por su belleza femenina adornada de todas las culturas, sino la esposa-modelo, la madre-maestra, la patriota que en todo momento haga holocausto de sus fuerzas y de su vida misma ante los destinos de la Patria" (Ichaso Vásquez 1927: 61) [not only the social ornament who succeeds because of her feminine beauty adorned by culture, but also the model-wife, the mother-teacher, the patriot who at all times makes a sacrifice of her strength and even of her very life in accordance with the Homeland's destiny]. Woman's natural role as the moral caretaker of the country, the priestess of the home, the bearer and guide of future citizens was thus consecrated.

La niña de sus ojos reproduces the same ideology of womanhood and its underlying notion that the "true" woman is a wife and mother. Moreover, it deliberately affirms an exclusionary "measure of womanhood" to shift desirability away from the criolla of the oligarchy, who can command both wealth and a prominent family name, by casting her as a mere "social ornament" notable for being frivolous and morally bankrupt, hence "less than" female. The superficiality of the upper-class woman is personified in Hercilia, one of Domy Perales's classmates:

era muchacha elegante y bonita, pero tonta y orgullosa, imbuída de prejuicios y pretensiones sociales y muy pagada de su persona y de su fortuna; indiferente y desdeñosa para el estudio, pero, eso sí, consagrada exclusivamente a dar el campanazo con sus trajes de última moda y de demasiado precio para una simple colegiala. (Díaz Villamil 1956: 27)

[she was an elegant and pretty girl, but also foolish and arrogant, imbued by social prejudices and pretensions and very pleased with herself and her luck; indifferent toward and disdainful of her studies, but, of course, devoted exclusively to causing a sensation with her dresses of the latest fashion and of too high a price for a mere schoolgirl.]

This description of Hercilia deflects the reader's gaze away from her body and toward her character. Her frivolous nature and love for material objects can be traced directly back to an indifference and disdain for her studies. In contrast, by focusing on Domy Perales, the narrative locates erotic desire in a physical beauty that is heightened by psychological depth of character, moral virtue, and racial difference. Her excellent academic career further affirms the shift of desire from woman-as-ornament to a femininity in which the maternal and the teacher are conjoined to foreshadow her subject position as the "mother/teacher" in the rural indigenous school.

The novel introduces Domy as she is about to take her final oral examination before graduation. The excitement she feels as she is called in to the examination heightens her beauty. Just as the exam will confirm her position at the top of the class, her physical beauty validates her femininity and individuates her from the other students, all of whom are from aristocratic backgrounds. The reciprocal relationship between education and femininity is made clear when the reader's eyes are first directed to the curvaceous shape of her body that is apparent in spite of, or because of, the severe cut of the school uniform. The imaging of Domy's body within the narrative is neither static nor neutral; instead, it engages and positions the reader with respect to it. For instance, the reader's gaze is next guided to Domy's breasts, "las deliciosas prominencias de los senos turgentes" (18) [the delicious protuberances of her turgid breasts], which, like fruit, "incitan a la gula" [incite one to gluttony]. Drawing from Kaja Silverman, I read Domy's femininity as being constructed upon a body that has been carefully organized and "made to bear meaning, a meaning which proceeds entirely from external relationships, but which is always subsequently apprehended as an internal condition or essence."[9] Indeed, the narrator concludes the description of Domy precisely by drawing attention to her feminine essence or alluring "*no sé qué*": "En todo su conjunto esa figura de encantadora mujercita, en medio de toda su aristocrática distinción, guarda en el fondo algo de excepcional particularidad, de raíz nativa, de secreto racial, que es lo que le confiere mayor atractivo por cierto sello incógnito e indefinible" (19) [As a whole, that enchanting young woman's form, in the midst of all its aristocratic distinction, protects deep down at heart something of an exceptional particularity, of native roots, of a racial secret, which is what confers upon it an even greater charm because of a certain undefinable and unknowable sign]. By equating femininity and sexuality with the mestiza body, the novel evokes the question of race to underscore irrevocably Domy's difference from her classmates. At the same time, by constructing racial difference as an undefinable *"no sé qué,"* a "racial secret," the novel suggests that Domy heralds a future perfect citizen of a country where the indigenous peoples have been literally reduced to nothing more than a "nostalgia."[10] Domy's innocence and virtue protect her from self-knowledge; consequently, she is unaware of the fact that her body is offered to the reader as a promise or guarantee of political and economic reform. Thus the narrative represents desire as if it were innocent and subjective as well as unaffected by the workings of political history.[11]

The inscription of desire on Domy's body draws the reader in to gaze at her with pleasure and to linger especially on the "delicious protuberances" of her eroticized breasts. The adjective "delicious" and the accompanying simile that compares them to fruit links them to consumption, and so they invite the reader to partake of them to the point of gluttony. By means of the adjective and simile, Domy's youthful, eroticized breast is linked to the maternal breast where the infant eats to the point of satiety. This conflation of eroticism and the maternal inscribes desire within a patriarchal, capitalist economy. First, Domy's eroticized breast marks her as an appropriate woman for male sexual choice. This choice is absolutely necessary for the success of the reformist project of *mestizaje.* Secondly, as this chapter will later demonstrate, the maternal breast of the westernized mestiza becomes a symbol of modernity articulated as economic incorporation and racial integration of indigenous peoples (through educational reform and miscegenation) into a national monetary economy as consumers and producers.

In *La niña de sus ojos,* the representation of woman relies on the continuous reinforcement of hierarchies of race and class. Not surprisingly, then, the reader can only be seduced into the vision of femininity elaborated in the narrative once Domy's physical beauty and moral character are proven superior to those of her mother. Because of this the novel next targets the urban *chola* and working class with even greater censure than it does the upper-class elite in order to highlight education's ability to forge the new mestiza, who has emerged from the "worst possible" circumstances. The novel asks us to link poverty and inadequate living conditions to the immoral behavior of urban *cholos* and their tradition of "wasteful" spending on the fiesta, rather than to an unjust economic system and racist society. Therefore, Domy Perales only "becomes" a woman once she has turned away from her cultural and racial heritage. Her successful cultural transformation from *chola* to mestiza is due to the fact that she lived away from home in an elite boarding school for twelve years. Domy characterizes her life at school as a "a path of roses," where she lived surrounded by affectionate teachers (Díaz Villamil 1956: 22).

In contrast, she remembers her real home as a hovel on the outskirts of town. The dark and squalid rooms were always filled with the noise from the patio "donde a diario se alojaban caravanas de indígenas y de asnos que traían para el negocio de su madre los cargamentos de fruta" (21) [where caravans of Indians and donkeys bringing the loads of fruit for her mother's trade were lodged each day].

Just as Domy's beauty reflects her refined moral character, her mother, Doña Saturnina, is bestialized in direct proportion to the degree in which she strays from the complex of values that make up the ideology of womanhood. Physically and morally she is "less than" woman. In particular, she deviates from the "normal" family model that privileges woman as "mother-teacher" the moment she absents the home to enter the public workforce. While still the object of the reader's gaze, the female body of the *chola* is not constructed as the multiple site of male pleasure. She is more monster than woman, starting with the way in which her seated position on the ground symbolically mutilates her:

> Esta manera de sentarse daba la impresión de que Doña Saturnina y todas sus "camaradas" del mercado eran personas mutiladas de las extremidades inferiores y cuyos cuerpos sólo emergían de cintura para arriba de una inmensa col que les sirviera de curioso pedestal. En cambio, parecía que toda la vitalidad motriz de las fruteras se hubiera concentrado en las manos. Pues era de admirar su destreza para manejar las frutas, tomando hasta cinco naranjas en cada mano y, luego, con un movimiento lleno de donaire, lanzarlas desde su elevado sitio, con impulso certero, hasta la canasta o bolsa del comprador. (10)

> [This way of sitting gave the impression that Doña Saturnina and all of her market "colleagues" were mutilated people missing their lower extremities, and whose bodies only emerged above the waist out of an immense cabbage which served them as a curious pedestal. In contrast, it seemed like all the driving vitality of the fruit sellers was concentrated in their hands. Their skill at handling the fruit had to be admired, taking up to five oranges in each hand and, then, with a movement filled with elegance, throwing them from their elevated location with accurate aim, into the buyer's basket or bag.]

Unlike her daughter, Saturnina is "cut off" at the waist, without sexual organs. Instead, the lower half of her body is reduced to a vegetable by her *pollera*. In this instance one signifier of her culture and race, the skirt, is not a "racial secret" that allures; instead, it dehumanizes her and transforms her into a freak, half vegetable, half woman. Her hands, those of a working woman, take on a life of their own to constitute her source of energy and further desexualize her. Just as Domy's petite features mark her socially and racially, so too does her mother's body similarly position her. For example, Domy's hands are petite, dimpled, and immaculately cared for; she would never be able to juggle five oranges in each hand like her mother (10). Numerous references to Domy's hands emphasize their whiteness. In contrast, her mother's hands are enough to make a caballero recoil from their enormous, hence "deformed" size.[12]

Through her work the mother is further constructed racially and sexually. Although she is portrayed as an astute businesswoman who is extremely successful in what she does, her success is attributed to an underlying eroticism that frames a potential sale. Thus her overture to the wealthy, foreign client is replete with sexual overtones: "saca a relucir sus más exquisitas atenciones, sonríe con sonrisa de sirena; toma una palta, le hunde la uña, levanta un trozo de la corteza y se la ofrece coquetamente, diciendo:—¡Ay, caballero! Bien ricas siempre están mis paltas" (11) [she displays the most pleasing and courteous attention, smiling like a siren. Picking up an avocado, she sinks her fingernail into it and lifts up a piece of the rind to offer it to him flirtatiously, saying:—oh, gentleman! My avocados are very delicious]. Doña Saturnina's sirenlike sexuality deliberately beguiles the client much as if he were a potential john. If her coy sales pitch, "bien ricas siempre están mis paltas" [my avocados are very delicious] similarly associates her breasts with fruit, this time the reference to their fruitlike form links them not to the maternal but to prostitution because of the transactional context in which they are invoked. Ultimately, there is no metonymic link between her breasts and motherhood. The portrait of the *chola* as first desexualized, almost monstrous, and later the embodiment of sexual titillation suggests the "spectrum of representation" to which she is subject (see Carby 1987: 21–22). If the "physical mutilation" she undergoes as a consequence of her work marks her as "less than" woman, the sexuality she exudes during a business transaction characterizes her as morally suspect at the same time as it maligns her competence as an astute businesswoman.

If the *chola* is more aligned with sensuality than with the maternal, the foreign mother is similarly dismissed from the text on moral grounds. Liliana, the lovely French wife of Domy's true love, Joaquín, is the primary obstacle standing between Domy and happiness. Like Hercilia, Domy's aristocratic classmate, Liliana is exceedingly pretentious. Furthermore, because she is foreign, she is eternally an outsider.[13] Domy's friends are quick to remind each other that Bolivian women lack neither beauty nor civilization. Of important note, however, is that her friends judge both according to the measure of distance between themselves and racist stereotypes: "[Liliana] es bastante joven y bonita—corroboró Susy—. Pero, hija, de eso a que quiera pasar por reina y exagerar sus pretensiones. . . . ¡Aquí, donde tampoco nosotras andamos vestidas de plumas! ¡Ni tenemos caras de quitar el hipo!" (Díaz Villamil 1956: 161) [[Liliana] is indeed quite young and pretty, corroborated Susy. But, girl, she wants to be taken for a queen and flaunt her pretentions. . . . Here! where we don't walk around dressed in feathers either! Nor do we have faces that scare away the hiccups!].

Liliana's character flaws manifest themselves shortly after she becomes pregnant. Her most egregious shortcoming is that she lacks a fundamental element of motherhood—self-sacrifice. Instead, during her pregnancy Liliana is reduced to childish whims [*caprichos pueriles*], and if not satisfied, she becomes monstrous. The seemingly "childish whims" originating with the pregnancy involve Liliana's request to return to her home country to give birth. Joaquín reveals to Domy that Liliana's desire to leave Bolivia is evidence of a discontent that goes far beyond the expectation to give birth in familiar surroundings. Instead, her desire to abandon her husband's country is grounded in the irrational and borders on madness. Joaquín's explanation to Domy leaves little doubt about his wife's "maternal nature": "—[Liliana] siente repugnancia por nuestro país. Me lo ha dicho a gritos, con tremenda franqueza y con una cólera incontenible: '¡Preferiría ahogar a mi hijo en el vientre antes de que nazca en esta miserable tierra de indios!'" (187) [[Liliana] feels repugnance for our country. She has told me that at the top of her lungs, with dreadful frankness and with an uncontrollable rage: "I would rather kill my child in the womb than have it be born in this wretched land of Indians!"].

First of all, her cries, uncontrollable rage, and willingness to abort her baby undermine any credibility she might have and leave the reader more than convinced of her madness. Secondly, the narrative is bent on demonstrating that, because she is an outsider, Liliana cannot see beyond the idea of Bolivia as a primitive backwater to imagine the country's enormous potential that can easily be fulfilled once the proper road to civilization has been laid out. The situation does not improve after the birth of the baby, and Joaquín tells Domy of the incredible suffering he has undergone because of his wife's monstrous behavior toward the baby: "se había negado hasta a darle el seno materno" (251) [she had gone so far as to deny it the maternal breast]. The denial of the maternal breast, the last straw, heralds the disappearance of the foreign woman from the narrative and highlights once and for all the national, mestiza mother.

To withhold the maternal breast from the young baby is to fly in the face of the dominant ideology of womanhood and motherhood in Bolivia during the 1920s, 1930s, and 1940s. Indeed, self-sacrifice is an essential link in the chain of signifiers connecting motherhood and the nation. The mother who untiringly gives of herself to her children exemplifies the ideal citizen who gives of himself to the nation. As I noted in Chapter 1, if self-sacrifice establishes a parallel between motherhood and patriotic duty, it similarly links motherhood and instruction. Thus, educational manuals described the teacher's role with metaphors that resounded with maternal significance.

The conjunction of mother and teacher is exemplified in Domy Perales, who, upon her return home after graduation, tries to be a civilizing example for her parents, teaching those who should be teaching her. In spite of her best efforts, they are unable to "cross over" and follow their daughter's example. Before long their behavior betrays their inability to inhabit the refined spaces of their own home, such as the newly refurbished dining room, redone so that it would be a place suitable for a *señorita*. In spite of Domy's efforts to model proper civilized behavior, her parents will not sit in chairs at the table during a meal, preferring instead to squat. Nor will they use silverware. Her patience comes to an end when her parents let out loud belches "como la cosa más natural del mundo en las propias narices de su hija" (184) [like the most natural thing in the world, right in their daughter's face]. Domy runs from the room and up to her bedroom crying out: "Soportar esto está por encima de mis fuerzas y de mi naturaleza" (184) [It is beyond my strength and nature to bear this].

In summary, Domy's education has apparently triggered a mutation of her "*naturaleza*" or "phenotype," in Fanon's words (1967: 19), which suggests that she has acquired "a new race." [14] She is virtually unrecognizable as the daughter of her mother. Domy's body shape is not only different from that of her mother, but it is privileged *because* of that difference. She no longer carries the burden of race since it is only the Other who is ethnic, it is only the Other who has color (Fuss 1989: 75). Ironically, the certain racial "*no sé qué*" that the narrator both perceives and finds seductive in Domy (Díaz Villamil 1956: 19) can only be a result of the wedge that education has driven between Domy and her indigenous heritage. No longer threatening, this "mood of nostalgia makes racial domination appear innocent and pure" (Rosaldo 1989: 68) and, in the context of this novel, seductive.

According to the dominant ideology of womanhood constructed in the novel, Doña Saturnina is most responsible for her daughter's distress because from the beginning she forsook the home for the public market and thus never modeled proper gender behavior for her daughter. From the first pages of the novel, Doña Saturnina is revealed to be a "failed" mother.[15] If Doña Saturnina has already been erotically disinvested in the narrative, her alleged failure as a mother triggers a process of rupture and irrevocable separation between the daughter and the mother. By annihilating the mother-daughter recognition, the novel makes it increasingly difficult for Domy to use the word "mother" when talking to Saturnina because it is no longer appropriate:

> Pero, al sentirse a sí misma pronunciar la palabra "mamá," la encontró inadecuada, porque hubiera querido que a esa invocación tierna de su cariño correspondiera no una mirada y un gesto tan ingenuos y plebeyos como los de aquella chola que estaba a su vera, sino una dama distinguida, una matrona dulce e inteligente, apta para acogerla y comprenderla tal como correspondiera a las inmensas y exquisitas delicadezas de su corazón. (180–181)

> [But, when she heard herself say the word "mamá," she found it to be inadequate, because she would have liked for that tender invocation of her affection to correspond, not to the naive and unrefined look and expression like those of the *chola* who was at her side, but to a distinguished lady, a sweet and intelligent matron, able to welcome and understand her in the way consistent with the immense and exquisite refinements of her heart.]

Domy's dissociation from the working-class mother in favor of an imagined mother who is "refined" and "distinguished" marks her irrevocable entry into the Symbolic (the "civilized" or modern world), an entry that definitively separates her from her mother who is the Other, the *chola*.

Separation from the mother is traditionally represented in Freudian terms as a loss that initiates desire. The fetishist is one who substitutes the desired lost object with another, thereby engaging in a process of loss, substitution, and, finally, identification (Chow 1991: 26). Rey Chow's discussion of the fetish departs from Freud to consider a different reading of fetishism as the "process of a belated consciousness, a consciousness that comes into itself through memory substitution, and representation" (26). Moreover, she continues, "we see how the experience of 'dismemberment' (or 'castration') can be used to describe what we commonly refer to as 'Westernization' or 'modernization.' Typically, as the history of the non-West is divided into the classical/primitive and the 'modern' stages, modern non-Western subjects can be said to be constituted primarily through a sense of loss—the loss of an attributed 'ancient' history with which one 'identifies' but to which one can never return except in the form of fetishism" (26–27).

The fetishizing process is doubly complicated by the fact that, on the one hand, the subject identifies with the ethnic culture, and on the other hand, the person might at the same time have a "strong sense of complicity with the 'dismembering' processes that structure those imaginings in the first place" (Chow 1991: 27). Chow's insightful discussion of fetishism is germane to the story of femininity narrated in *La niña de sus ojos*. The loss of the working-class *chola* mother, a symbol of urban ethnic culture, initiates a process of substitution that ultimately propels Domy into the position of the fetishized mother in whom eroticism and identification are conjoined (Silverman 1988: 137, 149–150).

Doris Sommer has noted that Latin American foundational fictions legitimate the "nation-family through love." Furthermore, she writes, "this natural and familial grounding, along with its rhetoric of productive sexuality, provides a model for apparently non-violent national consolidation during periods of internecine conflict" (Sommer 1990: 76). In *La niña de sus ojos*, it is the fetishized conjunction of eroticism and identification that results from modernization or cultural and ethnic dismemberment that will enable the reformist ideal of the mestizo nation-family to become a reality. Consequently, at the same time that this conjunction fetishizes the mestiza mother, it represses all other mothers—the criolla, the *chola*, the indigenous. The representation of Domy as the idealized "mother-teacher" is crucial to the literal and symbolic reproduction of this process of fetishization because, as "mother-teacher," she heralds a future "perfect" nation racially and culturally.

The impact of Domy's fetishized role as "mother-teacher" hinges on her departure from the urban center, where she inhabits a liminal space suspended between two hostile worlds—"el de arriba, presuntuoso y perverso, y el de abajo, torpe, ignorante y repulsivo" (Díaz Villamil 1956: 212) [the one above, presumptuous and perverse, and the one below, clumsy, ignorant, and repulsive]. First of all, her literal and metaphorical journey away from the limitations of the city and toward the promise of the rural countryside marks the final stage of her personal growth and development as a woman. Although Domy has crossed both physical and cultural distances to reach the indigenous village of Collamarca, she has, in a sense, "come home" to a place that heralds "una nueva fe, más humana y fraternal, en que a cada uno, rico o pobre, le correspondiera un sitio y un beneficio, según la capacidad de hacer el bien con el talento, el músculo o la virtud del corazón" (215) [a new faith that is more human and fraternal, in which there corresponds a place and benefit for everyone, rich or poor, according to each person's ability to do good with their talent, strength, or the virtue of their heart]. This metaphorical homecoming is significant because according to the dominant ideology of womanhood, the home is woman's "natural kingdom," where she rules supreme. Thus, in the countryside, Domy "innocently" occupies her "natural" place. The characterization of the indigenous peoples completes this idealized picture because they are depicted as childlike, eagerly anticipating the long-awaited arrival of the "mother-teacher" who will put their house in order. Most importantly, then, Domy's homecoming endows her position with maternal significance. The innocent simplicity of this initial scene obscures the fact that the representation of Domy's arrival as a homecoming grants her certain rights and privileges that legitimize her authority over the indigenous people of Collamarca.

This authority empowers Domy with the ability to "understand" otherwise unfamiliar surroundings. For example, on her first evening in Collamarca, as she is readying herself for bed, she hears the faint strains of a flute:

> Al escuchar esa música elemental y primitiva se sintió apta para comprenderla. Ese instrumento, con su gama pentatónica le causaba una sutil añoranza por algo misterioso y desconocido que existía en su alma. Quizá era el mensaje de algún lejano abuelo aimara que desde lo remoto de los tiempos le enviaba al corazón de la pampa indígena a redimir a sus descendientes. Le pareció que su sangre mestiza golpeaba más fuertemente en el corazón, como si fuera un motor que estuviera probando su potencialidad para emprender un sostenido esfuerzo (220).

> [Upon hearing that elementary and primitive music she felt capable of understanding it. That instrument, with its pentatonic scale, gave her a subtle longing for something mysterious and unknown that existed in her soul. Perhaps it was the message from some distant Aymara grandfather who from the remote past sent her to the heart of the indigenous plain to redeem his descendants. It seemed to her that her mestiza blood pounded more strongly in her heart, as if it were a motor testing its potential to undertake a sustained effort.]

Domy interprets the "innocent nostalgia" evoked by the music to be a message that is comprehensible to her because the music reveals a kinship or blood bond between herself and the sender, an ancient Aymara grandfather. Even though the message is at once knowable and other, Domy understands that she has been sent to save her grandfather's descendants. This knowledge, which invests her with the responsibility to do what is "best" for the residents of Collamarca, legitimizes a nascent westernized authority in the indigenous community.

Domy's first task as the community "mother-teacher" is to put her own home in order. Within hours of her arrival Domy has accomplished the seemingly impossible. Thanks to "la gracia de una mano femenina" [the charm of her feminine hand], she easily transforms her primitive living quarters. Once she has put away her personal belongings and hung pictures on the wall, she has brought color to an otherwise gray place; her clothing and other belongings perfume the room, erasing "el olor a caverna" (219–220) [the cavelike odor]. This early transformation of squalid conditions into a homey space portends the kinds of changes Domy will bring to Collamarca.

Again drawing from Rey Chow's work, I propose that these metaphors linking domesticity and the maternal with the indigenous countryside suggest an important theoretical move whereby "'femininity' as a category . . . include[s] . . . fictional constructs that may not be 'women' but that occupy a passive position in regard to the controlling symbolic" (Chow 1991: 18). If entry into the Symbolic in *La niña de sus ojos* is necessarily marked by the rupture or dismemberment that results from the process of westernization or civilization, the Bolivian rural countryside is constructed as outside the Symbolic, a feminine space that is at an "eternal standstill" (Chow 1991: 9), outside history and civilization. Collamarca, the small indigenous village where Domy will reside, is frozen in an atemporal, prehistoric space where the houses smell like caves and clothing is hung on llama bones. The indigenous people inhabiting this pre-Symbolic, feminine space is correspondingly infantilized, metonymically represented by a raggle-taggle band of children who have never seen anyone like their new teacher: "empujados por la curiosidad, se aproximaron a contemplar con ojos azorados la, para ellos, exótica figura de la joven, pero al advertir que ésta avanzaba hacia ellos para hablarles y demostrarles su complacencia, retrocedieron amedrentados, hurgándose la nariz con los dedos o rascándose las polvorientas e hirsutas cabezas" (Díaz Villamil 1956: 218) [urged on by curiosity, the children moved closer to look with frightened eyes at the figure of the young lady who, for them, seemed very exotic; but once they realized that she was coming toward them to speak to them and show her pleasure, they retreated fearfully, picking their noses with their fingers or scratching their dusty and shaggy heads]. The infantilization of the Indians further sanctions Domy's newfound authority as the "mother-teacher" who oversees the child's (read: community's) development along the lines of acculturation and, ultimately, economic integration.

Within two months of her arrival, the schoolchildren are well on the road to progress as they flourish under Domy's guidance: "Los chiquillos, bajo la influencia casi maternal de aquella mujer alegre, graciosa y sagaz, habían dejado ganarse íntegramente para su obediencia y predilección" (223) [The kids, under the motherly influence of that happy, charming, and astute woman, had let themselves be totally won over, obeying and favoring her]. Like Domy's own parents, the parents of Collamarca do not understand the actual significance of Domy's work, but they can appreciate the changes she has made in their children, who no longer resemble the band of disheveled urchins that first greeted her. To cite one example, Domy instructs the children in table manners; at each meal, they correctly use their silverware and napkins and generally display "proper" behavior. The scene begs comparison between the schoolchildren and Domy's parents, who quite simply were incapable of learning by example. As the children become westernized, the gap between themselves and Domy lessens. Thus Domy's curriculum exemplifies what Paulo Freire would later term the banking concept of education, whereby the teacher deposits knowlege into the students as if they were empty, inert vessels waiting to be filled (Freire 1989: 58).

The narrative suggests that to the degree the children emulate westernized behavior, they proportionately leave racial and cultural differences behind. However, their advancement is couched in ambivalence. If, on the one hand, racial and cultural differences are increasingly masked as they progress toward the Symbolic, on the other hand difference is always already inscribed in their skin color. Thus Joaquín's young son articulates what Homi Bhabha calls the "'everyday' colonial scene" (Bhabha 1983: 28) when Pablito points to the indigenous children sitting at the same table with Domy, his father, and himself and questions why they eat together. Domy hastens to explain to him that they sit together because they are all equals. Not convinced, Pablito asks, "—Y, entonces, ¿por qué son de color tan oscuro y visten como nuestros sirvientes?" [Then, why are they so dark-skinned and why do they dress like our servants?]. She gently teaches Pablito that the other children dress the way they do and are a dark color because they work "en el campo, en medio del viento, del frío y del sol para mandarte a la ciudad lo que tú comes en tu mesa" (256) [in the countryside, in the midst of the wind, the cold, and the hot sun in order to send to you in the city what you eat at your table].

This "primal scene" whereby Pablito looks first at the indigenous children and back again at Domy to return to a point of identification is critical. He perceives racial difference between the indigenous children and himself both because of the way they dress and because of the color of their skin. Domy nonetheless disavows racial difference between Pablito and the other children at the moment she attributes their skin color to their work outdoors and constant exposure to the harsh elements. Said another way, the scene suggests that underneath the dark skin and native clothing there lies another, whiter body that anticipates liberation from its darkness. According to Bhabha, "In the act of disavowal and fixation the colonial subject is returned to the narcissism of the Imaginary and its identification of an ideal ego that is white and whole" (1983: 28). Within this dominant Imaginary where all difference is repressed, Domy metaphorically replaces the children's real mother because the indigenous mother has been unequivocally eradicated by this act of disavowal and fixation. This replacement is "natural" because, as Kaja Silverman's analysis of Freudian psychoanalysis has demonstrated, "distance from the mother is the precondition not only of subjectivity and language, but of desire itself" (Silverman 1988: 160). Therefore, the children can enter into the Symbolic, a westernized, Spanish-speaking world, only after they have been distanced from the indigenous mother.

Nevertheless, an uneasy ambivalence continues to resurface even at the moment of metaphorical replacement because, as Bhabha indicates, there is a "simultaneous play between metaphor as substitution (masking absence and difference) and metonymy (which contiguously registers the perceived lack)" (1983: 27). If Domy, as the teacher, displaces the indigenous mother, the latter nevertheless continuously figures within the narrative precisely because of her absence. The indigenous mother threatens the imagined nation of the counterelites because she unceasingly poses the problem of resistance and separation—the possibility of the "Other" nation heralded by indigenous resistance throughout the 1940s. Thus the indigenous mother suggests an alternative relationship with the controlling Symbolic, one analogous perhaps to that which Freud termed the negative Oedipus complex.

Silverman analyzes the negative Oedipus complex with insight to argue that it is not typically Oedipal in that "the girl's aspiration to occupy the place of the mother does not imply the latter's exclusion from her erotic economy, but the endless reversibility of their relative positions" (1988: 153). Thus for the female the negative Oedipus complex is the "conjunction of identification and eroticism" which Silverman perceives to be "the 'censored, repressed element of the feminine'" (151). Within this erotic economy the third term is no longer the father but the child whom the daughter "both wishes to give to the mother and to receive from her" (153). In the context of this study the erotic economy of the negative Oedipus complex that disavows separation and dismemberment suggests a very different paradigm whereby the indigenous mother and child are both recuperated *and* reproduced in their endless reversibility and mutual recognition. This model unequivocally problematizes the reformist ideological discourse "nation–anti-nation" precisely because it undermines the supposed homogeneity of purpose on which the term "nation" was ideologically constructed. Instead, this alternative model links indigenous identification back to activity and agency rather than to the passivity generally attributed to indigenous peoples by the dominant discourses and institutions (Rivera Cusicanqui 1984: 15–22). This agency has historically manifested itself as collective resistance to colonial domination and reconstitution of traditional indigenous values.[16] Consequently it is not surprising that during the 1940s and 1950s, the counterelites would unremittingly attempt to repress this Other erotic economy through the "peaceful" promotion of *mestizaje* and the elimination of all things indigenous, including the word "*indio*" from the national vocabulary.

A SUBALTERN ECONOMY OF DESIRE

Warisata, the most famous rural experimental school from the 1930s, offers one pertinent illustration of how the figure of the indigenous mother symbolized the conjunction of identification and eroticism within the history of indigenous resistance to criollo dominance. The year 1940 marked the end of a decade of experimentation with rural indigenous education in Bolivia. Founded in 1931 by the Aymara teacher Avelino Siñani, Warisata was internationally acclaimed for its pathbreaking methodology that privileged communal indigenous autonomy over dependence and servitude. This approach wholeheartedly rejected the dominant theory of education from the first two decades of the century that defended "domestication" of the Indian in order to "convertirlo en 'un servidor eficaz pero sumiso'" (Carlos Salazar Mostajo, cited in Martínez 1991: 26) [convert him into "an efficient but submissive servant"]. Instead, Warisata imparted traditional Andean ethical values, thereby reproducing and revalorizing communal indigenous identity and culture as well as traditional forms of governance (Claure 1989: 99–100). With its reproduction of indigenous institutions and values Warisata epitomized indigenous resistance to dominance and repression. According to writer and teacher Carlos Salazar Mostajo, Warisata was "la casa de los explotados, símbolo vivo de la lucha por la justicia y la libertad, emblema de todas las antiguas rebeldías del indio, jamás extinguidas" (Martínez 1991: 26) [the house of the exploited people, a living symbol of the struggle for justice and freedom, emblem of all the ongoing Indian rebellions that have never been extinguished].

In this context it is not surprising to learn that the name used to refer to the school was "Taika" [Mother]. Juan Luis Martínez draws from Salazar Mostajo when he observes how the word "Taika" brought together reproduction and resistance in the symbol of the indigenous mother: " . . . Taika, esto es 'madre,' seno fecundo y nutricio, encarnación de la Pachamama, amparo en la adversidad, impulsor de las luchas, en suma era el verdadero complejo vital que circunda al hombre, su relación social con su medio ecológico, con su lógica organizativa, con su espíritu libertario" (27) [. . . *Taika,* which means "mother," the nutritious and fertile breast, the incarnation of Pachamama, protection in adversity, instigator of struggles; in sum, she was the true vital complex that surrounds man, his social relation with the ecological environment, with its organizing logic and libertarian spirit]. In a similar vein Elizardo Pérez, Warisata's mestizo-criollo director, recognized how, "[m]ás allá de la simple alfabetización, el indio warisateño acabó por ver en la escuela que se levantaba, el símbolo redentor por excelencia, y de ahí el nombre de 'Taika' (madre) con que solían designarla" (Pérez 1962: 94) [in the end, the Indian from Warisata viewed the school that was being built as much more than a mere vehicle for literacy: it was a symbol of redemption par excellence, and from there came the name "Taika" (mother) that they frequently used to refer to it]. Thus the indigenous mother's fetishized breast, the "seno fecundo y nutricio" [the nutritious and fertile breast], symbolized the recuperation and reproduction of an Other nation, one separate and distinct from the nation imagined by the intellectuals of the criollo oligarchy.

Díaz Villamil was certainly familiar with both Warisata and Elizardo Pérez because in 1939 the two men traveled to Mexico to participate in the Congreso Indigenista, Pérez as a representative of Warisata, and Díaz Villamil as vice president of the Consejo Nacional de Educación (Pérez 1962: 338). At the time, Pérez explains, the Consejo Nacional de Educación was opposed to Warisata and the theory of education for which it stood, and so its representatives in Mexico blocked a move on the part of Doctor José Antonio Encinas to applaud Bolivia for its many projects on behalf of the Indian. Although Díaz Villamil was present at the time, Pérez reports: "No sé qué parte de responsabilidad le tocaría al señor Díaz Villamil en esta tenebrosa cuanto antipatriótica conjura; sus

FIGURE 2.2.

No nos dejen morir. *Original drawing by Eusebio Víctor Choque Quispe.*

intervenciones fueron, más bien, favorables a nuestra causa" (341) [I don't know what responsibility Mr. Díaz Villamil played in this dark and unpatriotic conspiracy; rather, his interventions were favorable to our cause]. Within two years of the trip to Mexico, Warisata and other similar schools had been closed due to alleged infiltration by "subversive elements" and to supposed mismanagement by administrators of the curriculum, schools, and teachers. In the effort to discourage future Warisatas, many of the indigenous teachers were jailed, murdered, or sent into exile (Claure 1989: 55–60; Choque Canqui 1986b: 62–63).

Questions surrounding Díaz Villamil's role in the Bolivian government's public dissociation from Warisata in Mexico appear to be answered with the publication of *La niña de sus ojos*. Domy's curriculum affixes progress to a westernized moral code of acculturation rather than to indigenous autonomy. Consequently, it is Collamarca's moral progress, symbolized by the banning of alcohol and the adoption of "civilized behavior," that leads to economic integration, symbolized by the communal purchase of a tractor. As time passes, Domy increasingly exercises more authority within the community to the point that she completely eclipses the indigenous leaders. Five years later, when Joaquín, now divorced from his French wife, finally shows up to take Domy away with him so they can be married and live happily ever after in the city, the indigenous community becomes distraught with grief and anger at the unexpected appearance of a "rival." Domy is torn between her love for Joaquín and her duty to the indigenous community. Her sense of maternal duty is foregrounded when the parents and leaders communicate their fear that without her guidance the community may very well lapse back into the primitive state in which she found it. Domy acknowledges that she cannot forsake the community for her own personal desires; therefore she asks Joaquín to remain with her in Collamarca where, together, they will work on "esta bella obra" (Díaz Villamil 1956: 270) [this noble deed].

Clearly, then, at the same time the narrative argues that the Indians can be "reformed," it drives home the precarious nature of this progress to claim that the guiding hand of the educated mestiza will always be a necessary presence to prevent the community from slipping back into the grip of primitivism. This ambivalence is at the heart of the colonial fantasy which, according to Bhabha, constructs a teleology whereby "under certain conditions of colonial domination and control the native is progressively reformable" (Bhabha 1983: 34–35). At the same time, however, this teleology "effectively displays the 'separation,' makes it more visible. It is the visibility of this separation which, in denying the colonised the capacities of self-government, independence, western modes of civility, lends authority to the official version and mission of colonial power" (35). As a consequence of this ambivalent positioning, the counterelite project of national consolidation reconfirms racial and cultural hierarchies within its imagined utopia at the same time as it supposedly eradicates them.

This ideological ambivalence emerges with an unexpected intensity in the final scene of the novel, where the promise of Domy and Joaquín's marriage becomes a promise of national consolidation. The narrative comes to a close as Domy and Joaquín, holding hands, walk off together in the direction of the school, surrounded by affectionate Indians. Joaquín's young son follows closely behind: "Detrás, Pablito, el niño rubio, rodeado cordialmente por los chiquillos y tomado de las manos por dos 'imillas,' siguió a su padre hacia su nuevo hogar de Collamarca" (Díaz Villamil 1956: 271) [Pablito, the little blond boy, cordially surrounded by the [Indian] kids and holding hands with two "*imillas*" (Indian girls), followed along behind his father toward his new Collamarca home]. Pablito, "the blond boy," is clearly differentiated from the two "*imillas*," both because he is named while they remain anonymous, locked in the Other through the use of the word "*imilla*" [Indian girl] and because he occupies the center of the circle of attention that maintains the indigenous children eternally at the margins. This scene would appear to herald the new mestizo nation. After all, Pablito, the little white boy, is holding hands with two Indian girls. In addition, however, Pablito's presence as a miniature white "Father" who comes between the two indigenous girls interrupts the erotic economy of the negative Oedipus complex to signal the return of the classic (positive) Oedipus complex. This interruption and return realigns the indigenous peoples with the dominant values of the hegemonic Symbolic Order and enables narrative closure to take place at the point of separation between races, a separation that continually reinscribes the necessity of criollo dominance.

∽

THREE

DISMEMBERED HOUSES

∽

Critical studies on the relationship between motherhood and the home in Bolivia, written by middle- and upper-class essayists, have changed little throughout the twentieth century. As I observed in previous chapters, these accounts confirm the notion of an essential feminine nature that is fixed and unchanging, one that is biologically determined by woman's reproductive activities.[1] According to this prevailing representation, the domestic space of the home constitutes the core of womanhood. Hegemonic depictions of the private, domestic realm emphasize a logic of interiority, a unified spatial order that is enclosed and timeless, where stasis, nostalgia, and security are troped in the figure of the criolla mother.[2] Thus, the essence of womanhood, and therefore also of motherhood, is inextricably linked to the socio-spatial arena that is the home.

In his study of Bolivian housing, *El problema social de la vivienda* (1949), Alberto Cornejo elaborates on the metaphorical relation between motherhood and the home, claiming that both can be linked to the notion of origin. Cornejo frames his argument by citing at length from the work of Ramón Clarés. Clarés, in turn, appears undoubtedly to have been influenced by Freud, who, in his essay on "The Uncanny," defines humankind's original home as the mother's womb (Freud 1955: 245). On motherhood, Clarés writes: "Madre es pues, síntesis viva de espacio y tiempo. . . . Más allá de la madre, el infante no siente la vida, porque madre es origen. . . . La madre es la mujer fundamental, simbólicamente llamada la casa, en el místico lenguaje de los libros sagrados" (Clarés, cited in Cornejo 1949: 6) [Mother is the living synthesis of space and time. . . . Beyond the mother, the infant does not feel life, because mother is origin. . . . The mother is the fundamental woman, symbolically called the "house" in the mystical language of the sacred books]. Premising his thesis on Clarés's ideas, Cornejo foregrounds the link between the foundational role of the house and motherhood in the development of humankind to contend that both influence the quality and condition of human character and of life itself (5–6).

Cornejo argues that legislators must address Bolivia's housing shortage, a shortage that already constitutes a problem in 1949 because of the increasing growth of urban populations and economic limitations that prevent many people from buying their own homes (Cornejo 1949: 5). According to Cornejo, the solution to the problem is, simply put, more affordable housing. However, he cautions, the houses should be constructed according to certain specifics that would enable the reorganization of urban society: "Los barrios donde el conventillo ofrece capacidad de vivienda para multitudes policromas, va siendo proscrita por las necesidades sociales. Porque, no sólo basta construir casas, sino que ellas deben responder a las necesidades y finalidades de la vivienda" (18) [The districts where low-income projects offer housing for the polychromatic multitudes, these projects are becoming outdated due to social necessity. It is not enough to build houses; rather, these should meet the needs and objectives of a home]. If mother equals origin equals home, Cornejo clearly advocates a House (Mother) through which the polychromatic poor can be eliminated, thereby establishing a decisive link between motherhood, the home, and the racial formation of the modern nation-state.

In recent years, critical work in architectural theory drawing from the practices of Derridean deconstruction, psychoanalytic theory, and gender studies has begun to interrogate the political, cultural, and spatial order of the house. For example, Mark Wigley (1992) analyzes the production of gender by examining the spatial, structural, and psychic operations of the house. This work, in turn, has carried over into a detailed reading of the ways in which western metaphysics constructs a "domestic regime" (Wigley 1993). This analysis can be productive for the understanding of hegemonic representations of modernity in Bolivia, which, I will suggest in this chapter, are organized according to an architectural logic that structures dominant understandings of race and gender relations. The equation of a particular kind of house with the formation of acculturated (mestizo) citizens suggests that, like clothing, architecture fashions the body politic.[3] Consequently, the house constitutes both the gateway to citizenship and the condition of its possibility, functioning literally and symbolically in a continuous trajectory of identity formation.

As an overdetermined cultural and political site, the house is central to both hegemonic discourses of domesticity and counterhegemonic indigenous practices that continually resist criollo efforts to delimit the boundaries of the familiar and the selfsame. This chapter will plot an itinerary of houses, a route making its way from Domy (Perales) to Domitila (Barrios de Chungara).[4] In Collamarca Domy Perales directs the construction of houses that privilege the scene of recognition and identification between indigenous peoples and western forms of political and cultural authority. In contrast, Domitila Barrios de Chungara's depiction of mining camp houses in her *testimonios,* essays, and interviews highlights misrecognition and the broken social contract between the miners' families and the state. She calls attention to the singularity of the miner's house as a space that has been designed specifically to keep workers in their place, domesticated.

Both Wigley and Anthony Vidler refer to the violence of the house that is structured through the very act of domestication; domestication, in other words, delimits the realm of the familiar at the same time as it represses the unfamiliar, the unhomely. The critical interrogation of the house from the point of view of its architecture and the implications this has for understanding social, political, and economic relations becomes a useful lens through which it is possible to read the racialized and gendered boundaries of modernity in the context of Bolivia. These current debates unequivocally indicate that hegemonic depictions of modernity in Bolivia are structured through a rhetoric of domestic space; the house functions as a spatial metaphor through which the "unruly play of representation" can be controlled precisely because it defines and differentiates the (modern or civilized) inside from the (uncivilized) outside (see Wigley 1993: 106–107).

The architectural rhetoric that is deployed insistently by criollo discourses through the anxious reiteration of boundaries suggests that this domestic regime constitutes both the condition and the very possibility of the hegemonic state itself. Dominant depictions of the house, emphasizing enclosure, the privatization of space, and individualization, become an important mechanism with which hegemonic discourses repeatedly attempt to order and discipline the racially heterogeneous social body throughout the second half of the twentieth century. So-called "normative" houses domesticate individual bodies and families by forcibly bringing them into the realm of the familiar; therefore, the physical layout of hegemonic houses structures processes of ethnic and racial acculturation at the same time as it organizes dominant constructions of gender. The door of the house serves as a threshold metaphor, one that marks the limit of the racialized space of the selfsame (see Silverman 1996). Moreover, because normative houses insistently delineate a series of boundaries be-

FIGURE 3.1.

Untitled. *Sculpture by Eusebio Víctor Choque Quispe. Photograph by Cheryl Kelly and Shannon Snyder.*

tween inside and outside, it soon becomes apparent that racially diverse groups position themselves and are positioned differently in relation to these same boundaries. Indeed, different or nonhegemonic houses suggest competing positions about boundaries.

The analysis in this chapter goes beyond current debates in architecture because it introduces the question of racial formation. Indeed, while recent architectural discourse has enriched the understanding of the operations of gender construction, to date it has remained largely silent on race. If, however, the House is "a metonym of the prototypical Mother," as critics Heidi J. Nast and Mabel O. Wilson maintain (1994: 49), this chapter suggests that the prototypical mother in Bolivia who inhabits the normative house is either white and from the upper class or an acculturated, westernized mestiza. Consequently, the state constitutes itself through specific constructions that not only produce traditional gender roles but also promote racial assimilation by privileging white, western norms. Nonhegemonic or resistant homes, therefore, have implications not only for gender roles but also for racial and political identities.

HOME-WOMAN-STATE: THE MODERN FORMATION OF THE SELFSAME

In their discussion of Minnie Bruce Pratt's work, Biddy Martin and Chandra Mohanty have suggested that a monolithic representation of home guarantees its own repeatability (or fixity) because it participates in and reproduces a series of "exclusions and repressions which support the seeming homogeneity, stability, and self-evidence of 'white identity,' which is derived from and dependent on the marginalization of differences within as well as 'without'" (Martin and Mohanty 1986: 193). This tension between representation and repression is what Homi Bhabha identifies as the paradox that is central to fixity, precisely because, as a sign of difference in the "ideological construction of otherness," it connotes both "an unchanging order" and "disorder" (Bhabha 1983: 18). The discussion in Chapter 1 foregrounded this same paradox: when urban working-class indigenous and *chola* women circulated freely outside the home, as in the instance of the militant Federación Obrera Femenina (FOF) of the 1930s and 1940s, their bodies threatened the social order because they were out of place (the home) and in the streets. According to the criollo oligarchy then, these disorderly, hence polluted and polluting, racialized, female bodies were identified with (political) instability and consequently subjected to surveillance and discipline. By the 1960s and 1970s, hegemonic womanhood continued to be constructed according to a racial and economic logic that was spatially organized according to the constellation of signifiers ranging between "order" and "home" (property). The process is reminiscent of what French feminists have identified as the continuum of meanings between *propre-propriété*.[5]

For Hélène Cixous, the multiplicity of meanings embedded in the continuum between propre-propriété[6] is inextricably bound up in the construction of the economy of masculine desire and the assurance of its repeatability: "The opposition appropriate/inappropriate, proper/

improper, clean/unclean, mine/not mine (the valorization of the self-same), organizes the opposition identity/difference. Everything takes place as if, in a split second, man and being had propriated each other. And as if his relationship to woman was still at play as the possibility—though threatening, of the not-proper, not-clean, not-mine: desire is inscribed as the desire to reappropriate for himself that which seems able to escape him" (Cixous and Clément 1986: 80).

In an influential study examining the reciprocal relationship between gender and architecture, Mark Wigley argues that this economy of masculine desire for the selfsame, expressed through the play of meaning in *propre-propriété*, is produced and reproduced spatially through the actual physical structure of the home, the house. In other words, the house's "primary role is to protect the father's genealogical claims by isolating women from other men. Reproduction is understood as reproduction of the father. The law of the house is undoubtedly no more than the law of the father. The physical house is the possibility of the patriarchal order that appears to be applied to it" (Wigley 1992: 336). The possibility of the patriarchal order depends on woman's sexuality being confined within the bounds of the house. Therefore, Wigley continues, "The house then assumes the role of the man's self-control. The virtuous woman becomes woman-plus-house or, rather, woman-as-housed, such that her virtue cannot be separated from the physical space" (337). One might note that Peter Stallybrass has similarly commented in another context (Renaissance England) that close watch and supervision of women emphasized "the mouth, chastity, the threshold of the house. These three areas were frequently collapsed into each other" (Stallybrass 1986: 126). The law of the father, understood as the reproduction of the selfsame, requires, then, that the boundaries of the house be maintained and protected through a complex system of surveillance which includes controls that are both tangible (walls, doors, closed windows) and intangible (dress, manners, legal and cultural codes) (Wigley 1992: 338). For Wigley, the law of the father is therefore always already architectural because "It is itself understood as the intersection of a spatial system and a system of surveillance" (339).

Whereas Wigley's essay convincingly analyzes the complicity between architecture and the construction of gender, Peter Stallybrass's work links the relationship between architecture and gender to the production and maintenance of state structures. Drawing from Bakhtin, Stallybrass suggests that the predominant signs of Woman include "the enclosed body, the closed mouth, the locked house" (Stallybrass 1986: 127). Therefore, "normative 'Woman' could become the emblem of the perfect and impermeable container, and hence a map of the integrity of the state" (129). The architectural rhetoric that enables these metaphors of containment, enclosure, and interiority to slide between Home-Woman-State, is one that fosters notions of safety and security, the condition of being at home and all that that implies (the familiar, family history, nostalgia) (see Vidler 1992: 17); this rhetoric is therefore grounded in the recognition of the selfsame and bolstered with the deployment of multiple boundaries that necessarily reinforce differences between inside and outside.

A similar notion of Woman, the Home, and the State as bounded, constituent identities is a fundamental concern of an unusual Bolivian publication from 1950, Lola Mercedes Terán de Pohl's *Anticomunismo*. *Anticomunismo* chronicles the author's founding in 1949 of the Organización Femenina Democrática Nacional (OFDN), a supposedly apolitical women's anticommunist league, the slogan of which was *"Dios-Patria-Hogar"* [God-Fatherland-Home]. Deploying a rhetoric of enclosure and exclusion, the book claims that the integrity of the Bolivian state is being threatened from outside its borders by communism. Religious leaders quoted in the opening pages offer their full support to the organization, exhorting Bolivian women to join together to form a united barrier that will send a clear message to the communist threat lurking just beyond national boundaries: "No penetrarás" (Terán de Pohl 1950: 16) [You will not penetrate]. Terán de Pohl urges women to take heed because communist "penetration" specifically targets Bolivian womanhood with its promise to expropriate the home. The words of Monsignor Paul Yuping, the archbishop of Nanking, therefore strike an ominous chord when he places his blessing on the incipient OFDN, stating: "Es muy importante que la mujer se organice contra el comunismo, porque es la que más sufre en un régimen de esa naturaleza, pues el comunismo le quita a la mujer lo que más quiere en el mundo: su Hogar, que condensa su Dios y su Patria" [It is very important that woman organizes against communism. She is the one who suffers most under this kind of regime because communism takes from her what she most loves in the world: her Home, in which her God and her Fatherland are condensed].[7] This perceived threat to the Home and concomitantly to Bolivian womanhood is especially foreboding precisely because expropriation or loss of the Home, the space in which God and Country intersected, signifies the ruin of what the author calls the Catholic-Democratic State.

Terán de Pohl argues that the Home is the target of communism because it encloses the (feminine) matrix of the timeless ideals of the ordered, civilized, Christian nation. Her description of the home reads: "Ese núcleo pequeño pero vital de la sociedad; esa columna fundamental de la Nacionalidad; ese emporio de ternuras, de renunciamientos, de sacrificios; ese manantial perene [*sic*] de amor y perdón, ese cofre donde se guarda límpida la tradición y el sentimiento católico-democrático de los bolivianos" (Terán de Pohl 1950: 24) [That small but vital nucleus of society; that fundamental pillar of Nationality; that emporium of tenderness, of renunciations, of sacrifices; that perennial source of love and forgiveness; that coffer where the Bolivians' limpid Catholic-democratic traditions and sentiments are kept]. The metaphors she employs are both architectural and, as I will show later, economic. By describing the house as a nucleus, an emporium, and a coffer, her narrative places emphasis on an essential, feminine interiority as well as on the structures that create and control order, what Wigley has called the "advertised presence of the masculine" (Wigley 1992: 376). The space or building as enclosed is what establishes and preserves the image of order; the (feminine) inside becomes subordinated to the visible (masculine) outside. Furthermore, the metaphor of the house as pillar serves as an example of how, through architecture, Terán de Pohl props up her argument, elevating the authority of her interpretation "to a transcendental level" which then makes it "appear as an enduring system of meaning."[8] In this manner, then, the house constitutes a dominant signifier in the atheist-Communist/ Catholic-democratic binary because only through its ordering and ordered structure can the ideals of the civilized, Christian world be reproduced and made seemingly "timeless."

Terán de Pohl's text invokes communism as a dangerous phenomenon that has the power to infiltrate and contaminate the ordered unity of the Bolivian state. The author warns her readers that if communists succeed in forging ideological inroads among the nation's population, they will exert the greatest influence on the working-class poor and indigenous communities:

Pues sabido es que la mayoría de los afiliados o con pensamientos comunistas, son aquellos cuyo nivel de vida está por debajo, realmente, de lo humano-cristiano y que encuentra, por tanto, en la prédica comunista, al menos un refugio momentáneo y una esperanza futura,—claro está que irrealizable—de que todo lo que vé de bello, de grande, de comodidades, de abundancia, será repartido entre ellos . . . (Terán de Pohl 1950: 27)

[It is known that the majority of members affiliated with the Communist Party or those who hold communist thoughts are people whose standard of living is truly below the human-Christian level; as a result, they find at least a momentary refuge and a future hope in communist preaching—one that is obviously unattainable—that all that they see as beautiful, great, comfortable, and abundant will one day be apportioned among them . . .]

For the author of *Anticomunismo,* the working-class and indigenous peoples are already outside (i.e., under) the human-Christian realm. For this reason, there exists a greater likelihood that they will be adversely influenced by communists. Although Terán de Pohl opens her work with a call for increasing surveillance of national boundaries, the major part of her book addresses *internal* reforms in land distribution, wages, education, and so on, suggesting that the deployment of an anticommunist discourse apparently masks another anxiety that lies underneath: an anxiety that results from a more widespread crisis of interiority and the destabilization of oligarchic structures.

As early as 1935, Terán de Pohl published an article calling for the construction of "Casas para obreros" [Houses for workers] and foregrounding the importance of the house in the formation of well-adjusted citizens:

Estemos seguras de que cuando el obrero tenga una vivienda confortable y no habite, por necesidad pequeñas pocilgas incubadoras de microbios, . . . será el ciudadano consciente de sus deberes. . . . Será ya el "obrero hombre" que irá deseando más bienestar cada día, y costeándose comodidades con el fruto de su trabajo. Sabrá imprimirle a su hogar hasta un aspecto burgués, matando radicalmente sus vicios, como natural resultado de su cambio de vida y aspiraciones en ese nuevo ambiente. (Terán de Pohl 1950: 93)[9]

[We [ladies] can be certain that when the worker has a comfortable home and does not inhabit, by necessity, small pigsties, incubators of microbes . . . that he will be a citizen aware of his obligations. . . . At last he will be the "worker-man" who desires greater well-being each day, paying for amenities with the fruit of his labor. He will even know how to create a bourgeois look in his house, radically putting an end to his vices as the natural result of his change of aspirations and lifestyle in this new environment.]

Terán de Pohl's philanthropic as well as paternalistic goal of better housing for the working class is based unequivocally on an environmental determinism. Comfortable, inhabitable, bourgeois homes produce the proper citizen, whereas filthy shacks become breeding grounds of disorder or the improper. This paternalism can be linked to a need for social control through housing as well as to the promotion of the interests of economic liberalism (compare Mitchell 1993: 116, 121). In other words, the physical construction of the house is indispensable to the production and repeatability of the oligarchy because it disciplines the individual body in ways that are acceptable politically and socially. While depicted as representing Order, the house, in fact, represents a specific criollo order (see Wigley 1992: 380). Returning to Terán de Pohl's description of the house as coffer and emporium, the house can be understood as a mechanism of savings (Cixous), underwriting the economy of the selfsame. Property (individual possession), order, the proper, all are values necessary to the maintenance of the liberal state, embodied in the *obrero-hombre* now supposedly prepared to participate in a market economy. The modern house, identified as bourgeois in Terán de Pohl's writings, thus emerges as the very foundation and frame of the criollo state.[10]

The link between the house and the state is similarly foregrounded in novels from the 1940s, such as Antonio Díaz Villamil's *La niña de sus ojos* (1948), where the central theses of economic modernization and racial acculturation are constructed by and through predominant representations of the house. Because the novel continually reminds the reader of Domy's suitability as a future perfect mother of the modern nation, as argued in Chapter 2, it must necessarily underscore the centrality of home. The reconstruction and remodeling of houses punctuate Domy's homecoming from boarding school and the events surrounding her life as a rural school teacher. This emphasis on house renovation suggests that the novel architecturally plots its major themes to emphasize representations of (political and economic) stability while undermining those that are seemingly unstable. The house does not merely enclose these arguments, but is, instead, produced by them.[11] Therefore, these newly constructed buildings function as a kind of covering or clothing for similarly transformed bodies. In other words, like clothing, houses do not merely cover bodies; they shape and define them by gendering and racializing them.

Domy's parents, working-class *cholos,* decide to remodel the upper portion of their home in anticipation of their daughter's return from boarding school. They plan for Domy to live in the newly refurbished rooms, moving their own living quarters downstairs into the "obscuras y desmanteladas habitaciones de la planta baja" (Díaz Villamil 1948: 32) [dark and dismantled rooms of the first floor]. Upon her arrival, Domy finds the new quarters to be lovely, redone and decorated in a fashion that she once considered impossible for such a run-down house: "Al ser encendidas las luces, la muchacha recibió la más grata sorpresa. Jamás había sospechado que sus padres, por mucho que fuera el cariño que le profesaran, hubieran podido preparar y complementar aquellos elegantes cuartitos en una casa de tan tosco y primitivo conjunto" (75–76) [When the lights came on, the girl had the most pleasant surprise. She never suspected that her parents, however great the affection for her they might profess, could have readied and finished those elegant little rooms in such a rustic and primitive house]. Domy's mother and father feel awkward and out of place in the new area even after they change into their Sunday best to join their daughter in the dining room. Their visits upstairs gradually decrease in frequency until they seldom intrude upon the newly modernized space of the house. In spite of their absence, the physical contrast between the remodeled upstairs with its fresh white walls and the old downstairs with its chipped and cracking dirty walls, continually points to the precarious foundations of this renovation project. Even though Domy manages to shut out the rest of the house by closing her door on it, she never feels at home here; her parents cease being her parents. Cultural and ethnic differences between Domy and her parents become increasingly evident and progressively intolerable because they are, quite literally, structured architecturally by the dividing walls between the upstairs and the downstairs. Differences are too close for comfort, sharing common walls and thresholds as it were. The binary logic of the parents' house, marked by the opposition white walls/dirty, chipped walls, is organized and sustained through architecture and so, as a result, there can be no single, unitary subject inhabiting this space. The upper floor functions merely as a dissimulating cover that masks another underlying truth.

This partially veiled truth emerges painfully during a party hosted by Domy's parents when a drunken young man takes advantage of her momentary inattention to kiss her sloppily on the mouth. Horrified, Domy becomes angrily indignant. The man, smiling, asks her why she is so offended: "¿Acaso no eres una cholita con vestido?" [Aren't you simply a *cholita* wearing a dress?].[12] Domy's anger fades as she faces the truth of his question: "Toda su cólera se desarmó con esa frase cínica, pero que, después de todo, encerraba la verdad. Y, esa verdad, esa tremenda verdad que ayer la humilló entre la gente bien, ahora, entre los de su propia casta, era la más sangrienta realidad" (117) [All of her anger vanished with this cynical statement, but which, after all, contained the truth. And, that truth, that terrible truth which yesterday humiliated her in the midst of the upper class, now, among those of her own caste, was the most offensive reality]. The truth that Domy cannot gainsay and that literally sickens her is the ambivalent truth of her parents' house, at once hidden and recognizable. In other words, the architectural split that distinguishes the top floor, Domy's quarters, from the bottom, her parents's space, similarly clothes a split subjectivity. The renovated house that is not *really* renovated because it maintains the original foundation, is irreparably divided by the partition between the upper white walls and the lower chipped, dirty surface. In that house, Domy can only be a "*cholita*" (her foundational self) dressed in a "*señorita*'s" clothing. Clearly, Domy cannot "find herself" until she has left this space.

The second portion of the novel similarly hinges on operations of construction and renovation. Upon her arrival in the indigenous village of Collamarca, Domy is saddened by the physical condition of the school and the shacks [*casuchas*] in which the inhabitants live. Part of a long-term renovation plan that she undertakes includes designing a new school and, ultimately, a new Collamarca. Under her direction, all of the families of the village eventually rebuild their own homes. By the end, each house has been given a fresh coat of whitewash so that from a distance the town gives the appearance of cleanliness, order, and unity: "Cada casita correspondía a un estilo semi-colonial muy apropiado para el crudo clima de la puna. Las paredes estaban enjalbegadas con estuco, lo que, desde la distancia daba al caserío el aspecto de una pequeña villa moderna, muy diferente a las miserables aldehuelas de la altiplanicie" (234) [Each little house corresponded to a semi-colonial style very appropriate for the harsh *puna* climate. The walls were whitewashed with stucco, which, from the distance, gave the little village the appearance of a small modern town, very different from the wretched hamlets of the high plain]. The "semi-colonial" style that characterizes each house points to a blending of colonial and Andean architectural forms, an architectural miscegenation of sorts. The salient characteristics that emerge as a result of this mixing are predominantly European, and they are marked by the authority of the modern white walls.

These white walls do not mask an interior (darker) difference; they embody the truth of a new internal order as well. If, when Domy first comes to Collamarca, she is dismayed by the "promiscuidad en que vivían esas gentes, en moradas tan estrechas y desaseadas" (225) [indiscriminate mingling in which these people lived, in dwellings so cramped and filthy], the renovated house completely reorders the family's internal, communal living space to emphasize western notions of privacy. Instead of one central living area typical of Andean houses of the *puna*,[13] each house's interior is divided into separate bedrooms (one for the parents, and one or more for the children), a living room, and a kitchen; the storage areas for animal feed, tools, rabbit pens, and so on are placed apart from the living area. The redefinition of the interior space of the house along the lines of western notions of privacy and functionality links the ordering of the modern body to questions of race, gender, and economic integration.

Díaz Villamil's novel suggests that modern understandings of order are connected to the spatial organization of the body as well as to its gendering and racialization. These processes, in turn, cannot be separated from their economic consequences. According to Wigley, the architectural control of privacy through the management of bodies necessarily required architecture's detachment from the body: "Order in general depends upon an ordering of the body, which is to say, a detachment from it. It is this detachment that makes the individual subject possible. Architecture was used to effect it as the agent of a new kind of modesty and in so doing played an active part in the constitution of the private subject. It clothed the body in a way that redefined it, at once constructing the body as dangerous and containing that threat" (1992: 345). For Wigley, the containment and management of the body is but "an extension of the traditional disciplining of the cultural artifact 'woman,' authorized by the claim that she is too much a part of the fluid bodily world to control herself" (345). Thus, the white coat of paint that clothes the newly ordered, acculturated (masculine) subject of Collamarca stands in stark contrast to indigenous peoples who occupy the disordered space of the eroticized feminine Other, remaining eternally outside the social contract.

Carlos Medinaceli's novel *La Chaskañawi* (1947) similarly foregrounds the colorfully dressed *chola* as the embodied sign of the eroticized feminine Other. During carnival street festivities, all (criollo) eyes become riveted on the flamboyant entrance of the *cholas:* "Todas [las cholas], elegantemente trajeadas de polleras y corpiños de claros colores, como en una fiesta pagana o en una kermesse flamenca, presentaban el espectáculo de un vivo cromatismo" (Medinaceli 1955: 118) [All [the *cholas*], elegantly dressed in brightly colored *polleras* and bodices, as in a pagan celebration or a Spanish flamenco dance, presented a show of vivid chromaticism]. At the height of the carnival dance, the *chola* Claudina stands out from the rest of the women, tantalizing the *señorito* Adolfo with her sensual yet socially forbidden body: "Ruborizada y jadeante por el baile, con un cálido relampaguear de dionisíaca voluptuosidad en los ojos, se destacaba de la pandilla por la dulzura de su canto y la gracia de sus movimientos y requiebros al bailar" (118) [Flushed and breathless from the dance, with an ardent gleaming of Dionysiac voluptuousness in her eyes, she stood out from the group because of the sweetness of her song and the grace of her movements and flirtatious allure when dancing].

In spite of the *chola*'s fascination, however, criollo men distrust her, fearing that prolonged relations with her will ultimately destabilize their own identity. Adolfo's friend and relative Fernando warns him to take care, reminding him that while the *chola* might be fine for those occasions when "need" arises, gentlemen must always take heed not to fall under her spell: "En primer lugar, si nosotros vamos donde cholas, es donde tipas como las *Rancheñas* o la Macacha, que son cholas de tres al cuarto, que uno las toma por necesidad y después las deja, pero no nos dejamos atrapar por ellas, como el pobre Aniceto" (92–93) [First of all, if we seek out *cholas,* we look for trollops like the Rancheñas or like the Macacha slut who are of little importance, to whom one goes out of need and later drops, but we don't let ourselves get caught by them, like poor Aniceto]. Indeed, once the character Aniceto Díaz falls under the erotic power of the mannish *chola* Petrona Rodríguez, his mental and physical condition deteriorates such that Adolfo likens him to an abandoned house (20). When Adolfo first meets Petrona, he is somewhat taken aback, apparently because of her masculine behavior and the dirty environment in which she lives: "[Petrona], con desenfado, con aplomo, le extendió la mano. Una mano gruesa, varonil, sucia. Le apretó con fuerza:—Petrona Rodríguez, señor, para servir a usted" (20) [[Petrona], with assurance, with aplomb, extended him her hand. A thick, mannish, dirty hand. It gripped his with force: "Petrona Rodríguez, sir, at your service"]. Life with Petrona in her house, described as a "narrow, run-down tent," with an "uneven, dirt floor" (19), transforms Díaz into an unkempt, emasculated shell of his former self; virtually stripped of his masculinity, his dismembered identity is laid bare for all to see. To his friends' dismay, he has become, literally, "*encholado*" [cholified].

Commenting on Díaz's miserable condition, Fernando observes: "Desde que cayó en poder de 'La Wallpa,' está hecho un degenerado, el pobre ya no tiene ni pantalón que cambiarse" (93) [Ever since he fell under the power of "La Wallpa," he is like a degenerate; the poor guy no longer even has a change of pants]. The implicit comparison between dirt and disorder throughout this scene anticipates Mary Douglas's observation that "absolute dirt" does not exist, that dirt is, instead, "essentially disorder" (Douglas 1992: 2). The novel suggests that gender and race have become disrupted or disordered here, the symptomatic sign of which is the criollo man transformed into the "*encholado*," "castrated" by a butch *chola*. In contrast to the new homes of Domy's Collamarca that clad the promise of racial acculturation in white walls, the *chola*'s house threatens because of its otherness, warning *señoritos* against following Aniceto's example.

In my reading of these novels, I am suggesting that it is only through the control and privatization of sexuality (the feminine), that the individual, male subject is produced; indeed, subjectivity itself is understood to be masculine and, in Wigley's words, is "specific to that privatization. The new conditions of privacy mark a new subjectivity rather than simply modify a preexisting one" (Wigley 1992: 345). This new, masculine subject is, importantly, also racialized: it is insistently white. Consequently, the white, masculine (individual) subject can only be produced by and through the control and management of the indigenous feminine collectivity.

Throughout Díaz Villamil's *La niña de sus ojos*, the narrative links the privatization of sexuality with the proper ordering of bodies in the house, racial acculturation, and the economic integration of indigenous peoples. The new subject specific to privatization and heralded by the novel's project of modernization is one who has become acculturated to western socioeconomic practices and therefore is ready to enter the social contract (citizenship) and embrace a liberal market economy. These are the characteristics of the modern (civilized) citizen. For this reason, the act of privatizing indigenous communally held lands, an act that accelerates the formation of citizens according to hegemonic economic and political discourses, also has racial implications. For example, Aymara historian Carlos Mamani Condori maintains that Aymara identity is produced and reproduced through the unity of space and time called *pacha*. The rupture created by colonialism fragmented this *pacha*, bringing to a standstill Aymara control over their own history and disrupting historiographic practices that had flourished in Tawantinsuyu (Mamani Condori 1992: 9). According to Mamani Condori, the recuperation of history can only be accomplished in the space of the *ayllu* (the community), not in private, nuclear homes:

> La ruptura colonial no puede ser respondida sino mediante una recuperación de nuestro destino histórico truncado. Y ésto sólo puede, a su vez, hacerse a partir de los espacios en los cuales se desenvuelve nuestra vida colectiva: los ayllus que, aunque fragmentados, permanecen como espacio vital de nuestras prácticas sociales y culturales, y de nuestro vínculo con la naturaleza y con nuestros antepasados. (9–10)

> [The colonial rupture cannot be contested except by means of a recuperation of our truncated historical destiny. And this, in turn, can only be accomplished starting from the spaces in which our collective life develops: the *ayllus* that, even though fragmented, remain a vital space of our so-

cial and cultural practices, and of our lasting connection to nature and our ancestors.]

Mamani Condori's work underscores how the privatization of communal indigenous lands is instrumental in the dismantling of indigenous identities.

Large-scale systematic attempts to seize indigenous lands first took place in the nineteenth century and were accompanied by Positivist rhetoric that equated participation in the market with civilization: "La incorporación del indio al mercado aparece como una medida humanitaria para lograr su incorporación a la sociedad 'civilizada'" (Platt 1982: 96) [The incorporation of the Indian into the market appears as a humanitarian measure in order to achieve his incorporation into "civilized" society]. Historian Tristan Platt argues that the first agrarian reform in Bolivia took place not in 1952 but in 1874 with the enactment of the Ley de Exvinculación [Law of Expropriation]. This law legalized the abrogation of the *ayllu* and implemented a new system of taxation. Platt indicates that although the first commissioner [*Revisitador*], Narciso de la Riva, was largely unsuccessful in his attempts to implement the law,[14] the commissioner nevertheless argued in his final report that

"la bondad de la Ley (de Exvinculación) es innegable": aunque las tierras "estatales" se encuentran "secuestradas" por los ayllus, el Estado—mediante "la más elevada filantropía"—ha concedido al indio un derecho enfitéutico perfecto, y ahora ha dispuesto la Revisita para que pueda convertirse en propietario pleno, abriéndose de esta manera al "cambio, que es el instrumento más poderoso en el desarrollo del trabajo." "La parte esencial . . . de la ley consiste en la exvinculación de las tierras de orijen, con el fin de disolver esos grupos de individuos rezagados" (los ayllus). (cited in Platt 1982: 96)

["the generosity of the Law (of Expropriation) is undeniable": although the *ayllus* have "confiscated" "State" lands, the State—by means of "the most noble philanthropy"—has granted to the Indian the perfect right to lease the land and now, the Commission, so that the Indian can become a property owner in full, opening himself up in this way to "change, which is the most powerful instrument in the development of work." "The essential part of the law consists in the expropriation of originary lands,[15] the objective of which is to break up those groups of individuals lagging behind" (the *ayllus*).]

De la Riva envisioned the law as a vehicle enabling a particular kind of "coming out," a passage across household thresholds: "[La Ley de Exvinculación es] un instrumento esencialmente móvil, que semejante al mar produzca flujos y reflujos, con cuyo poder el aboríjena salga de las grutas donde habita, se interpole con las masas ilustradas del país, y despierte a la vida del progreso" (cited in Platt 1982: 96) [(The Law of Expropriation is) an essentially dynamic instrument, which, like the sea, produces rising and ebb flows; empowered by it the aborigine can come out of the caves where he lives, mix in with the country's enlightened masses, and wake up to the life of progress].

For de la Riva, the Indians that came forth out of their primitive houses (caves), entered into knowledge and the realm of the civilized. This "outside/inside" location in which de la Riva's discourse positions indigenous peoples calls to mind Diana Fuss's observations regarding the particular situatedness of gays and lesbians today: "to be out . . . is precisely to be no longer out; to be out is to be finally outside of exteriority and all the exclusions and deprivations such outsiderhood imposes. Or, put another way, to be out is really to be in—inside the realm of the visible, the speakable, the culturally intelligible" (1991: 4). De la Riva's commentary on the 1874 law suggests that an Indian could enter the "realm of the visible," the "speakable," and the "culturally intelligible," only by stepping "outside of exteriority" or crossing over the threshold of the Andean house into the criollo world.

Importantly, however, as Platt (1982) and Rivera Cusicanqui (1984) have rigorously documented, indigenous resistance to the Ley de Exvinculación prevented the legislation from being systematically enforced. By the mid 1940s, the counterelites, the writers and intellectuals who would constitute the heart of the MNR, pressed for similar reform of the indigenous communities (see Salmón 1986). At the time of the publication of *La niña de sus ojos* in 1948, the same logic of inside/outside continued to be deployed architecturally. In order to take up residence in modernity's newly renovated white house, Indians had to traverse willingly or by force the threshold of their dark cavelike dwellings [*grutas*].

As both *La niña de sus ojos* and Terán de Pohl's writings emphasize, the modern subject can be unified and made whole only through a genuine or true process of acculturation, from the ground up. Therefore, Terán de Pohl equates the changing of clothing with a completely refurbished house. She predicts that, given a new home, indigenous women and *cholas* would undergo an ontological transformation as they occupied a heretofore unfamiliar space; as evidence of this, their clothing, like the house, would similarly be refashioned: "Ahora en cuanto al elemento femenino se refiere (del pueblo) podríamos adelantar, que en homenaje a su cambio de 'residencia y ambiente' sería capaz, de su parte—de cambiar su clásica indumentaria, por encontrarla, sencillamente fuera de lugar" (Terán de Pohl 1950: 93) [Now, as for the female element (of the people) to which we are referring, we could anticipate that, in honor of her change of "residence and environment" she would be able, on her own, to change her traditional clothing, finding it simply out of place]. Thus, for Terán de Pohl, the modern house does not merely contain the subject; it produces and shapes it. Old ways, such as the use of native Andean clothing, can and should be refashioned as they become, quite literally, out of place.

THE ARCHITECTURE OF RESISTANT MEMORY

At this point it would help to shift perspectives from a critique of criollo ideology to a consideration of Aymara forms of resistance conditioned by the house and clothing. Beatriz Colomina's work on modern architecture reminds us that architecture is "a system of representation, or rather a series of overlapping systems of representation" (1994: 13). Therefore, it is possible to comprehend the house, for instance, as a "mechanism of representation," a "'construction,' in all senses of the word" (13–14). The house emerges as a signifying text, one that can be read as tissue, texture, textile (see Barthes 1975: 64). The connection between architecture and textile is not a new one. Mark Wigley observes that the nineteenth-century German architect Gottfried Semper had already identified this relationship: "Building originates with the use of woven fabrics to define social space. Specifically, the space of domesticity. The textiles are not simply placed within space to define a certain interiority. Rather, they are the production of space itself" (Wigley 1992: 367). This deconstruction, as it were, of an essential interiority is what Roland Barthes has in mind when he emphasizes the etymological link between text and textile: "*Text* means *Tissue;* but whereas hitherto we have always taken this tissue as a product, a ready-made veil, behind which lies, more or less hidden, meaning (truth), we are now emphasizing, in the tissue, the generative idea that the text is made, is worked out in a perpetual interweaving" (Barthes 1975: 64). The importance of the relationship "textile/text" among Andean cultures has been noted by many.[16] Textiles do not fix an essential indigenous identity or interiority; rather, they map identity spatially across the variety of weaving techniques employed, the pattern and colors of the design, and the use of supplementary ornamentation. By "reading" these texts/textiles, it is possible to identify the wearer's *ayllu* and community (Arze 1988: 24–28).

Among the Aymara there also exists a literal and symbolic relationship between the woven cloth and the house. The house as a complex text/ textile, a perpetual interweaving of social and cultural identities, is foregrounded in Denise Arnold's influential study of the Aymara dwellings of the Qaqachaka *ayllu*.[17] Arnold's essay examines the way in which the very operations of construction link the house and the newly married couple who will inhabit it to Aymara cosmological and *ayllu* socioeconomic practices. Following the pattern of *ch'allas,* libation rites that celebrate each stage of the construction process, Arnold divides her essay into two broad themes which include the "house as cosmos" and the "house as the method or practice of memory (*arte de la memoria*)." Her rigorous investigation of each theme reveals how the operations of construction as well as the festivities celebrated during the final roofing ceremony weave the house into an elaborate network of cosmological, kinship, and gender practices. By upholding these traditions, the couple, with their land and animals, becomes an integral part of the larger socioeconomic structures of the *ayllu*. At this time, moreover, the husband and wife are officially recognized by the state because, as owners of a house, they must pay taxes and provide labor to public works projects (Denise Arnold 1992: 78).

The Qaqas build their houses in relation to the agricultural cycle, putting them up during the period following the final harvest and before the next planting season. This means that the roofing ceremony generally coincides with Day of the Dead festivities (Denise Arnold 1992: 36). Each year thereafter, the Qaqas commemorate the anniversary of the roofing ceremony at the same time as they remember the land and mountains:

Al compartir la memoria del proceso de construcción de una casa en cada una de estas ocasiones, los Qaqas reconstruyen no sólo el espacio sino el tiempo, en la medida en que recuerdan el pasado, las genealogías ancestrales y sus orígenes míticos e históricos. La casa sirve de trasfondo mnemotécnico sobre el cual se superponen las memorias colectivas de los ancestros y los muertos. (38)

[While sharing the memory of the process of the construction of the house on each one of these occasions, the Qaqas reconstruct not only space but also time insofar as they remember the past, the ancestral genealogies, and their mythical and historical origins. The house serves as a mnemonic backdrop against which the collective memories of the ancestors and the dead are superimposed.]

Within this matrix of relations, the house can be seen structurally and symbolically as the union of space and time for the Aymara, a coming together expressed in the word *nayrapacha*. For Carlos Mamani Condori, the phrase "Qhiparu nayraru uñtas sartañani (mirando atrás vamos a ir adelante)" [looking back we will go forward] best describes the Aymara understanding of *nayrapacha:*

> Mirar atrás, hacia el pasado, conocer nuestra historia, saber cómo ha vivido y luchado nuestro pueblo a lo largo de los siglos, es condición indispensable para saber cómo orientar las acciones del futuro. Pacha y nayra son por eso pasado, presente y futuro; uniendo las dos palabras tenemos nayrapacha: tiempos antiguos. Pero no son antiguos en tanto pasado muerto, carente de funciones de renovación. Implican que este mundo puede ser reversible, que el pasado también puede ser futuro. (Mamani Condori 1992: 14)

> [Looking back, toward the past, knowing our history, how our people have lived and fought over the centuries, is an indispensable condition of knowing how to direct future actions. *Pacha* and *nayra* are for that reason past, present, and future; combining the two words we have *nayrapacha:* ancient times. But they are not ancient in the sense of a dead past, one without the potential for renovation. They imply that this world can be reversible, that the past can also be the future.]

Mamani Condori's essay suggestively points to the dominant role that the critical practice of memory plays in weaving the Andean past together with its present and future.

The actual practice of remembering emerges as a focal point during the libation rituals [*ch'allas*] that celebrate the roofing ceremony. According to Arnold, drinking is inextricably linked to memory, such that the partaking of drink initiates the shared practice of remembering. Together, men and women drink in order to stimulate memory's vertical and horizontal paths [*sendas*] that enable the family, literally, to re-member their genealogical and cosmological past with the present. These paths of memory, symbolically configured through the construction of the house, differ according to gender, whereby men remember the "path of semen" and women the "path of blood." Neither path of memory can be complete in and of itself but is, instead, always contingent on the other partner as well as on its continuation by future generations.[18] Arnold cites one woman who explained the practice thus:

> "El recuerda el lugar de nacimiento de su padre, los hombres siempre recordarán a sus padres. Nosotros estamos recordando la senda de la sangre." De manera que los hombres recuerdan como recordaban sus padres, y las mujeres recuerdan como recordaban sus madres. Las hijas también escuchan cuidadosamente a las ch'allas de sus madres, porque continuarán recordando el orden de su genealogía carnal, así como lo seguirán haciendo las hijas de sus hijas. "Así tomaba mi madre," diciendo, "hasta ella va a continuar tomando, hasta ella así va a parir nomás también, y luego hasta sus hijas va a seguir tomando nomás también así. Así somos. Esta es nuestra senda." (1992: 106)

["He remembers his father's birthplace, men always remember their fathers. We [women] are remembering the path of blood." So men remember how their fathers remembered, and women remember how their mothers remembered. The daughters also listen carefully to their mothers' *ch'allas* because they will keep on remembering the order of their family genealogy, just like the daughters of their daughters will continue to do. Saying: "my mother drank in this way;" "up to her she will continue to drink, up to her mother in just this way she will give birth also. And then up to her daughters she will also continue drinking just like this. That's the way we are. This is our path."]

During the *ch'allas*, these gendered paths of memory likewise follow the construction of the house as each and every material used to build it is affectionately remembered and nicknamed as well as gendered. For example, the adobe bricks forming the walls are made from a tough (masculine) mud mixture, while the water blended with the softer mud of the mortar suggests the damp earth following a rain and female menstrual blood (Denise Arnold 1992: 53). The many gendered building materials and structures similarly refer to the sun and moon of the cosmos as well as to the Inca foundational blocks of stone that anchor the house to the ground. The house is therefore symbolically configured and literally remembered as a complicated weave of gendered and cosmological signifiers which are always contextualized, maintaining a relational position, each one to the other (87). References to the house as both a nest and as a weaving or bundle [*tejido* or *atado*] (55–56) further emphasize its dense texture of overdetermined signs.

FIGURE 3.2.

Aguayo. *Original drawing by Eusebio Víctor Choque Quispe.*

Qaqachaka women describe the house's influence and power as a "madre nido de envolturas concéntricas, enteramente asignado al género femenino" (Denise Arnold 1992: 56) [mother nest of concentric wrappings, assigned entirely to the female gender]. The house, as a "mother nest," takes on metaphorical significance linking it to woman's reproductive capabilities:

Las madres que amamantan describen como un nido al montón de tejidos que envuelven al pequeño infante durante los tres primeros meses de su

vida en los que no se le permite ver el sol, estando enteramente cubierto y
en sombra debajo de una gruesa capa de tela. Sólo después de tres meses,
cuando la guagua ya es un poco más grande, se dice que "deja la madre
nido por primera vez." (56)

[The mothers who are breastfeeding describe as a nest the pile of woven
cloth used to wrap up the small infant during the first three months of its
life when it is not permitted to see the sun; the infant is completely covered
and shaded underneath the heavy layer of cloth. Only after three months,
when the baby is a little bit bigger, they say that "it leaves the mother nest
for the first time."]

Employing the metaphor of weaving, the women of Qaqachaka invoke
what Arnold calls a "discourse of seams," one that locates power in the
edges or borders of different cloths joined together. This discourse of
seams rejects dominant notions of closure (domestication) that mask
edges and borders and, in so doing, appear to be seamless. Rather, it suggests a threshold space between "two woven elements" "pregnant" with
"la inminente posibilidad de generar desde dentro y de crear riqueza futura" (56) [the imminent possibility of generating from inside and of creating future wealth]. Wealth, in this context, does not signify monetary
power or private capital. Instead, it is tied to the communal accumulation
of agricultural products, animals, and land with which the *ayllu* will continue to prosper. The possibility of production and reproduction becomes structured architecturally through the use of simile as the seam
of the house/textile is likened to the "mother nest" or "house-as-tied-
bundle [*atado*]," as well as to the seam of the woven bags in which food
is stored (56).

The physical and symbolic structures of the Qaqachaka house problematize the western binary inside/outside, emphasizing instead relatedness and contextualization. As a weave of signifiers, the spatial and structural logic of the house continually reproduces Aymara social, cultural,
and economic practices. At the same time, it also intersects with state
structures as the young couple readies itself to contribute to tax and labor obligations. Nevertheless, because the symbolic logic of the house
continually alludes to indigenous ancestors and deities, it resists hegemonic processes of acculturation (101).

One of the clearest examples of negotiation and resistance occurs
when the Qaqa utilize imported rather than Andean materials to build
the house. The Spanish words used to identify these non-native products
undergo transformation when pronunciation and meaning are renego-

tiated through intricate language games: "Los nombres de brindar, o nombres cariñosos, de todos los materiales de construcción son extraordinarios en su creatividad sincrética. Es como si las leyes de construcción de casa, impuestas por los españoles, con su terminología española acompañante, . . . en un momento histórico preciso, fueran confrontadas por los préstamos y juegos de palabras de este arte verbal local" (Denise Arnold 1992: 65) [The names used during the libation offerings, or affectionate names, of all the construction materials are extraordinary for their syncretic creativity. It's as if the laws regarding the construction of a house, imposed by the Spanish, with its accompanying Spanish terminology, in a precise historical moment, were confronted by the borrowings and word games of this local verbal art]. For instance, Arnold describes the adoption of *"calamina"* for the roof which in many areas replaces a form of straw prevalent throughout the altiplano. During the *ch'allas* celebrating the roofing ceremony, then, people drink to remember the Japanese factory where the *calamina* was made, the money earned in the mines to purchase it, its long journey across the ocean, and its arduous transport over the mountains to reach finally the *ayllu* (66). However, through the use of homophones, the Qaqa link *calamina* to the words *kalamila* and *kalawira*—*kalamila* being an Aymara-adapted form of the Spanish word for "carnation" [*clavel*], a flower associated with mountain cliffs, the fertility of the herd, and the dominant animal that leads the flock (66); *kalawira*, on the other hand, derives from *calavera*, the skull that symbolizes the roof of the house and the ability to communicate with the dead ancestors (66). All three words (*calamina, kalawila*, and *kalawira*), therefore, negotiate both Aymara and Spanish meanings. In this context, linguistic borrowings do not suggest replacement, an "either/or" act of acculturation; instead they signify both "this and that," such that meaning becomes increasingly textured and nuanced.

THE VIOLENT THRESHOLD

In contrast to the Aymara logic of relatedness expressed symbolically and materially through the house as text/textile, a logic that resists the binary either/or, inside/outside, hegemonic criollo notions of modernity emphasize the dividing line that marks the passage from the Aymara house to the interior space of the criollo home. For young Aymara women and girls, this passage generally takes place for reasons of economic necessity, as they migrate to the city in search of work as domestics. Ana María Condori's *testimonio, Nayan Uñatatawi: Mi despertar* (1988), provides a compelling account of this journey across thresholds, from her parents' house located in the rural province Carangas to that of her employers in the city of Oruro and, later, La Paz.

Condori's first job is cast as her entrance into the socio-symbolic contract when her father leaves her in her employer's house after having been assured by the *señora* that she will be treated just like another member of the family: "Nosotros le vamos a tratar como a una hija, no le va a faltar nada, ni comida ni ropa. Todo lo que comen mis hijos ella ha de servirse, el trato va a ser muy bueno" (Condori 1988: 56) [We will treat her like a daughter, she will not lack anything, neither food nor clothing. Everything that my children eat she will help herself to as well; the treatment will be very good]. Disregarding the sociocultural and economic differences that constitute the employer-employee relationship in this instance, the woman of the house emphasizes instead familial and homely relations which will supposedly determine their interaction. The passage across thresholds therefore is presented as continuous and unfragmented; Condori was a daughter in her parents' house and she will be a daughter in her employer's house.

As Anthony Vidler has observed, the homely house is associated with domesticity and the sense of being "at home" (Vidler 1992: 17–44). The seemingly secure and innocent space of the house becomes, therefore, in Wigley's words, a "paradigm of interiority" (Wigley 1993: 104). Nevertheless, as I argued earlier, the criollo house domesticates precisely because it insistently structures inside and outside spaces, thereby determining those places that are proper (the familiar and selfsame) and improper (the unfamiliar, the unrecognizable). What is more, not all interiors are equal, nor does everyone inhabit the interior in the same way. As Condori's *testimonio* demonstrates, one can be both inside and outside simultaneously. In contrast to the Qaqachaka house which problematizes oppositional structures to affirm Aymara subjectivity and agency, Condori's *testimonio* of her life as a domestic worker in the city discloses a Bolivian-criollo version of the "drama of instituting and revealing the proper" (Ingraham 1988: 10). Thus, what at first appears to be a seamless transition between houses increasingly gives way to the violence of domestication as Condori begins to learn her proper place:

Al principio yo me imaginaba que almorzaría y cenaría con ellos en un solo lugar y que el plato también iba a ser de los que usaba toda la familia, pero después vi que yo tenía que comer en la cocina, separada de todos, que para mí el plato era reservado: "Este va a ser tu plato, ésta va a ser tu cuchara, éste tu jarro." Así, un jarrito de la peor categoría que ni en mi casa usábamos.

Nosotros tenemos platitos de barro, pero son pues buenos, de lo mejor . . .
(Condori 1988: 59)

[At first I imagined that I would eat dinner and supper with them in the same place and that my dish would be from the set used by all the family. But later I saw that I had to eat in the kitchen, separated from everyone, and that for me there was a reserved plate: "This is going to be your plate, this is going to be your spoon, this your cup." Just like that, a little cup of the worst kind, that we didn't even use in my own home. We have earthenware dishes, but, well they're good, of the best quality . . .]

Not only must Condori learn to eat apart from the others, she also discovers that she cannot sit on the family's chairs, nor on the sofa, nor on any of the beds; she may not use their shower nor their soap. Paradoxically, even when she occupies her proper place she is always already improper: "Ellos creen que porque una es campesina es cochina, sucia y por eso dicen: 'No te sientes, no uses, me lo vas a ensuciar'" (60–61) [They believe that because you're a *campesina* girl you're a pig, dirty, and so they say: "Don't sit down there, don't use that, you're going to get it dirty"]. This interior, therefore, is not a homogeneous space inhabited equally by all. Within the house, Condori becomes further restricted to certain spaces such as the kitchen, beyond which she ventures only to clean and order the other rooms. The phrase "la empleada tiene que estar en su lugar" [the maid has to be in her place] resonates like a litany throughout the pages of *Mi despertar*.

Condori's new place is also marked by a hitherto unfamiliar language, a language exemplified by the phrase, "set the table": "Después, 'pon la mesa' me decía, pero yo no sabía qué era poner la mesa. En el campo estaba acostumbrada a comer parada o sentada en cualquier lugar, porque hay que estar a la expectativa de los rebaños para que no se vayan al pastizal reservado para el invierno o a la chacra" (57) [Then, "set the table," she told me, but I didn't know what set the table meant. In the countryside I was used to eating while standing up or seated anywhere, because you have to be on the lookout for the flocks of sheep so that they don't wander into the grazing pasture reserved for the winter or into the garden]. Little by little, she explains, she had to learn this new language. Nevertheless, it is not a language to which she comes as a speaking subject. She herself cannot utter the phrase, "set the table." Instead, Condori need only learn enough so that she can be commanded. She is always only this language's object, its other, and she will never occupy the place of subjectivity; she can never be "at home" in this language of domestication. Reflecting on her silence, Condori locates its origin in her upbringing:

> Lo positivo del niño campesino es que conoce su realidad, está integrado al trabajo de la familia y además no se cría muy mimado de los padres; aprendemos a soportar muchas cosas. Pero lo negativo es que a veces uno se acostumbra a no protestar. Así era yo al principio: no decía nada en mi trabajo; calladita nomás aceptaba, tenía miedo de hablar de lo que quería. (60)

> [The positive thing about the *campesino* child is that she knows her reality; she is integrated into the family work and besides she is not raised by her parents to be spoiled; we learn to endure many things. But the negative thing is that sometimes one becomes used to not protesting. That's the way I was at first: I didn't say anything at work; with my mouth shut I accepted. I was afraid to talk about what I wanted.]

If the relation between language and silence she remembers from her own home was rooted in processes by which the child is brought into familial and communal practices, her silence in the employer's house results from a different structure of power relations. Analyzing her (im)proper place as a domestic worker, Condori recognizes that this supposedly familiar, homey interior is, in fact, unfamiliar and unhomely:

> Ya no esperaba comer con ellos; me di cuenta de que me hubiera sentido incómoda, de que se hagan la burla de mí: de lo que como, de mi manera de hablar. Sentarse en la misma mesa con ellos no es lo mismo que estar con un amigo o un familiar, sino que es tener que comer delante del patrón, del que manda. (60)

> [I no longer expected to eat with them; I realized that I would have felt uncomfortable, that they might make fun of me: of what I eat, of my way of speaking. Sitting at the same table with them is not the same as being with a friend or a family member; rather, it's having to eat in front of the boss, of the one who commands.]

She can never forget that her (im)proper place, that of economic dependence and racial difference, is apart from the familiar and the familial.

When Condori does speak up, at the end of her time working as a domestic employee, it is to talk back to the *señora*. bell hooks defines "talking back," the transition for the oppressed from silence to speech, as a "gesture of defiance that heals, that makes new life and new growth possible. It is that act of speech, of 'talking back,' that is no mere gesture of empty words, that is the expression of our movement from object to subject—the liberated voice" (hooks 1989: 9).[19] Condori tells of how she argued with the *señora* over a period of two hours about her salary, which had been withheld from her for the past few months. The *señora* attempted to silence her on several occasions by crying out "Esta india . . ., ¡vos eres una campesina que no sabes nada!" (Condori 1988: 103) [This Indian [girl]! . . . you're a *campesina* who doesn't know anything!]. The *señora*'s repeated use of the phrase "this Indian," calls attention to racial differences and constitutes an attempt to highlight Condori's impropriety within the house. Condori refuses to be silenced, however, and instead she continues to talk back, insisting on the relations that sanction economically and racially the *señora*'s property/propriety and her own supposed impropriety: "—Gracias a la india, gracias al campesino, tienes mercado aquí, que tienes donde comprar; gracias a todos los campesinos tienes toda la comodidad porque al final son ellos los que trabajan.—Así he empezado a hablar y ¡uhh! se ha desmayado" (104) ["Thanks to the Indian, thanks to the *campesino,* you have a market here, you have a place to go and buy; thanks to all the *campesinos* you have all the convenience because in the end they're the ones who work." That's how I began to speak and oh! she fainted]. The *señora,* clearly shocked by Condori's unwelcome positioning as a speaking subject, faints, and is thus herself rendered speechless.

Whereas Condori was invited into the house on the ground of propriety, as a daughter, her *testimonio* is about the breakdown of the proper and how the proper can only improperly domesticate. Wigley has argued that "[a]rchitecture is no more than the strategic effect of the suppression of internal contradiction. It is not simply a mechanism that represses certain things. Rather, it is the very mark of repression" (Wigley 1993: 209). Condori's *testimonio* also reveals the contradictory and repressive operations of the hegemonic criollo house. For example, Condori is repeatedly warned about the dangers facing a young woman who ventures outside the house alone. Domestic workers live like caged birds, she explains. The door to the outside is often locked to them, "y aunque la puerta esté abierta y una podría irse el rato que quisiera, hay muchos obstáculos que nos lo impiden: el desconocimiento, el temor, el aislamiento" (Condori 1988: 84) [and even if the door is open and you could leave the moment you wanted, there are many obstacles that impede leaving: the unknown, fear, isolation]. She admits that she was afraid to leave the house at first: "Era muy acomplejada siempre; tenía miedo que me pase algo, que pueda aparecer embarazada" (73) [I always had a lot of hang-ups; I was afraid that something might happen to me, that I could end up pregnant]. Her employers took advantage of her reluctance to go out because that way she worked even more for them. They affirmed her fears by contrasting the security of the interior with the dangers of the exterior: "Entonces ellos también me decían: 'No hay que salir . . ., no hay que tomar amistad . . ., no conviene porque con otras ha pasado que . . .' . . . Miles de cosas contaban y más me acomplejaban con eso" (74) [So they also told me: "You shouldn't go out . . ., you shouldn't make friends . . . it's not advisable because with other girls it has happened that . . ." . . . Thousands of things they told me and I felt even more afraid]. What she discovers, however, is that the real danger lies *inside* the house, where she is sexually harrassed on various occasions by the fathers of the families for whom she works. By revealing the fathers' attempts to assault her physically, Condori overturns hegemonic depictions of the house as a "paradigm of security" and as the "abode of the familiar" (Wigley 1993: 118). In this manner, Condori insistently calls attention to the necessary violence with which the hegemonic interior must be policed so that the law and propriety of the Father (the modern criollo state) prevail.

THE TYRANNY OF HOME:
THE MINING ENCAMPMENTS

Analysis of the relationship between domestic space and the Bolivian state would be incomplete without a reading of housing in mining centers.[20] Studies of Bolivian mining centers call attention to the complex weave of cultural and ethnic identities that structure their social formation. In his essay "Forma clase y forma multitud en el proletariado minero en Bolivia," sociologist René Zavaleta Mercado foregrounds the impact that the geographic specificity of the mining centers has had on the formation of the miner's identity, highlighting in particular the shared experience of migration from the Cochabamba valleys to vital enterprises such as Siglo XX in the Department of Potosí (1987a: 222–223). This process of migration and relocation was critical because it created a geographic rupture and cultural break from the miners' original indigenous roots.[21] By the 1960s and 1970s there existed two and three generations of this mining proletariat, giving rise to communities with a distinct social and political fabric (224). Although most scholars agree that many of the practices of everyday life continue to be rooted in native Andean rituals and traditions, Zavaleta's essay emphasizes how geographic dislocation initiated a transformation of consciousness, a process he refers to as *"descam-*

pesinización," understood as the (gradual) undoing of *campesino* identity. For Zavaleta, *descampesinización* was fundamental to the formation of the new working-class miner's identity; he argues that this process of rupture and transformation enabled the miners to emerge in the political scenario as a powerful, organized collectivity (223–224).[22]

This network of political and economic relations that converged in the mining centers was also a complex and shifting terrain of ethnic and class relations. The emphasis on the spatiality of socioeconomic and political relations, as Doreen Massey reminds us, suggests that "what is at issue is a geography of power relations in which spatial form is an important element in the constitution of power itself" (1994: 22). The spatial interrelatedness of the mining enclaves and the rural countryside was manifested through the continual reinscription of traditional colonial structures of power. For example, Xavier Albó calls attention to the persistence of dominant structures when he observes that "the mining proletarians of Bolivia often consider themselves the 'civilized' with regard to the 'little Indians' who surround their camps" (1993: 22). Due to these spatialized racial relations, the ontological process of *descampesinización* heralded by hegemonic working-class discourse was considered crucial to the cultural and economic modernization and politicization of the indigenous *campesino*. The separation from the indigenous past identified with the rural countryside and the subsequent entry into the working-class labor union—denoted by the space of the mining center—was marked by the fact that the miner was generally referred to as a mestizo even if Quechua or Aymara continued to be the language spoken at home. (See also Harris and Albó 1976; Delgado 1989).

Although the unions' political and philosophical underpinnings were an outgrowth of liberal citizenship and cultural *mestizaje,* marking thus their difference from indigenous peoples (Rivera Cusicanqui 1993: 105–106), the state could neither embrace nor recognize the miner as an embodied symbol of modernization/modernity (the selfsame). Rather, as Zavaleta argued, from the 1940s [to the 1980s], Bolivia's history could be understood as an ongoing confrontation or duel between the military and the working class whereby the military represented the heart of the state and the working class the heart of civil society (Zavaleta Mercado 1987a: 222, 222 n. 12.; 1987b; 1990).

Domitila Barrios de Chungara's portrayal of daily life in the mining centers brings to light experiences rooted in a specific politics of location during the 1950s, 1960s, and 1970s. Insisting on the historical and economic circumstances of the Bolivian miners' living and working conditions, she focuses on the regional context that led to the development of a radical Bolivian working-class consciousness. In Barrios de Chungara's writings, the contradictory (and violent) relationship between the miners and the state is frequently played out through the house, which serves as both a metaphorical and a literal site of confrontation. Consequently, her discussion necessarily raises fundamental questions concerning the place or position of women in working-class discourse and practices of resistance. Through her critique of the quality and practice of the distribution of housing units in mining centers, she debunks the notion of the house as an unchanging, secure, and homogeneous space, and at the same time she foregrounds the interconnected relationship between the house and the production and reproduction of labor in a capitalist, market economy.[23]

In her *testimonios* and essays, Barrios de Chungara highlights the state-owned mining company's underlying practice of social control and the fostering of worker dependency when she describes the unstable and discontinuous characteristics of the miner's house. The availability and distribution of housing corresponds neither to need nor income; instead it is treated as a reward to the deserving worker. Throughout the 1960s and early 1970s, corporate-owned housing was so limited that houses were held out like carrots to the miners who worked hard and caused no trouble. Although distribution of housing was supposed to be carried out according to a point system that considered the miner's longevity with the company, the difficulty of his work, the size of his family, and so forth, a miner generally had to work five to ten years before the company would provide him with a home (Barrios de Chungara 1987: 22–24).[24] Frequently, two families had to share the cramped one- or two-room space that made up each unit. If the miner retired, fell ill and could no longer work, or died, the family had ninety days to vacate the premises (22). Given the short life span of the miners, many never lived to reside in their "own" borrowed space (24). As a result, neither the sense of worker satisfaction nor the feelings of independence from the company associated with homeownership (see Mitchell 1993: 118) were ever within the grasp of the miners. Barrios de Chungara explains, "los trabajadores mineros, que en gran parte sustentan la economía del país, al fin y al cabo ni su casita pueden tener" (Barrios de Chungara 1987: 25) [the mine workers, who in large part support the country's economy, don't even have a little house in the end] (Barrios de Chungara 1978: 26).[25]

Throughout the history of western architecture, the unified structure of the house has traditionally been likened to the human body and, by extension, to the social body, with emphasis being placed on the proper order and regular arrangement of the different parts in the construction of the integrated whole (Kolbowsky, Hawkinson, and Smith-Miller 1994: 60–61; Vidler 1992).[26] When the various "limbs and torso" of the house "are situated where they *belong,* in familiar proportions and positions in relation to one another, the body functions nominally, as it is supposed to, in the name of 'family life' and all that this currently entails—as an ideal and as the drama of abjection that often scripts its persistence and its frequent undoing" (Kolbowsky et al. 1994: 61; emphasis in the original). The "normative" house, as it is constructed in dominant discourses, then, apparently fulfills a primary role in oedipal and imaginary impera- tives. This role is what Nast and Wilson have in mind when they contend that the house "disciplines the practices of the ideal nuclear family and body politic along politically and sociospatially acceptable channels." Similarly, it is caught up in the imaginary because "it presents a viewer . . . with visual icons and ideals 'out there' that cannot be perfectly grasped" (1994: 52). Domitila Barrios de Chungara's depiction of the mining en- campment house as a space that has been fragmented and dismembered runs counter to these prevailing representations of the house as a clean, unified body.

In her accounts written during the 1960s, 1970s, and early 1980s, she characterizes the miner's house as being in a state of disrepair or "dis- memberment" as various of the different "limbs" of the structural body— bedrooms or bathrooms, for example—were missing or "out-of-order." The general condition of the structures was one of shocking deteriora- tion. Many were falling down or virtually in ruins, while others needed new roofs because, whenever it rained, portions of the house flooded or caved in (Barrios de Chungara 1987: 24).[27] Separate bedrooms, a struc- tural feature insisted on by criollo elites bent on refashioning rural in- digenous houses, were unthinkable in this instance, where the living units were impossibly small to begin with.[28] Parents, children, and other rela- tives had no option but to sleep together in one room, with children crowded side by side on beds and under them. Because space was at such a premium, Barrios de Chungara had to convert the kitchen into a bed- room and set up a cooking space outside the building under an added- on roof or *calamina* (1987: 24).[29] The thin walls of the row housing units further hindered western notions of privacy. Anthropologist June Nash observed that everyday conversations as well as family altercations could be heard in the next unit: "When a worker is fired, neighbors share their own food because, as one woman told me when her neighbors were left in this condition, 'We could not bear the sound of the children cry- ing with hunger at night'" (Nash 1979: 94). Illness spread as easily as news from one unit to the next (94).

Because the row housing lacked plumbing, the miner's home pos-
sessed neither showers nor toilets; family members had to stand in line to
use the showers, men one day, women the next, because there were only
ten for each neighborhood. Ten latrines similarly served an entire vicin-
ity: "Muy rápido se ensucian y no hay agua corriente. En la mañana hacen la limpieza los trabajadores de la empresa que están destinados para
esto; pero después, todo el día tiene que estar así sucio. Y si falta el agua,
durante varios días. Sobre esto, sobre esto, tenemos que ocupar las letri-
nas. Así" (Barrios de Chungara 1987: 23) [They get dirty very fast and
there's no running water. In the mornings the company workers assigned
to the job clean them; but afterward, all day long they're very dirty. And
if there's no water, they're dirty for several days. Even so, we have to use
them. Just like they are] (Barrios de Chungara 1978: 24). During her
stay in the mining camps in 1970, Nash observed that there were no
sanitary facilities of any kind, nor any regular supply of drinking water:
"Dust and garbage mingle on the bare ground surrounding the mine
buildings, rising up in swirls as the harsh winds of autumn and winter increase in the late afternoon" (Nash 1979: 93).

As I suggested earlier, Terán de Pohl's narrative highlighting the relationship between housing and citizenship placed emphasis on the exclusion of the abject as a necessary precondition for the formation of proper
and orderly citizens. In sharp contrast to Terán de Pohl's work, which differentiated between the enclosed, uniform space of the bourgeois house
and the so-called dirty pigsty of the working class, Barrios de Chungara's
testimonios locate the abject literally in the center of each neighborhood
and each home, identifying it as a consequence of economic exploitation. These dismembered houses destabilize the boundaries between the
clean and proper (civilized) subject and the symbolic's excluded Other.
Ironically, even as the state-owned mining corporation used housing
to discipline and domesticate the miners and their families, the results
tended to be much more equivocal precisely because of the ambiguity of
the house's boundaries. Bodies moved fluidly between the interior and
exterior of the house, in excess of its physical confines, continually trans-
gressing the threshold between the inside and outside, the private and the
public, the domestic and the political. As a result, due in large part to the
precarious conditions in which they lived, the miners and housewives
were always already (improperly) outside the social contract.

The inability of the house to domesticate, or hold things and people
in their place, cuts the ground from under hegemonic foundations of
(gendered) subjectivity. Recalling Terán de Pohl's text for a moment, one
of her greatest concerns originated with the fear of women being un-

housed by civilization's Other, communism. In the mining centers during the 1960s and 1970s, ironically, many of the women were unhoused literally due to the shortage and poor quality of company-owned housing. With the destabilization of the space of the home, the identity of the miner's housewife, defined by dominant discourses as "woman-plus-house," underwent similar transformation. If the woman was no longer recognizably a "house"wife, she and her family's relational position to the socio-symbolic contract became more uncertain. Given this situation, the (military) state arbitrarily and repeatedly revoked the rights and privileges guaranteed all citizens, a practice carried out with impunity in the mining centers during these two decades. For example, in one military assault, women from the Housewives' Committee were specifically targeted when they enforced a miners' strike by guarding the opening of the mine shaft. The military officers leading the aggression refused to recognize the protesters as women and commanded the reluctant soldiers forward: "'¡Estas son comunistas y hay que destrozarlas! ¡Para ustedes aquí no hay mujeres, no hay niños, no hay nada!'" (Barrios de Chungara 1987: 247) ['These women are communists and we've got to destroy them! Those aren't women, those aren't children, nothing like that!'] (Barrios de Chungara 1978: 222). As the soldiers marched the women outside the mine, however, the housewives responded in defiance by singing the popular *cueca* "Viva mi patria Bolivia." With their song, the women reclaimed the right to position themselves inside the social contract. The soldiers, nonplused, could not move against them: "Y era tan impresionante la escena, me dijeron, que el ejército no fue capaz de hacer nada" (1987: 248) [And the scene was so impressive, they tell me, that the army couldn't do anything] (1978: 222). Barrios de Chungara's *testimonios* suggest that the housewives of the mining encampments were particularly vulnerable to abuse by the military precisely because they transgressed the socio-spatial mechanisms of the house that discipline women as women; their mobility implied a feminine excess that could not be contained by the house. This understanding of the housewives as the personification of an unbounded and therefore potentially dangerous mobility carried important resonance for strategies of repression and resistance.

For Terán de Pohl, the success of the (male) worker could be judged by his house and its "bourgeois appearance," what we might understand as visual signs of material success and consumerism, broadly categorized as decoration, furnishings, ornamentation, and so on. In his discussion of architectural ornamentation, Wigley notes its association in the writings of Leon Battista Alberti (15th c.) with excess and, consequently, with sensuality (Wigley 1992: 352). Ornament, as a form of representation, constitutes a possible danger because of its potential to deceive the eye of the beholder through the manipulation of the surface (354–355).[30] Like the feminine, ornamentation (artifice) can seduce the (masculine) beholder with its sensuality: "The risk of ornament is an impropriety in which the sensuality of the body confuses the mind that seeks to control it. As always, reason is threatened by the fantasized sexual mobility of the feminine" (355). The (masculine) economy is, therefore, "no more than the control of the veneer, the representational surface exposed to the eye" (356). Stallybrass has similarly noted the etymological relationship between "decoration" and "decorum," whereby "decorum" refers to the order that must be brought to personal and class conduct through decoration (i.e., appropriate dress) (Stallybrass 1986: 125). Just as with woman, then, ornament must be controlled and immobilized, domesticated: "The practices of ornamentation are regulated so that ornament represents and consolidates the order of the building it clothes, which is that of man. It is used to make that order visible" (Wigley 1992: 357). It is not so much ornamentation itself that matters but the *control* of it because ornament holds the potential to both reiterate and destabilize hegemonic order.

Whereas Terán de Pohl's text links citizenship to participation in a market economy, thereby positing the acquisition of this "bourgeois appearance" as the standard according to which the working-class male's successful entrance into the socio-symbolic contract can be measured, Barrios de Chungara's writings point instead to the paradoxical nature of the social contract itself when she highlights the state's contradictory relationship to these same processes of consumption (ornamentation). A central principle of liberalism, as Mary Dietz has observed, is that of equal access to the market for all individuals: "under liberalism, citizenship becomes less a collective, political activity than an individual, economic activity—the right to pursue one's interests, without hindrance, in the market-place" (Dietz 1992: 67). However, Dietz emphasizes that when it comes to understanding the reality of equal access, context becomes everything; we need to unveil the relations of power that affect who we are and the choices we make (63, 67). In Bolivia, Silvia Rivera Cusicanqui argues, historically the social contract (citizenship rights) has been alternately extended and revoked when deemed necessary by the (military) state (see Rivera Cusicanqui 1993). This paradoxical deployment of the social contract signals an underlying anxiety, an anxiety that becomes apparent in the surveillance and suppression of the very same processes of consumption and ornamentation called for in hegemonic discourses.

Nash's fieldwork revealed that, due to high rates of inflation, miners and their families tended to buy consumer goods whenever possible rather than save their money. For example, she tells of one woman who had purchased three sewing machines to use as a dowry for her daughters (Nash 1979: 242). In an interview from 1980, Barrios de Chungara gives an account of García Meza's military government, indicating how this form of consumption was frequently policed in the mining centers: "There have been many military raids on my house, everything I have ever had they have taken. If I had a radio, they took it. If I had a new pair of shoes for my children, they took them. Now, there is only my house, so they will have to take that. . . . The only things I have left are my children" (McIntosh 1981: 310). Decoration, furnishings, personal belongings, all become suspect under military authoritarianism. Ornament, in other words, signifies deception in the hands of the working class; a seductive surface that masks another truth behind it. Goods such as radios, sewing machines, and shoes surely fall under the category of the kinds of commodities Terán de Pohl presumably had in mind that the worker would purchase with the fruits of his labor. In addition to newspapers and military force, the radio served as a principal means by which the government conveyed its message to the nation. In this context, the radio can be understood as an example of ornamentation that upholds hegemonic order. Paradoxically, however, the miners' radio also broadcasts a variety of oppositional programs in support of workers' issues as well as shows on popular education and liberation theology. Indispensable to the organization of resistance during military occupations of the mining centers, the miners' radio stations consistently were one of the first targets to be hit with force.[31] The radio provides a compelling example of ornamentation's duplicity as it simultaneously upholds and destabilizes the practices of control and order. Given this fluidity of representation, then, ornament, like the feminine, had to be viewed with intolerance and violently suppressed.

In her analysis of Habermas's critical social theory, Nancy Fraser argues that neither the role of the worker nor the role of the consumer is simply an economic concept; rather, they are "gender-economic" concepts because each has an "implicit gender subtext" (Fraser 1989: 128). According to Fraser, the consumer maintains a decidedly feminine subtext because, in a complementary role to that of the male worker, she assumes the duty of "purchasing and preparing goods and services for domestic consumption" (125). Guillermo Delgado's work on the survival strategies adopted by the Bolivian miners' housewives suggests, however, that these gender subtexts are also racialized: "Indeed, I would argue that the more impoverished the household, the more pronounced the tendency to maintain peasant strategies" (Delgado 1985: 163). In other words, Delgado's analysis reveals that the poorer a woman and her family tend to be, the more likely it is that she will engage in communal indigenous practices of exchange and reciprocity, drawing upon *ayllu* traditions of extended kinship relations. Thus, it is not uncommon for women to pass from one household to another items such as a "'borrowed bone' for soup," a practice referred to among rural indigenous communities as *mañay* (164). So, too, many women continue to make the freeze-dried potato or *chuño,* which they can trade for necessary products from other areas (167–168). These practices, rooted in long-standing Andean traditions and ways of life, in conjunction with occasional possibilities for sharecropping on indigenous communally held lands, help the poorest women make ends meet. Because they cannot afford to participate in the marketplace to the extent that Terán de Pohl had envisioned, women are likely to preserve ritual kinship obligations and other cultural ties that link them more closely to indigenous identities rather than to the proletarian, class-based identities of the (male) miners (Delgado 1985: 166–168). Consequently, these practices allow poorer women to control somewhat the degree to which they become proletarianized and domesticated. Because western gender roles have little meaning for indigenous women, the more closely a woman aligns herself with communal practices the less apt she is to identify herself as a "housewife": "es decir, más india, menos ama de casa; menos india, más ama de casa" [In other words, the more Indian a woman is, the less housewife she is; the less Indian, the more housewife].[32]

One of the most effective forms of control over the workers and their families in the mining centers, nonetheless, is the control of access to foodstuffs and other goods that the women purchase for their families. By regulating the items available for consumption, the mining company can influence the worker's entire family. Women would appear to be especially targeted in this manner because their time and energy become wholly directed to the acquisition and preparation of necessary provisions. Barrios de Chungara tells of the long lines women form in front of the *pulpería,* or state-subsidized store, from very early in the morning and throughout the day to obtain meat and other scarce items (Barrios de Chungara 1987: 32–35; see also Nash 1979: 91–92). Moreover, Nash tells of the cycle of debt and dependency structured through the *pulpería* that eliminates more favorable prices and access to a wider range of goods (Nash 1979: 239–245). As there are few options for the women, they become dependent on the store as a primary source of food. It is to the advantage of the mining company to create and sustain this general dependency because, at the first sign of union unrest, the stores can be shut down. In this manner, the company normally controls not only what the women buy but also when and in what circumstances they buy it. Moreover, by forcing the women to spend a large percentage of their day standing in line, the company prevents them from engaging in other, more subversive, activities. Nash observed that "Management is more aware than the union leaders of the potential force the mobilization of women might have in providing an independent supply base and in the public demonstrations which had an effective appeal to the wider population" (243). Ironically, however, it is often while standing in line that many of the women become organized and involved with the political activities of the Housewives Committees (243).

THE POLITICS OF THE HOUSE

Because the women of the mining centers were unable to fulfill their role as it had been traditionally defined, they found it imperative to challenge the boundary that separated the personal, domestic sphere from the political and economic dimensions of the public realm. In 1961 prolonged food shortages in the *pulperías* propelled the women—wives, widows, daughters of miners—from three mining centers into the political arena (Ardaya 1992: 99). This crisis situation, brought about by the lack of foodstuffs, the withholding of salaries for over three months, and the arrest of political leaders, culminated in the mobilization of 150 women who traveled to La Paz as a group to speak directly to the president of the Mining Corporation of Bolivia (COMIBOL). They demanded of him the immediate release of the jailed workers, the payment of overdue salaries, and food and supplies to be sent straightaway to the mining centers (Barrios de Chungara 1987: 77–79; Ardaya 1992: 99). Their petitions were met with repressive measures, so the women, accompanied by their children and infants, initiated a twenty-day hunger strike that received overwhelming support from numerous labor unions, university students, and housewives from other mining regions. When one of the women died, the government had to meet the strikers' demands to prevent the situation from escalating further (Barrios de Chungara 1987: 79; Ardaya 1992: 98–99).

This dramatic incident illustrates how the housewives, when pushed to the limit, were compelled, in bell hooks's words, to "move out of their place" (see hooks 1990: 145), to leave their homes and travel to La Paz in protest. By articulating a series of demands in such public forums as the meeting with the president of COMIBOL and, later, with the hunger strike, the housewives sought to give political status to demands that otherwise had been depoliticized through their domestication as private, familial needs (see Fraser 1989: 168–171). Just as Nancy Fraser has argued in her work on needs interpretation, the housewives' protest in La Paz "contest[ed] the established boundaries separating 'politics' from 'economics' and 'domestics'" (171).

The housewives soon found themselves caught in a double and triple bind, however, because the miners also expected the women to remain at home. If the housewives' success in La Paz resulted from the public formulation of their needs as political, this initial victory did not lead immediately to the opening up of what Fraser terms "new discourse publics" within the radical labor movement through which the women might continue to articulate a "politics of need interpretation" (171, 163). Upon their return from La Paz, these women decided that it was imperative that they form a permanent group that would enable them to join the struggle for change in solidarity with the miners. However, the women's transgressive act of "moving out of their place" and their subsequent entrance into a politicized discursive arena as speaking subjects did not meet with support from the labor unions. Barrios de Chungara recounts how the men reacted to the housewives' initial efforts to organize:

> Por ejemplo, en la primera manifestación que hubo en Siglo XX después que ellas volvieron de La Paz, las compañeras subieron al balcón del Sindicato para hablar. Los compañeros no estaban acostumbrados a escuchar a una mujer junto a ellos. Entonces gritaban: "¡Que se vayan a la casa . . . ! ¡a cocinar!, ¡a lavar!, ¡a hacer sus quehaceres!" Y les silbaban. (Barrios de Chungara 1987: 80)

> [For example, in the first demonstration in Siglo XX after they came back from La Paz, the compañeras went up on the balcony of the union hall to speak. The men weren't used to hearing a woman speak on the same platform as them. So they shouted: "Go back home . . . ! Back to the kitchen! Back to the washing! Back to your housework!" And they jeered and booed them. (1978: 74)

Even as the housewives began to protest publicly the state's political and economic policies that prevented them from carrying out their domestic responsibilities, the women quickly discovered that they would have to confront their own husbands and partners as well because these men likewise resisted women's participation in the struggle for change. What's more, many of the miners perceived the feminine domestic realm as an essentially apolitical space. Not surprisingly, then, when one mine worker identified a "politics of the house," he considered only the adequacy of *his* earnings to make ends meet so that his family could be fed and clothed and the children could receive some education: "So in balancing all these responsibilities, I would say that there exists a politics of the house. Politics is not only an international feature, but also something that one finds in the family. And in the family politics, the B$10 that I earn daily has to be stretched over the month" (quoted in Nash 1979: 238–239). This miner's notion of the "politics of the house" apparently did not encompass woman's role in the household dynamics as an unpaid laborer nor her strategies in the distribution of extremely limited resources. Instead, it reinforced hegemonic constructions of gender relations that depicted women's relationship to money and power as peripheral at best (see Fraser 1989: 118–122). Drawing from Barrios de Chungara's first *testimonio*, sociologist Moema Viezzer observes how this particular "politics of the house" is incomplete in its scope:

Si el minero tuviera como única fuente de ingreso el salario que percibe y si tuviera que pagar, de este salario, los servicios de que necesita para sí y para su familia, estaría totalmente imposibilitado de hacerlo en las condiciones de trabajo actuales.

Gracias a todas las tareas que la mujer realiza en el hogar sin retribución financiera (cocinar, lavar, planchar, cuidar de los niños) y las otras formas de trabajo suplementario (tejer, vender comida en la calle, etc.), ella facilita la reproducción de la fuerza de trabajo de su esposo. (Viezzer 1980: 95)

[If the miner had as the sole source of income the salary that he gets and if he had to pay, from that salary, the services that he needs for himself and for his family, he would be totally unable to do so under his current working conditions.

Thanks to all the housework that the woman does with no financial recompense (cooking, washing, ironing, childcare) and the other forms of supplementary work (knitting, selling food in the street, etc.), she facilitates the reproduction of her husband's labor.]

Nancy Fraser has effectively traced the relationship in a patriarchal, capitalist society between the worker and masculinity, arguing that "Masculinity is in large part a matter of leaving home each day for a place of paid work and returning with a wage that provides for one's dependents. It is this internal relation between being a man and being a provider that explains why in capitalist societies unemployment is often not just economically but also psychologically devastating for men" (Fraser 1989: 124). What Fraser describes as the "masculine subtext of the worker role" (124) is vital not only to understanding the construction of gender in the mining encampments but also to discerning how the state (generally via the military) appealed to dominant notions of masculinity among the miners themselves as a way of suppressing the housewives' activism outside of the house.

While scholars and activists of the Left have enhanced our understanding of ethnic and class-based identities in Bolivia, gender as a category of analysis tends to be overlooked, at times even dismissed. Historically, the Left discounted gender-specific issues, arguing that patriarchy was a product of capitalism and therefore would disappear when the working-class revolution triumphed. For example, Domitila Barrios de Chungara remarked in 1980:

> al luchar entre hombre y mujer, le estamos dando gusto a esos capitalistas que han sido los que han creado el machismo, que quiere decir que el hombre no acepta la participación de la mujer y de esta forma nos están dividiendo para que no podamos luchar juntos, unidos. Por eso también los capitalistas han creado el feminismo, es decir, que las mujeres peleen contra los varones. (Barrios de Chungara 1980: 25)

> [by fighting between men and women, we are pleasing those capitalists who are the ones that created chauvinism, which means that the man does not accept the woman's participation. In this way they are dividing us so that we can't fight together, united. For this reason too, the capitalists have created feminism: in other words, so that women might fight against men.]

There was no arena for dialogue between different expressions of resistance because the working class and the state privileged their oppositional stances, claiming them to be absolute and irreducible (see Lazarte Rojas 1988: 7–8). This positioning calls attention to the anxiety that emerges with the repetition of hegemony (see Bhabha 1983), an anxiety that is evident among the miners when they call for the women to come down off the platform and go home. In order to reaffirm its own authority, the radical Left constructed itself as the *only* space for the representation and engagement of a true oppositional subject position. As a result, the logic of Bolivia's hegemonic working-class ideology was unable to make the connections between its own oppositional standpoint and that of other marginal groups, including indigenous peoples and working-class women.[33]

MINING AND MASCULINITY

Although the Left dismissed gender as a category of analysis, a close reading of the dynamics of identity formation in the mining centers reveals that gender could be separated neither from the consolidation of the politicized working-class subject nor from the signifying system of the mine shaft itself as a political and socio-symbolic space.[34] Fundamental to the understanding of the interior mine shaft [*interior mina*] as an over-determined space that founds and secures identity is the fact that the mine shaft is always gendered as a masculine space. With few exceptions, the mine shaft is a site that, historically, has been prohibited to women.[35] The (phallic) verticality of the mine shaft literally and metaphorically re-produces an array of relations which exclude women. In particular, the iconographic figure of the *Tío* [literally "Uncle," a devil figure], generally located just inside the entrance of the mine, acts as a kind of guardian to this space, representing a hyperbolic masculinity with his "larger than life" erect penis.[36]

This masculine/feminine binary, continually reinforced by the di-chotomy *interior mina/exterior mina* [inside/outside the mineshaft], is visually striking in Jorge Sanjinés's film, *El coraje del pueblo* (1971). His long takes of the assembly of miners, students, and political leaders gath-ered inside the mine underscore woman's absence from the place where crucial political decisions were debated and adopted. The mine shaft was thus a paradoxical space in that it was at once a radical space of resistance for the working class and a masculinist geography that continually rein-scribed the exclusion of women.[37] Those women who worked in the border zone between the *interior mina/exterior mina*, the *palliris*— women who sort through the slag piles for ore—were poorly paid, had no benefits, and received no attention from the unions. Gloria Ardaya observes how throughout the 1960s the labor unions, especially those formed in the mining centers, elaborated a political discourse that increas-ingly disregarded women:

> Tanto en la representación como en los objetivos de las nuevas organiza-ciones sindicales nacionales, éstas heredaron de la política la mentalidad vertical de que eran depositarios de cara a las mujeres. Concebían a todos

sus miembros como iguales formalmente y a la política como totalidad sexualmente neutra, finalmente masculina, donde no había cabida para las mujeres trabajadoras y sus reivindicaciones específicas. (Ardaya 1992: 92)

[The new national labor organizations, in their representation as well as in their objectives, inherited a vertical mentality from politics which they preserved right in the women's face. They viewed all their members as essentially equal, and politics as a whole, sexually neutral—in other words, masculine; there was no room for working women and their specific demands.]

The mine was a homosocial space, a political place forbidden to women. As such, the production of gender was central to the process of identity formation within the mine shaft. The mine, as the space in which identity, politics, and place converged, was literally and symbolically embodied in the miner—the mature, political speaking subject who enunciated the powerful, ideological discourse of the radical Left that irradiated outward from the mining centers (Zavaleta 1987a). For this reason, forging one's identity as a miner was a correlate to becoming a man. The linkage between mining and masculinity also surfaces in June Nash's study of Bolivian mining communities. For example, in one interview, a miner responded to Nash's question of whether or not he felt fear when working in the mine shaft by stating the following: "I don't have any fears. I was born to be a miner! I like the mine. I like the excitement of putting myself in danger to prove my manhood and my capacity . . . I like the comradeship. I believe we all ought to live like brothers in a family, the way we workers feel inside the mine" (Nash 1979: 12).

Although the mine shaft was a place of erasure for women, nevertheless, Woman figured dominantly, integral to its signifying system. The mine shaft took on feminine attributes through an array of symbolic associations that alternated between virginity and fecundity (Nash 1979; Taussig 1980). As an icon of virginity, the brute space of the mountain (Nature) had to be "penetrated" by the miner, a performative act of culture according to which each time the miner forged the mine shaft he reenacted his masculinity.[38] On the other hand, the symbolic correlation of the mine shaft as a virginal space gave way to representations of fecundity because it birthed the precious ore *and* the working-class male. In a third instance, the mine shaft metamorphosed into an aggressive and devouring female presence, the "hembra maligna que cobra en sangre lo poco que se deja arrancar en mineral" (Mansilla T. 1978: 9) [malignant female that taxes in blood the little ore that she lets be torn out from her]. As the inverted symbol of virtue and fertility, the mine shaft symbolized a *vagina dentata,* one that demanded a blood sacrifice in exchange for her labor. Paradoxically, then, at the same time the mine shaft was represented as changing and dynamic, it was also a place securely enclosed and bounded, where meaning was *fixed* as masculine, and oppositionally constructed in relation to a feminine Other/Outsider (see Massey 1994: 168). To put it another way, the feminine Other "serve[d] as matrix/ womb for the subject's signifiers" (Irigaray 1985: 101). Within this system of symbolic representation, the miner was (en)gendered according to a spatial logic that delimited the condition of his possibility and which could not be reterritorialized outside the mine. As a result, the closing of the mines in the mid-1980s and the relocalization of the miners generated a process of identity deconstruction, referred to by some as "la desarticulación de los mineros" [the dislocation of the miners] (see *Por la vida* 1986), with the result that in a few short months they had become "ex-miners," stripped of their political power and masculinity (see Javier Sanjinés 1991; 1992b; 1992c).

According to the dominant ideology of womanhood in Bolivia, a woman's identity could only be fully realized as a wife and mother within the confines of the domestic realm of the house. The miners who belonged to the labor unions and political committees constructed a parallel discourse of womanhood when they repeatedly emphasized the platitude, "Con un revolucionario en mi casa basta" (Barrios de Chungara 1980: 44) [One revolutionary in my house is enough]. The housewives therefore were being positioned (domesticated) as apolitical reproductive units by dominant discourses, including those articulated by the powerful labor unions. Consequently, the union members perceived the first women who began organizing the Housewives Committees as well as those who ventured into the male-run union meetings as either lazy— they would rather "play" at being political rather than fulfill their domestic responsibilities—or promiscuous because they moved "freely" outside of the house (Barrios de Chungara 1980: 6–8; 17–26). Even other women accused the members of the newly formed committees of organizing to avoid housework: "No van a conseguir nada, dijeron. E incluso hablaron que nosotras éramos ociosas, para perder nuestro tiempo así, y que ellas tenían obligaciones que atender en sus hogares" (Barrios de Chungara, cited in Viezzer 1977: 33) [You're not going to achieve anything, they said. And they even remarked that we were loafers, wasting our time like that, and that they had obligations to attend to in their homes].

Nevertheless, while the miners' housewives originally mobilized around a set of needs directly linked to their roles in the home, the women's choice of the name "Housewives Committees" [*Comités de amas de casa*] emphasized a *political* relation between the house and the larger community of resistance. The name "Housewives Committees" created an oxymoron that juxtaposed the domestic sphere with the radical political arena of the miners' unions (or committees), thereby throwing into question the boundary that otherwise separated the two spaces. Consequently, the Housewives Committees directly contested the dominant gender ideology of the state at the same time as they challenged the gender politics of the overwhelmingly male, working-class labor unions.

In *Si me permiten hablar,* Barrios de Chungara underscores the paradoxical way in which the state interpellated the women as housewives and mothers within the dominant social contract. The prevailing ideology of womanhood constituted a political and cultural standard according to which, if the women did not "measure up," the state, via its military or police, could "legitimately" enact violence against them. For example, one of the first times Barrios de Chungara was arrested, the police attempted to blackmail her by threatening to kill her children if she did not cooperate (Barrios de Chungara 1987: 129–147). Thus, the military forced her into a limit situation where she had to choose between motherhood (the house) or a political stance. Taking up a political stance outside the house signified, literally, the loss of motherhood through the violent death of her children. When she refused to buckle under the pressure to sign a blank piece of paper, one of the women present cried out, "Te dije, te dije. Si así son esas herejes, así son esas comunistas. . . . ¿Qué clase de madre es usted que no quiere defender a sus hijos? . . . ¡Qué barbaridad, qué horror, qué asco de mujer!" (Barrios de Chungara 1987: 140) [I told you, I told you. That's what these heretics are like, that's what these communists are like. . . . What kind of mother are you that you won't defend your own children? Ay! How horrible, how terrible, what a disgusting woman!] (1978: 128). The second time the military took Barrios de Chungara, now almost nine months pregnant, into custody, the jailers literally beat the child out of her. One of the sergeants who attempted to help her afterwards asked her, "¿A qué te atienes, hija? Vos, siendo mujer, estando embarazada, ¿por qué no te callas? . . . Las mujeres, ¿por qué son así de rebeldes?" (1987: 165) [What are you up to, girl? Being a woman, being pregnant, why didn't you just keep quiet? . . . Why are women so rebellious?] (1978: 150). On each occasion, the military represented the violence inflicted upon her as the result of her own doing when the police asked Barrios de Chungara repeatedly what kind of woman would sacrifice her children in such a fashion. In the eyes of the military authorities (the guardians of the law), a woman can only reproduce the law of the father (the state) through motherhood by be-ing housed (domesticated). The woman who freely (improperly) leaves the house as a speaking subject can be neither a woman nor a mother but a monster, and appropriate action should be taken to put an end to monstrosity.[39]

The managers of the Siglo XX mining company, seconded by the military, appealed to dominant notions of masculinity in the effort to suppress the housewives' organized resistance. For example, Barrios de Chungara recounts how her husband, René, was brought before the company authorities and threatened with the loss of his job as a conse-quence of her political activities:

> Mira. Te estamos retirando de la empresa por culpa de tu mujer, porque tú eres un cornudo que no sabes amarrarte los pantalones. Ahora vas a apren-der a dominar a tu mujer. Primero: tu mujer ha estado presa, y en vez de estar callada, ha vuelto peor: sigue agitando, sigue metiendo cizaña entre la gente. Por eso te estamos retirando de la empresa. No es por vos, es por culpa de tu mujer. Segundo: Mira, ¿Para qué vas a necesitar tú de una mujer política? Andá, pues, botala por ahí . . . y yo te voy a devolver tu trabajo. (Barrios de Chungara 1987: 150–151)

> [Look. It's your wife's fault we're firing you from the company, because you're a sissy. You know who's wearing the pants in your family. Now you'll learn to control your wife. First of all, your wife's been in jail and instead of shutting up she's worse than ever now: she's still making trouble, she's still getting everyone all riled up. That's why we're firing you. Not because of you, but because of your wife. In the second place, what do you want with a political wife? Go ahead, give her up . . . and then I'll give you your job back.] (1978: 137)

By calling him a "*cornudo*" [literally, a cuckold] and casting doubt on his masculinity, the manager incites Chungara's anger against his wife; at the same time, he promises to bring Chungara back into the (masculine) fold of workers if he learns to wear the pants of the family and keep his wife in line. In other words, it is due to his own "weakness" rather than state and corporate oppression that Chungara has lost his job. Because of her involvement in politics, Barrios de Chungara's femininity also be-comes suspect. As I noted earlier, hegemonic representations of woman turn on signs of silence and enclosure within the house. Order hinges here on the reinforcement of enclosure. Within this signifying system, the housewives are disorderly by definition because they have "strayed" from their proper place. The image of order can only be recovered if the housewives are subordinated once again to the house. The house thus functions here, in Wigley's words, as a "mechanism of political order by both representing the possibility of order itself and enforcing specific orders" (Wigley 1992: 380). In his warning to René Chungara, the manager exclaims that because of Domitila's unruly behavior, she no longer even seems like a woman; what's worse, her actions provoke the loss of the house:

> Una mujer así no sirve para nada. Digamos que mañana, con el sacrificio de tu trabajo vas a conseguirte una casita—¿quién no sueña en hacerse una casita?—. Pues te compras una. Pero, como tu mujer es política, pasado mañana el gobierno la va a confiscar. Entonces, tu casita, para nadie la tienes, ni para ti. ¿Por qué eternamente vas a estar arruinado con esa mujer? Ahora que estás retirado, no tienes quien te mantenga. Pues, a ver si escarmienta esa mujer. ¡Es demasiado esa mujer! Ni parece una mujer. (Barrios de Chungara 1987: 151)

> [A woman like that isn't any good for anything. Imagine, tomorrow, if you work really hard, you'll build a little house—who doesn't dream about a little house?—or you can even buy one. But, since your wife's political, the day after tomorrow the government will take it away. So your house isn't yours anymore. Why should you always be messed up by a woman like that? Now that you're fired, you haven't got anyone who'll support you. Well, let's see if that woman learns her lesson. That woman's too much! She doesn't even seem like a woman.] (Barrios de Chungara 1978: 137)

By linking the loss of both house and job to the worker's emasculation, the managers (backed by the military) imply that violent repression of the workers and their families would be less ironhanded if the women reconciled themselves to traditional gender roles.[40] Moreover, the managers construct a precarious bond between themselves and the miners as men who must stand together when threatened by a common enemy: monstrous women. In this way, the state-owned companies exert pressure on the men to discourage their wives' participation in the committees.

RECLAIMING AGENCY AS SPEAKING SUBJECTS

The leaders of the Housewives Committees were well aware of the dynamics of power relations in their own households. After one protest organized by the housewives in which more than five thousand women participated, members of the committee learned that many of the women had been beaten by their husbands upon their return home. The leaders decided that drastic measures were called for, so they went on the local radio station to denounce publicly these men, stressing their complicity with the state and accusing them of being government agents:

> Y cuando [las mujeres] volvieron a sus casas, muchos trabajadores las pegaron y dijeron que ellas eran amas de casa y que no tenían nada que ver con política y que su obligación era de estar en la casa. Hasta que, finalmente, nosotras dijimos que íbamos a hacer una crítica por la radio. Y la hicimos y dijimos: "Aquellos compañeros que pegaron a sus esposas deben ser agentes del gobierno. Sólo así se justifica que ellos estén en contra de que sus compañeras hayan pedido lo que en justicia nos corresponde."
> (Barrios de Chungara 1987: 84)

> [And when (the women) went back to their homes, lots of workers beat their wives and said they were housewives and had nothing to do with politics and that their obligation was to be at home. Until, finally, we said we were going to criticize them on the radio, which we did. We said: "Those compañeros who beat their wives must be government agents. That's the only thing that can explain the fact that they're opposed to their compañeras demanding what in all justice is ours.] (1978: 78)

Barrios de Chungara tells how, over the years, the men have become more accustomed to the women's activism. After all, she explains, even the capitalists' wives formed groups like the "Lady Rotarians" and the "Lady Lions." The wives of the working class must also organize (1987: 85).

Barrios de Chungara's account of the collective organization of the housewives of the mining centers and the women's concomitant politicization in the face of extreme repression provides insight into the corresponding relationship among needs, identity, and power. According to Barrios de Chungara, power and identity were closely linked to place or positionality and enunciation. For example, although the house or domestic realm was "woman's space," even there traditional gender roles restricted her voice. Barrios de Chungara explained that liberation for the working-class woman signified, therefore, the right to express an opinion outside *and* inside the home: "Porque a veces ni como madres podemos opinar ni corregir a nuestros hijos, porque ahí viene el papá, nos agarra a patadas y puñetes y nos quita la autoridad. Al final los hijos ya no nos respetan y cuando se muere el papá nos hacen callar y nos tratan de son-sas y todo ¿no es así?" (Barrios de Chungara 1980: 9) [Because some-times, not even as mothers can we give our opinion or scold our children, because then the father shows up, he grabs us, kicks us and beats us, tak-ing away our authority over the kids. In the end, the kids no longer re-spect us, and when their dad dies, they tell us to shut up, and they treat us as if we were idiots and all, isn't that so?]. Amy Conger Lind's work in Ecuador similarly documents how working class and poor women "rec-ognize that power is inherent in people's daily actions, speech, language, and movements. They have recognized forms of power in their interper-sonal and familial relationships and have made this politically visible by emphasizing 'democracy within the household'" (Lind 1992: 147).

The link between speech or "coming to voice" and the transformation of vertical relations of power both in the house and in the wider socio-economic arena is central to Barrios de Chungara's writings from the first title, *Si me permiten hablar,* to the final anecdote of *¡Aquí también, Domitila!.* Throughout her work and writings, the act of coming to voice, or speaking out, is contingent on woman's self-awareness and self-positioning as a political being inside and outside the home. Contrasting Barrios de Chungara's "voiceless" past before she joined the Housewives Committee to her position in the early 1980s as a speaking subject and leader of the committee, one neighbor observed: "Mírale a ver a esta 'habladora' lo que se ha vuelto. . . . ¡Quién iba a pensar que la Domitila iba a estar en Europa hablando! Si ella no sabía ni hablar, sabía llorar nomás" (Barrios de Chungara 1985: 280) [See? Take a look at what a chatterbox she's become. . . . Who would have thought that Domitila would be over in Europe speaking! Why, she didn't even use to know how to speak, she only knew how to cry].

Barrios de Chungara's writings as well as other documents by and about the Housewives Committees suggest, however, that the act of coming to voice was always already structured, at least in part, by the dominant political discourse of the miners' unions.[41] In order to legit-imize their standing as speaking subjects and agents who wanted to work for change in solidarity with the revolutionary mine workers, the women first had to position themselves discursively within the ideological frame-work of class consciousness. Otherwise, anyone who spoke solely in favor of women's rights ran the risk of being perceived as antagonistic to the liberation of the working class. For example, two fundamental texts, Barrios de Chungara's paper "La mujer y la organización" and the first publication of the Centro de Promoción Minera (CEPROMIN) series

"La mujer minera," entitled "La conciencia, el comité y el sindicato," represent the working-class housewife's political consciousness as the direct outgrowth of her realization that she is doubly discriminated against and exploited in capitalism as a worker and as a woman. The discursive space open to the Housewives Committees could be defined by the following parameters: "nuestra línea de acción principal es actuar en función de los objetivos de la clase obrera" (CEPROMIN 1990: 13) [our main strategy is to act in accordance with the objectives of the working class], and "la lucha de las mujeres no es antagónica a la de la clase obrera minera" (CEPROMIN 1990: 22) [the women's struggle is not antagonistic to the working-class miners' struggle].

What Barrios de Chungara had witnessed in Mexico City during the International Women's Year Tribunal led her to identify two, mutually exclusive, types of liberation: one that called itself feminism, advocating women's separation from men and the equal right to enjoy male vices like drinking and smoking; and a second kind that envisioned the liberation of the working class as men and women joined together to overthrow a common enemy. Thus, for Barrios de Chungara, the struggle for working-class women was the struggle to participate equally with the men: "Nuestra posición entonces no debe ser la pelea con nuestros compañeros o imitar los vicios del varón, más bien habría que imitar lo bueno que tienen nuestros esposos" (Barrios de Chungara 1980: 8) [Our position, therefore, should not be the struggle against our *compañeros* nor the imitation of the male's bad habits; rather, it should be the imitation of the good in our husbands].[42]

The terms of contestation which the Housewives Committees set up for themselves as speaking subjects within the working-class political sphere were mediated a priori by their position as an auxiliary committee of the miners' unions. Summarizing, Gloria Ardaya observes:

las mujeres del Comité de Amas de Casa asumen la posición que la izquierda boliviana tiene con respecto a la situación en que se encuentra la mujer; no niega que ésta se encuentra en situación de desventaja con respecto al hombre, pero considera que ello se debe a la explotación capitalista que sufre el país y que la solución al problema económico de la mujer vendrá cuando el proletariado conquiste sus objetivos históricos. (Ardaya 1989: 198–199)

[the women of the Housewives Committee adopt the position held by the Bolivian Left with regard to the situation in which woman finds herself; it does not deny that woman is in a situation disadvantageous to that of the man, but it considers that this is due to the capitalist exploitation that the country suffers and that the solution to woman's economic problem will come when the proletariat secures its historical objectives.]

In other words, during the 1960s and 1970s, the boundary between the domestic and the political, as a site of contestation, could not be reconstructed in a way that readily enabled the women to articulate their difference within the working-class struggle (see Alarcón 1990a: 254–255).

For example, in 1980 during the first Congreso de Mujeres Campesinas de La Paz, indigenous women discussed the urgent need for child care for those who worked in the fields. Reflecting on the debate, Barrios de Chungara admits, "Nosotros en el Comité nunca nos habíamos planteado tener una guardería, pero las compañeras campesinas decían: 'El trabajo en el campo es tan duro que nosotras necesitamos guarderías'" (Barrios de Chungara 1985: 86) [We in the Housewives Committee never thought of child care, but the *campesina compañeras* said: "The work in the fields is so hard that we women need child care"]. Barrios de Chungara's own writings make it plain that adequate child care facilities would have greatly assisted the majority of the housewives of the mining centers who frequently had to leave their children home unattended while they went out in search of additional work or while they stood in line for hours at a time to acquire basic foodstuffs and drinking water. The Housewives Committees were never in a position of power to participate fully in the definition of those issues which the unions would sanction or dismiss. Indeed, particularly during times of crisis, many of the policies and positions adopted by the miners were debated inside the mine shaft, a space forbidden to the women.

In spite of the limitations outlined above, the importance of the Housewives Committees cannot be overestimated. These women's organizations played a fundamental role in the working-class resistance movement, often during times of extreme repression by the military state or severe economic hardship. Their instrumentality in the demise of General Hugo Bánzer Suárez's dictatorship in 1978 will be discussed in Chapter 5. The Housewives Committees could be understood as a form of threshold or gateway to women's agency inside and outside the house because their positioning as speaking subjects threw into crisis dominant notions of social space as gendered, separate domains. The housewives' practices anticipate what feminist geographer Gillian Rose termed a double gesture, when, on the one hand, they claimed their identity as housewives as a ground zero for their participation in the larger working-class struggle. At the same time, however, they refused to be interpellated as Man's Other when they rejected hegemonic "exclusionary, territorial claims to identity" (Rose 1993: 154). On account of their agency and activism, therefore, the Housewives Committees gave impetus to the re-theorization of the relationships among gender, identity, and the terrain of working-class resistance.

✍

FOUR

FASHIONING THE
NATIONAL SUBJECT

Pedagogy, Hygiene, and Apparel

✍

In her book *Presencia de nuestro pueblo* (1976) criolla writer Elssa Paredes de Salazar tells the story of a man who, during his student years, officially "progressed" through three different racial categories. When he first migrated to La Paz as a child, he enrolled in a school that registered him as an Indian because of his appearance and the clothing that he wore. After years of struggle and perseverance, he obtained his high school diploma, which listed him as "mestizo." Later on, when he finished a university degree in engineering, his documents described him as being of the "white race" (1976: 31). Paredes de Salazar's account points to the important role educational institutions play in the formation of modern identities, suggesting thus that race is culturally rather than biologically determined.

This chapter will focus on pedagogy and the ways by which specific subjects of the curriculum, like hygiene, and topics of concern to criollo educators, like fashion, work together to produce racially acculturated, docile bodies. Docile bodies, according to Susan Bordo, are "bodies whose forces and energies are habituated to external regulation, subjection, transformation, 'improvement'" (1993: 166). By examining the intersections of pedagogy, hygiene, and fashion, it is possible to bring to light some of the organizing principles linking individual bodies to the modern Bolivian nation. Throughout the twentieth century, clothing and notions of dirt versus cleanliness have functioned as central, constitutive elements which stage cultural, racial, and gender differences. While seemingly unrelated, hygiene and fashion were frequently juxtaposed in normal school pedagogical manuals; both figured predominantly in the curriculum for rural indigenous and upper-class, urban girls' schools at the turn of the century. A critical reading that juxtaposes pedagogical manuals, women's journals, and Aymara testimonials suggests that fashion and hygiene discourses interpellate each group differently, often in contradictory and ambiguous ways.

At the beginning of the twentieth century, criollo educators believed that hygiene was one of the most important subjects of the new curriculum developed for rural indigenous schools; and even today it appears as a fundamental component of the rural school's plan of study. In 1940, the conservative Consejo Nacional de Educación maintained that "la cuestión educacional tiene que ser en primer término, principalmente entre los campesinos, de 'extirpación de piojos y de mugre'" (Consejo Nacional de Educación 1940: 5) [the educational issue, primarily among the *campesinos*, has to be first and foremost a matter of "exterminating lice and filth"]. As part of the curricular cultural politics, hygiene conscripted the body, positing it as a site of conflict between the authority of the criollo oligarchy and the indigenous Other;[1] therefore hygiene emerged as a principal ideologeme in the trajectory between the "normal" modern body and "disorderly" primitive bodies.[2]

Within the matrix of cultural and symbolic relations whereby the normative way of life was linked to political and economic power, the pathological body took on unprecedented importance. As Mary Douglas puts it, dirt is merely "matter out of place": "Where there is dirt there is system. Dirt is the by-product of a systematic ordering and classification of matter, in so far as ordering involves rejecting inappropriate elements" (Douglas 1992: 35). Emphasis on the new discipline of hygiene enabled the surveillance and management of bodies and spatial relations at the same time as it policed the "systematic ordering" of the normal (see Foucault 1980: 150–151). Dirt and pollution constituted racialized signifiers of disorder deployed by hegemonic discourses to designate the native Andean and working-class *cholo* peoples. According to the prevailing ideology, Bolivia was a disordered nation, a *pueblo enfermo*, because of its racial heterogeneity.

While many criollo intellectuals argued that racial differences were biologically determined and thus enfleshed, others believed that they were surface effects that converged in crucial ethnic signifiers such as clothing.[3] Certainly throughout the colonial period, clothing was instrumental in the fixing of racial and cultural differences (see Meléndez 1995). On the grounds that clothing could be changed voluntarily or by force, the vested interests of elite discourses focused on refashioning indigenous and *cholo* peoples in order to incorporate them into the imagined modern nation. Western clothing produced an image of modernity just as native clothing produced an image of barbarity. Writing on the relationship between modernity and reform dress, U.S.-based theorist Mark Wigley claims that "For all its ostensible functionalism, reform dress produced foremost an *image* of modernity that was actually understood as the very possibility of a modern life, rather than an adjustment to it or representation of it" (1994b: 10; emphasis in original). For criollo elites in the Bolivian context, western dress produced an image of a cohesive citizenry, a unified national body that ostensibly shared the common goal of one day becoming modern.

Because racial difference was marked most visibly through sartorial practices, traditional Andean clothing became synonymous with hegemonic conceptions of dirt, a primary trope of disorder. Both a change of clothing and the implementation of hygienic practices structured the modern imperative, constituting mutually consolidating facets of the process of rupture whereby subjectivities were transformed from Indians into acculturated mestizos (citizens). Olivia Harris similarly underscores the significance of rupture to the formation of "modern" western identities in the Andean region: "Full incorporation into the category of mestizos involved denial of one's identity, one's past, one's origins. This denial frequently involved—and still does—changing one's family name . . . and thereby distancing oneself from one's kinsfolk. Changing one's clothing, one's diet, and one's language were crucial indicators, and remain so today" (Harris 1995: 365).[4]

Even as the prevailing ideology enjoined indigenous peoples to conform to western standards of dress and hygiene, the possibility of the Indian's transformation became a source of anxiety for the upper class. A mere change of clothing seemingly enabled the Indian "Other" to pass as mestizo, rendering racial difference invisible. This ambivalence emerged with particular intensity in urban centers where the elites came into contact daily with Indians and *cholos*. For example, testimonials of female domestic workers describe both criollo and mestizo employers who, even today, continue practices that sustain racial differences, for instance, requiring that their maids wear *polleras* rather than dresses. Clothing, therefore, was vested with the paradoxical power to destabilize *and* resecure boundaries.

Because clothing could blur boundaries, it generated anxiety of another form. Liberalism emphasized the strengthening of market forces and patterns of consumption. One way in which upper-class girls and women could be drawn into modern consumerism was through the fashion industry. Like the Indian who buys soap, the criolla who buys a stylish dress is first interpellated and then showcased by modernity. Paulette Singley and Deborah Fausch address modernity's ontological and episte- mological boundaries through a critique of fashion. In their introduction to the anthology *Architecture: In Fashion,* they ask, "What exactly are the consequences of embedding fashion within modernism? Is it fashion's stark engagement in the commodity relationship which makes it such an apposite metaphor for modernity?" (Singley and Fausch 1994: 24). As cultural critics and theorists of fashion agree, women in particular have been targeted by the economy of clothing with the consequence that the act of consumption entices women to abandon the domestic sphere for the department store (see Felski 1995: 61–90). Fashion, therefore, comes dangerously close to psychosis (Singley and Fausch 1994: 24), as a "phe- nomenon which threatens the very stability of segregated zones: man/ woman, subject/object, the personal/political, reality/illusion" (Saw- chuk 1987: 62). When these boundaries break down, unleashed feminine desires threaten to run out of control: "The repressed feminine of aes- thetic and libidinal forces returns in the form of the engulfing, regressive lures of modern mass culture and consumer society, which trades inau- thentic pleasures and pseudo-happiness for acquiescence to the status quo" (Felski 1995: 5). Ironically, then, "the celebration of production" becomes opposed to the "pathologization of consumption" (Felski 1995: 69).

During the 1920s, Bolivian educators became alarmed, cautioning against the perils of fashion that "seduced" women by inducing them to leave their homes and squander their fathers' and husbands' money on the latest craze. They claimed that only by learning proper body man- agement and hygienic values would young girls comprehend the dangers of the public world and be content to remain modestly at home. In con- trast to fashion, hygiene figured as a vital instrument for the redrawing of gendered boundaries. My readings of hygiene and fashion, therefore, suggest that the ambivalence structuring the rhetoric of modernity in Bolivia derived from the continual production and reproduction of a bor- der logic endemic to its project.

FORGING THE NATION THROUGH EDUCATION

At the beginning of the twentieth century Bolivia had just begun to re- cover from the painful losses of the War of the Pacific (1879–1884) and the 1899 civil war between Liberals and Conservatives. This latter conflict evolved unexpectedly into a racial war when Aymara Indians under the leadership of cacique Pablo Zárate Willka rebelled, underscoring the precarious nature of Indian-criollo alliances.[5] In this context of civil strife and racial conflict, many criollos seized upon education as the remedy that would heal the sick nation and make it whole.

Leading intellectuals of the period turned to education as the most expedient means by which the Indian could be domesticated and transformed into a productive (mestizo) laborer (see Salmón 1986: 33–52; Soria Choque 1992: 49–59).[6] This unprecedented interest in schooling the Indian was posed rhetorically in discourses calling for a unified nation. For instance, in his study *La educación del indio: (Contribución a la pedagogía nacional)* (1919), educator Alfredo Guillén Pinto argued that Bolivia needed to forge a common national essence, a collective soul (Guillén Pinto 1919: 28). Only the school offered the appropriate "weapons" and "battle site" that such a project required: "Ferrocarriles, telégrafos, cañones, todo, todo podremos comprar con el oro de nuestras riquezas; pero un *alma boliviana, un carácter nacional único,* ¡no! Ni con plata ni con oro: con EDUCACION" (166–167; emphasis in original) [Railways, telegraphs, cannons, everything, we can buy everything with the gold from our wealth; but a *Bolivian soul, a unique, national character,* no! Neither with silver nor with gold: with EDUCATION]. Indeed, educators contended, if the Indian had the potential to become a "future citizen" (145), this transformation could only take place peacefully with the appropriate curriculum.[7]

Sentiment on educating the Indian varied according to different sectors of the criollo population. Many Liberals of the urban oligarchy firmly believed that education constituted the only humane way to civilize the Andean peoples and improve their economic productivity (Claure 1989; Salmón 1986; Mamani Capchiri 1992). In contrast, large landholders, many of whom were members of the Sociedad Rural Boliviana [Bolivian Rural Society], and mestizos who lived in rural towns ardently opposed schooling for the Indians, arguing that this was the way unrest infiltrated the countryside. This second group marshaled arguments based on racist discourses that claimed that the indigenous peoples were simply incapable of learning (Mamani Capchiri 1992: 81).

Ironically, however, even though both groups differed in their opinions on indigenous education, ultimately their objectives were less disparate. It was in the interests of each group to keep the productive and reproductive labor force of the Andean native peoples under the control of criollo elites. The debates over education therefore defined a complex paradox. Although education was hailed as the most prudent means by which Indians could be transformed into citizens, textbooks and pedagogical manuals of the time indicate that classroom strategies effectively recuperated and reinscribed racial difference. For example, Guillén Pinto steadfastly maintained that whites, Indians, and mestizos should be educated separately, "no por razones de casta sino por las opuestas aptitudes e inclinaciones" (Guillén Pinto 1919: 159; see also Salmón 1986) [not for reasons of race, but rather because of their opposing aptitudes and inclinations]. The debates over curriculum reform ultimately reiterated the Indian's difference from the criollo, thereby rendering racial hierarchies as the cultural norm. Moreover, because educators insisted that the Indian should be encouraged to remain in his rural milieu and not migrate to urban areas, they represented the native peoples in spatial terms that further exacerbated competing strategies of inclusion/exclusion.[8] The ambivalence surrounding the debates on indigenous education is foregrounded in recent studies by Aymara historians. Their investigations disclose how the move to reform the Indians through education was systematically accompanied by the parallel practice of aggressive extermination, one of the most notorious instances being the massacre in 1921 of the Indians from the Jesús de Machaca *ayllu*.[9]

Indians themselves played instrumental roles in the establishment of schools in rural *ayllus*. Many caciques appropriated incipient nationalist discourses to affirm their right to an education, publicly challenging conservative agendas that positioned Andean peoples as modernity's Other. For instance, in 1927, a group of caciques submitted a "*Memorial*" to Parliament protesting the denial of rural schools asserting that:

> los que tienen la culpa para que nosotros estemos en la ignorancia son estas autoridades que en vez de ayudar dan la contra, que a la fecha sabiendo leer la raza indígena hubiéramos sido útiles a la Patria, cada uno hubiera tenido su oficio ya sea sastres, carpinteros y labradores, que con conocimientos hubiera progresado Bolivia y la industria se hubiera fomentado, los que se oponen son los responsables del atraso de Bolivia, los curas, los corregidores, económicos y agentes, estos eternos enemigos de la raza indígena que nos quieren mantener en la ignorancia . . . (cited in Mamani Capchiri 1992: 88)

> [the ones who are to blame for our ignorance are these authorities who, instead of helping, actively hinder us, since by now, knowing how to read, the indigenous race could have been useful to the nation. Each one

would have had his own trade, be it tailor, carpenter, and farmer, because with knowledge Bolivia would have progressed and industry would have been promoted. Those who oppose [schooling for us] are the ones responsible for Bolivia's backwardness: the priests, corregidors, economists, and police, those eternal enemies of the Indian race who want to keep us in ignorance . . .]

Caciques appealed to the Liberal government's newly implemented laws, maintaining that there existed equality of rights for all citizens, including the right to be educated. Importantly, however, native Andean desire for the establishment of *ayllu*-schools was not based on any interest in the dominant pedagogic's supposed transformative power to create acculturated mestizos. Instead, the schools became an important vehicle with which the Aymara resisted repressive political programs.

In his work on schooling and popular education in England, James Donald contends that we must look beyond the official role of education in the constitution of subjectivities: "The strategies and discourses of governmental apparatuses tell only half the story. It is equally important to look at the unrecorded but resourceful improvisations of everyday life. Here the cultural norms are transgressed and reworked in the very moment they are instituted" (Donald 1992: 2–3). Donald's analysis calls attention to the potential for transformation of the pedagogic by the performative (2). Importantly, however, Aymara resistance to the dominant pedagogic cannot be understood solely in terms of spontaneous improvisation on the part of individual students. Aymara historians have compellingly determined that the Andean struggle for *ayllu*-schools transgressed hegemonic cultural norms, continually and systematically counterdeploying the pedagogic for purposes of resistance. The few rural schools that were established became strategic instruments in ongoing, collective practices of indigenous resistance (Mamani Capchiri 1992: 88). For example, Humberto Mamani Capchiri observes that Indians wanted to be educated, to learn to read and write Spanish, precisely because these skills aided them in their unremitting struggle to recover land that had been seized by criollos (84). Literacy in the Spanish language enabled the Indians to rely on their own scribes [*escribanos*] in the legal battles to recuperate communal territory (87). Traditional leaders (caciques) had *escribanos* read the Colonial land titles to them so that they could study the original boundaries of *ayllus;* these titles also allowed for traditional forms of communal governance, granting authority to the "*caciques de sangre,*" or descendents of colonial caciques (Soria Choque 1992: 44). Although actual gains were limited, Vitaliano Soria Choque emphasizes the ability of the indigenous movement to frustrate the ever-expanding interests of the rural oligarchy (45):

> La sociedad criolla representada por los hacendados y vecinos de pueblo usó todos los medios intimidatorios para obstaculizar los intentos de crear escuelas. Los testimonios nos muestran que los indios, a su vez, se valieron de todos los medios y establecieron todo tipo de relaciones—con sectores opositores, iglesia, dirigentes políticos—para conseguir su objetivo; además procuraron instruírse por su cuenta, aún a costa de arriesgar su libertad y hasta su vida. Esto muestra hasta qué punto, la escuela representaba una estrategia de sobrevivencia para las comunidades. (62)

> [Criollo society, represented by the landholders and the (mestizo) towns-people, used all methods of intimidation to block the efforts to create schools. The *testimonios* show us that the Indians, in turn, made use of every means possible and established all kinds of relationships—with op-positional sectors, the church, political leaders—in order to achieve their objective (of creating schools); in addition, they tried to educate them-selves on their own, and they did so at the cost of risking their freedom and even their lives. This shows to what extent the school represented a survival strategy for the indigenous communities.][10]

For the indigenous peoples, then, rural schools played a determining role in the ongoing struggle to reestablish and strengthen the *ayllu*.

Peter McLaren's work on critical pedagogy in the United States re-minds us that learning must be understood in terms of its relationship to the "production and legitimation of particular discursive positions" and that it "tak[es] place within historically situated practices involving polit-ical regimes of the body" (McLaren 1995: 45). For criollos, the curricu-lum for indigenous schools constituted a form of cultural politics that critically positioned individual, racialized bodies in relation to the ideal-ized, monolithic subject of the dominant symbolic.[11] The body, to use McLaren's term, was to become "enfleshed" through the pedagogic, as criollo curricular practices inaugurated a politics of body management rather than a politics grounded in land tenure. In contrast to Aymara em-phasis on the relationship between education and land rights, dominant pedagogical practices foregrounded the formation of individual, docile bodies at the same time as it actively worked against native movements to recuperate communal lands.[12]

For McLaren, enfleshment of the body involves a dialectical process

FIGURE 4.1.

The Public Handing Over of the Inkalipe Land Titles, *circa 1930*.
Photograph courtesy of Taller de Historia Oral Andina.

whereby the body both incorporates and produces cultural symbols and social structures (67): "Enfleshment can be conceived here as the mutually constitutive aspect (enfolding) of social structure and desire. Discourses neither sit on the surface of the flesh nor float about in the formless ether of the mind but are enfolded into the very structures of our desire inasmuch as desire itself is formed by the anonymous historical rules of discourse. It is in this sense, then, that the body/subject becomes *both the medium and the outcome of subjective formation*" (67–68; emphasis in original). In Foucauldian terms, the relationship between the individual body and the dominant socio-symbolic system is disciplined through the Normal: "In a sense, the power of normalization imposes homogeneity; but it individualizes by making it possible to measure gaps, to determine levels, to fix specialities and to render the differences useful by fitting them one to another" (Foucault 1979: 184). Individual bodies become the site of struggle through which the power of the Norm attempts to regulate and manage the social body. In Bolivian rural schools, these curricular processes of enfleshment mobilize conditions that continually measure primitive, racialized bodies against normative modern (white) bodies. Power individualizes and privatizes by calling attention to each student through dominant cultural practices of hygiene and fashion. Ideology thus masks itself, giving the illusion of freeing bodies from their own barbarism while dismissing vital questions of territoriality and indigenous autonomy.

A SUITABLE CURRICULUM FOR INDIGENOUS SCHOOLS

In 1910, Bautista Saavedra published the *Reorganización de la enseñanza primaria,* where he outlined the kinds of course subjects that should be taught in rural indigenous schools:[13] "idioma castellano, lecciones de objetos usuales a la vida civilizada, moral, enseñanza cívica y antialcohólica, nociones de higiene y agricultura, etc." (cited in Finot 1917: 89) [Spanish language, lessons on the usual objects of civilized life,[14] ethics, training in civics and antialcoholism, notions of hygiene and agriculture, etc.]. Although Saavedra's proposal was not immediately adopted, it functioned as a basic guideline for ongoing dialogues about the curriculum to be implemented in rural schools (Finot 1917: 89–90).

Of all the new subjects proposed, hygiene was one of the most important. Because educational manuals of the period increasingly correlated hygienic practices with modernization and its concomitant attributes of order and discipline, hygiene clearly signified more than "simply" being clean. It acquired obvious political and social meanings as it began to figure predominantly in the ordering of rural indigenous communities.[15] Criollo apprehension of dirt and filth, legitimated through new scientific research on microbes, focused on the bodies, clothing, and houses of indigenous families. For example, the Ministry of Education and Agriculture's 1928 publication *La reforma de nuestras escuelas rurales* emphasized the need to teach the proper way to cleanse the body, partitioning it into different zones, each of which required particular kinds of care and specific cleaning utensils. The teacher's job included daily inspections of the body and clothing to ensure that proper hygienic measures had been adopted: "aseo de las diversas partes del cuerpo; verificar revisiones rigurosas diarias en todos los cursos. El jabón, el cepillo para dientes, etc. Higiene de los vestidos. Lavar algunas prendas. Higiene de los útiles" (Ministerio de Instrucción Pública y Agricultura 1928: 13) [cleanliness of the different parts of the body; verify rigorous daily inspections for each grade. Soap, toothbrush, etc. Cleanliness of clothing. Wash some articles of clothing. Cleanliness of school utensils and tools].

Soap, water, and cleaning brushes inscribed social and cultural meanings and values onto the body's surface, thereby producing the difference between dirty/pathological/disordered bodies and clean/normalized bodies. Personal behavior was also to be cleaned up and strictly scrutinized for lapses in conduct; consequently, teachers taught children not to "llevar objetos extraños a la boca, mojar el lápiz, comer con las manos sucias, morder las uñas, pintarrajear las paredes, beber del mismo vaso que otro etc. (Todos estos y otros hábitos perjudiciales o desagradables, deben ser corregidos, así sistemática como ocasionalmente, sin dejar pasar una sola vez)" (13) [put strange objects in their mouth, wet the pencil with their mouth, eat with dirty hands, bite their nails, mark up the walls, drink from the same glass as someone else, etc. (All these and other harmful or disagreeable habits should be corrected, systematically as well as occasionally, without letting a single incident get by)]. Through mimicry and imitation, Indian children were drilled in hygienic practices such as washing their hands and brushing their teeth; their teachers also instructed them to introduce these habits at home so that other family members could learn the proper rituals of cleanliness.

It is important to note that these official documents do not provide any reference to or discussion of alternative Andean hygienic customs even with an eye to "correcting" them. What permeates these pedagogical manuals instead is the tremendous anxiety felt on the part of criollo educators as well as their enormous ideological investment in dominant cultural practices. Moreover, this anxiety points to the contradictory nature of hegemonic discourses that call for the "cleaning up" of primitive subjects and at the same time reiterate the impossibility of such a project; hence the need for constant review and drill in each class.

In this context, mimicry and repetition emerged as vital strategies of hegemonic power and knowledge (see Bhabha 1994: 85). Individual hygienic practices were linked to wider social codes and values when teachers encouraged the children to describe their own homes, the objects found within, and their general state of cleanliness, as part of the learning process emphasizing healthy mores (Ministerio de Instrucción Pública y Agricultura 1928: 15). Writing on the ways by which dominant ideologies become disseminated, black British cultural critic Kobena Mercer suggestively claims that they do not "just dominate by universalizing the values of hegemonic social/ethnic groups so that they become everywhere accepted as the norm. Their hegemony and historical presence is underwritten at a subjective level by the way ideologies construct positions from which individuals recognize such values as a constituent element of their personal identity and lived experience" (Mercer 1994: 103). The process of homogenization accordingly needs to forge positions from which individuals not only distinguish the norm but also appear to be complicit in its repetition. By publicly reporting on the state of their homes and families, school children identified those elements that had become part of their lived experience at the same time they ostensibly participated in the policing of the dominant ideologies.

As an ideologeme of hegemonic cultural politics, hygiene was strategic to identificatory processes throughout the 1920s, 1930s, and 1940s. The daily regulation and inspection of the body cathected the bonds of identification, channeling the path of indigenous desire and aligning it with the dominant symbolic.[16] In this paradigm of identification-counteridentification, to be unclean signaled moral and physical disease/disorder or desire gone awry (perverted). Given the significance of its symbolic capital, hygiene continued to play a contradictory role in indigenous education during the 1940s. The Consejo Nacional de Educación utilized hygiene as a measure against which it could blast radical experiments in indigenous education from the 1930s, such as the *ayllu*-school of Warisata for its implementation of a tripartite curriculum based on "el aula, el taller, y el sembrío" (Salazar Mostajo 1986: 91) [the classroom, the workshop, the planted fields].

For example, the Consejo's report, *El estado de la educación indigenal en el país* (1940), linked hygiene and identification by claiming that the *ayllu*-schools had failed in the efforts to forge a unified national identity because they had been unable to clean up the filthy bodies of indigenous schoolchildren: "Hay que declarar de una vez por todas, que no deben existir sino escuelas catalogadas por aptitudes, ramos y ciclos, desterrando las diferencias de clase y raza, peligrosas para un país donde se impone el imperativo patriótico de homogenizar la población, crear una verdadera nacionalidad, un bolivianismo puro, alentado por ideales y sentimientos unigénitos" (Consejo Nacional de Educación 1940: 4) [It is necessary to declare once and for all that the only schools that should exist are those classified according to aptitude, disciplinary areas, and grade levels. We must do away with racial and class differences that are so dangerous for a country where the patriotic imperative is necessary to homogenize the population, to create a true nationality, a pure love of Bolivia, encouraged by universal ideals and sentiment]. After having visited a number of *ayllu*-schools, the members of the commission observed with alarm that they could find no attempts either to modernize or to reform the Indians, primarily in the area of agricultural practices (4–5). Contrasting these findings with their own priorities, the Consejo asserted the need for indigenous schools, but not ones like those that fomented the "primitive" political and cultural practices of the *ayllu*. The report defended, instead, the Consejo's prerogatives, arguing that since it had assumed the administration of indigenous education, the government had invested large sums of money in school buildings, medicinal drugs, and soap (5).

The Consejo de Educación's commission investigated the controversial *ayllu*-schools with the intention of shutting them down. In particular, their report expressed alarm over the schools' seemingly careless attention to body management. The commission foregrounded this concern by focusing on the public display of uncontrolled bodily functions. For instance, Doctor Aliaga Suárez wrote the following description of one school inspected in Caiza:

Y sin tomar en cuenta la edad, los servicios higiénicos brillan por su ausencia, no tienen urinarios, ni retretes. Es una escuela según me dicen que tiene ya varios años de existencia y los niños y niñas realizan sus necesidades fisiológicas al aire libre y muy cerca de la escuela. Pero cuando se acerca la noche, o en la noche, antes de que fueran trasladados los varones a la sección nueva, las puertas de sus dormitorios y aún la de la Dirección, se transforman en urinarios y estercoleros. Teniendo los alumnos que realizar en la mañana el barrido. (cited in Consejo Nacional de Educación 1940: 61)

[And without taking age into account, sanitary facilities are conspicuous by their absence; there are neither urinals nor toilets. According to what they tell me, it's a school that's been around for some years and the boys and girls have to relieve themselves outdoors and very close to the school. But when nighttime approaches or is upon them, before the male students might be moved to the new section, the doors to their dorm rooms and even of the principal's office become changed into urinals and dungheaps. In the morning the students have to sweep up the mess.]

The report's emphasis on the students' anality draws attention to their perversion, or counteridentification. The uncontrolled profusion of urine and feces associated with the undisciplined indigenous body warns of the dangers of a racialized (i.e., premodern) desire run amok. This perversion, or turning away from the dominant symbolic, is further marked by the students' sexual promiscuity or racial "inbreeding." Doctor Aliaga Suárez continues:

> No fueron examinadas las niñas que hubiese sido muy conveniente en ese tiempo, pués, cortos meses después, llegó a dar a luz un robusto niño, una de las alumnas. . . . Veo como una necesidad imperiosa, que al indígena siempre hay que manejarlo con disciplina, darle mayor libertad y en el internado se desboca peor, como sucede hoy día, que el indio fruto de la escuela de Caiza, es elemento negativo. Existe promiscuidad de edades, cabe reglamentar la edad de los escolares y separar a los adultos tanto en varones como en mujeres (61–62).

> [The schoolgirls were not examined at that time, which would have been advisable, since, short months later, one of them gave birth to a robust boy. . . . I see it as a pressing need that the Indian be handled with discipline. If you give him greater freedom then, in the boarding school, he becomes even more unmanageable. That's what is happening today with the Indian who is a product of the Caiza school: he is a negative element. There exists an indiscriminate mixing of ages in the classroom, hence we must call for the regulation of the students by age, separating the adults, as well as the men from the women.]

According to the commission, these experimental indigenous schools, sites of perverse desire and moral contamination, needed to be "cleaned up," a euphemism for eradicated.[17]

The commission's report therefore expressed extreme dissatisfaction with the work accomplished in the *ayllu*-schools. Their review of the conditions found at one school is reflective of the spirit of the entire report;

lamenting the pervasion of filth, they unambiguously reiterated the link between the acquisition of western hygienic practices and modernization:

> Los alumnos indígenas carecen de hábitos higiénicos: sus vestidos, sus camas, y su alimentación no han variado fundamentalmente; los dormitorios, comedores y cocinas ocupados por aquéllos, siguen desaseados. No se nota ninguna irradiación social de los núcleos escolares para mejorar las condiciones de vida y de trabajo de las comunidades indígenas. Fuera de los cultivos primitivos que se realizan en algunos núcleos como Warizata, Vacas y Cliza no existe la menor intención de tecnificarlos, con semillas y abonos seleccionados, con utensilios e implementos agrícolas modernos. La cría de animales se reduce a tener uno o dos ejemplares ordinarios para el servicio de los núcleos. (107)

> [The Indian students lack hygienic habits: their clothing, their beds, and their food have not fundamentally changed; the bedrooms, dining rooms, and kitchens inhabited by them continue to be dirty. We cannot see any social outreach from the school center to improve the living and working conditions of the indigenous communities. Besides the primitive crops cultivated in some centers like Warizata, Vacas, and Cliza, there isn't the least intention to bring about their technicalization with selected seeds and fertilizers, and modern agricultural tools and implements. The raising of livestock is reduced to one or two ordinary examples for the centers' use.]

The commission's narrative moves from the filth of the individual body to the unwillingness to transform native clothing and eating habits. This chain of signifiers next connects individual refusal to remake itself with the community's rejection of modernity, manifested through the repudiation of improved agricultural techniques, seeds, and fertilizers.

Ultimately, the report continues, these unruly bodies lose sight of their "authentic" rural identity as they migrate to urban areas with the intention of taking up newly learned artisan trades: "Con la instalación de talleres de carpintería, herrería, sombrería [*sic*], tejería, etc., se corre el riesgo de que el indio olvide su destino de agricultor, convirtiéndose en artesano que emigrará a las ciudades forzosamente, como ya ha sucedido en Caiza por ejemplo" (107) [With the installation of workshops on carpentry, blacksmithing, hat making, weaving, etc., we are running the risk that the Indian will forget his destiny as a farmer to become an artisan who will unavoidably migrate to the cities, as has already happened in Caiza for example]. Although the commission calls for the modernization of indigenous peoples, the report makes it quite clear that they should not be encouraged to migrate to urban areas. Instead, schools should prepare them for their "destined" or "authentic" role in society as agricultural workers. In other words, even though education's role is to westernize the Indian, it should not make him into a mirror image of the urban criollo; there should always be a discernible (geographical) gap between Indians and whites.

Ironically, in spite of the commission's charges that the *ayllu*-schools were not addressing hygiene, the histories of these experimental learning centers written by criollo participants unequivocally emphasize the importance of teaching proper forms of cleanliness. Both Elizardo Pérez, the urban-raised, white director of Warisata, and his colleague and friend, Carlos Salazar Mostajo, identify the school's key role in introducing the concept of hygiene among the Indians. In contrast to the commission's report, however, Pérez's history does not evoke the argument of racial essentialism to suggest that some peoples are dirtier than others by nature. He implies, instead, that poor hygiene is an economic issue resulting from a lack of adequate resources. Discussing the practical way in which the school approached a community-based and collectively run endeavor, Pérez notes how teachers and students earnestly undertook the project of cleaning up the entire community:

> El aspecto sanitario e higiénico fue acometido también con gran decisión y entusiasmo. Iniciamos intensa campaña profiláctica en toda la comunidad. Equipos de alumnos entrenados para el efecto, con sus respectivos profesores, visitaban periódicamente las viviendas indígenas realizando en ellas una limpieza y desinfección generales. El jabón empezó a ser conocido y reclamado, y a pesar de la carencia de recursos, pudimos combatir algunos brotes epidémicos y repartir medicamentos. (Pérez 1962: 141)
>
> [The sanitary and hygienic issue was also undertaken with great determination and enthusiasm. We initiated an intense prophylactic campaign throughout the community. Teams of students trained to that effect with their respective teachers periodically visited the indigenous houses, carrying out there general cleaning and disinfection. Soap began to be known and demanded, and, in spite of a lack of resources, we were able to combat some epidemic outbreaks and to distribute medicine].

In addition, Pérez continues, the school taught the children the heretofore unknown pleasures of bathing (141). Like the commission's report, Pérez's commentary reflects a paternalism that emphasizes the need for

FIGURE 4.2.

Nosotros leemos también. *Photograph courtesy of Eusebio Víctor Choque Quispe.*

body management and the normalization of western hygienic practices. Salazar Mostajo similarly observes: "Con la Escuela, se introdujo definitivamente el uso del jabón y el jaboncillo, y estaba logrando igual resultado con los dentífricos y el cepillo respectivo. Los sábados en la tarde los niños iban al río a bañarse y lavar sus prendas personales. Quedó eliminada la sarna, tan común en sociedades pobres" (Salazar Mostajo 1986: 102–103) [With the School, the use of laundry and bar soap was definitively introduced, and it was achieving equal results with toothpaste and the toothbrush respectively. Every Saturday afternoon the children went to the river to bathe and to wash their own clothing. Scabies, so common among poor societies, was eliminated]. For Salazar Mostajo, liberation from perceived filth and mange rather than, say, emphasis on proper nutrition, is one of the first steps toward the liberation of a subjected people. With careful guidance and instruction from committed teachers, Warisata ultimately would have brought to light the class struggle taking place in the countryside (25). His depiction thus indicates a conflation of race and class to suggest that the liberated Indian will evolve into the enlightened revolutionary (123–133). For this reason, he maintains, the *ayllu*-school's demise was inevitable (26).

In sharp contrast to both the Consejo's report and the criollo accounts of Warisata, Aymara histories of the *ayllu*-schools do not mention hygiene at all; instead, they focus on the schools' role in the struggle to recuperate and retain communal lands. They downplay the role of men like Pérez to discuss instead the contributions of Aymara teachers, whose work often receives summary treatment at best in mainstream records. The silence with regard to hygiene and the insistence on Aymara autonomy suggests an ambivalence deliberately maintained by the Indians with regard to hegemonic identificatory processes and even toward the enthusiastic white teachers. This silence might encode another instance whereby indigenous peoples were willing to negotiate concessions with dominant groups in order to maintain a degree of independence (see Rivera Cusicanqui 1990a). In this context, mimicry of hygienic practices points to the presence of subaltern strategies of resistance, what Bhabha terms a "double articulation" insofar as imitation signifies both "reform, regulation, and discipline" and "difference or recalcitrance" (Bhabha 1994: 86).

MODERN BODIES AND SPACES

Following the Revolution of 1952 and the formation of the modern state, priority was given to modernizing the Indians (or *campesinos*, as they were now referred to) through agrarian reform and education programs that would prepare them to be consumers and producers.[18] With the publication in 1963 of the *Guía didáctica de educación rural*, it is apparent that hygiene and cleanliness continued to play a fundamental role in these transformational processes.

From the very first lesson taught, the *Guía* distinguished the modern body from the premodern body by its state of cleanliness. Zones of dirt and the potential for disease were mapped across the Indian student's body. The child was to learn that each area should be targeted for disinfection with a separate strategy, be it the comb, the toothbrush, the generalized use of soap, or DDT fumigations. A new vocabulary accompanied the reinvented modern body, to further distinguish it from its former dirty self: "Usar y fijar el nuevo vocabulario a razón de una o dos palabras por día: jabón, toalla, peine, cepillo, pañuelo, boca, nariz, oído, ojo, sucio, limpio, letrina, papel" (*Guía didáctica de educación rural* 1963: 5) [Use and ingrain into their new vocabulary at the rate of one or two words each day: soap, towel, comb, brush, handkerchief, mouth, nose, ear, eye, dirty, clean, latrine, paper]. The anxiety over the pathological, indigenous body could not be mitigated, apparently, as the same lessons on personal cleanliness were taught repeatedly at all levels and were incorporated into many different subjects. No bar of soap was big enough to do the job, as it were; the (racialized) stain of disease and contagion could not always be washed clean.

The increasing surveillance and control of indigenous schoolchildren and their families rendered first the body and second the interior of the house increasingly visible and knowable. Nevertheless, the discourse of modernity insistently inscribed new boundaries in the effort to order bodies in unprecedented ways. The operations of hygiene and body management unfolded in newly conceptualized spaces of containment that produced a public/private distinction. A modern sense of privacy was created in a variety of ways, beginning with the organization of a *"rincón de aseo"* [cleaning corner] at school (*Guía* 1963: 3). The children were strongly encouraged to create a similar cleaning corner in their own homes and to instruct their parents in its usage (4). The teachers also called upon the parents to assist in the construction of a latrine for the school (3). Purification of the modern subject thus became configured spatially and architecturally with the construction of new private spaces that could hide the excremental filth of premodern Indian culture. The schoolchildren learned to use the latrine at the same hour each day as well as how to clean themselves correctly. In addition, teachers taught them to "Echar el papel dentro de algún cajón para después quemarlo. Tapar la letrina. Evacuar el recto y la vejiga antes de acostarse" (3–4) [throw the paper into some container to burn it later. To cover the latrine. To evacuate the rectum and the bladder before going to bed]. The practices of hygiene required that the schoolchildren learn the western regulation of the division of space as well as of time.

The interconnection between the spatial organization of modern subjectivities and hygiene is at the forefront of architect Jorge Saravia Valle's study *Planificación de aldeas rurales* (1986). Saravia Valle contrasts a drawing of an alleged present-day rural house with a model of a proposed modernized house. In Figure 4.3, labeled *"Vivienda actual"* [present-day dwelling], the house depicted is run-down, in a state of advanced disrepair. The cracked walls, falling roof, and lack of a foundation suggest the fragility and permeability of boundaries that define and differentiate the interior from the exterior; the presence of a clay oven in the patio indicates that the woman carries out her domestic activities, literally, outside the confines of the house. A cow pictured in the front yard wanders

CUBIERTA EN MAL ESTADO

AUSENCIA DE VENTANAS

DEFECACIÓN

CORRAL

ANIMALES

CHARCOS

BASURA

MUROS
DETERIORADOS

ESTIÉRCOL

VIVIENDA ACTUAL

—————————— FIGURE 4.3. ——————————

Vivienda actual. *Architectural drawing courtesy of Jorge Saravia Valle.*

freely, leaving in its tracks a pile of manure. A man can be seen just beyond the wall of the corral, squatting and defecating. Next to the house there is a mound of garbage.

In contrast, Saravia Valle's proposed model house (Figure 4.4) has been emptied of all human and animal presences. The modern house underscores the importance of private rooms, the enclosed latrine, the contained corral, and a state of cleanliness missing in the first drawing. According to the architect, this model house illustrates how "el MEJORAMIENTO, con asistencia técnica que requiere la vivienda campesina tiene como objetivo principal, hacer de ella un 'ambiente' cómodo, higiénico, agradable y orgánico" (Saravia Valle 1986: 82) [the principal objective of IMPROVING the *campesino* house with technical assistance is to make it a comfortable, hygienic, pleasant, and organic environment].

During the 1940s and 1950s, while greater attention was being paid to the distinction between private and public spaces, gender roles were also targeted for transformation. In particular, teachers encouraged Indian women to self-identify as housewives. To this end, the teacher facilitated the organization of housewives' clubs. The *Guía didáctica* expressly laid out the following guidelines to the instructor:

a. Visitas de cortesía a los hogares, a los dirigentes, a los padres.

b. Promover interés por el bienestar rural entre las amas de casa, entre los jefes de la comunidad, entre los jóvenes.

c. Estimular, guiar, sugerir la organización del Club, señalando los objetivos claros: conocimiento de economía doméstica, de labores, de nutrición, costura, cuidado del niño y de la madre, capacitación cultural y alfabetización, etc.

d. Organización del Club: Redacción de sus estatutos. (*Guía didáctica de educación rural* 1963: 94)

a. Courtesy visits to the homes, to the leaders, to the parents.

b. Promote interest for rural well-being among the housewives, the community leaders, and the youth.

c. Encourage, guide, suggest the organization of the club, pointing out its clear objectives: learning about home economics, needlework, nutrition, sewing, care for the child and the mother, cultural training and literacy, etc.

d. Organization of the Club: draw up its statutes.]

The modern arrangement of gender required that indigenous women learn to assume the role of housewife; this role, as I suggested in Chapter 3, brought them one step closer to cultural *mestizaje,* an identity that was presumably class based rather than race based. Therefore, the fundamental communal principle of complementarity, embodied literally and symbolically in the Andean couple, *chacha-warmi,*[19] became reordered as

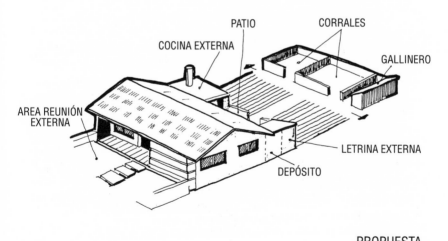

── FIGURE 4.4. ──

Propuesta. *Architectural drawing courtesy of Jorge Saravia Valle.*

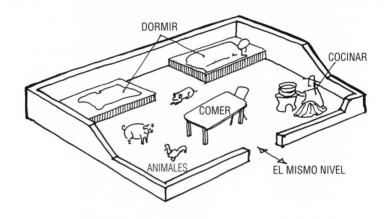

DORMIR

COCINAR

COMER

ANIMALES

EL MISMO NIVEL

VIVIENDA ACTUAL

FIGURE 4.5.

La vivienda actual. *Architectural drawing courtesy of Jorge Saravia Valle.*

the woman acquired a new identity with the unprecedented privatization of domestic space.

According to Elizardo Pérez and Carlos Salazar Mostajo, Indian schoolgirls attending Warisata were also taught that their primary responsibility was the home, thereby consigning newly acquired gender roles to the realm of the natural. Salazar Mostajo observes: "Las niñas, *como es lógico,* preferían las industrias domésticas, el tejido, la costura, el telar, la culinaria, la higiene del hogar. Algunas ya se interesaban en asistencia social, atención prenatal, pediatría, dietética, actividades que no pudimos desarrollar pues ya no hubo tiempo para ello" (Salazar Mostajo 1986: 108, emphasis added; See also Pérez 1962: 159–160) [the girls, *as is logical,* preferred domestic trades such as knitting, sewing, weaving, cooking, and house cleaning. Some girls were already interested in social welfare, prenatal care, pediatrics, and dietetics, activities that we were unable to develop as there was simply no time for them].

The process by which the Indian woman's identity undergoes transformation is illustrated in a second group of drawings by Saravia Valle. Figures 4.5 and 4.6 contrast the interior space of an "actual" Indian house with that of an "improved" dwelling. The "actual" house consists of a single room that serves household needs. An Indian woman squats on the floor, cooking, while another person sleeps. A pig, rooster, and dog share the same domestic space with the family. In contrast, the improved house once again stands out because of the absence of people and animals. Internal walls have been added to emphasize architecturally the containment and privatization of space; now the living room and the kitchen are separate from the bedrooms. The drawings suggest that as the house is modernized and improved, the racial identity of its inhabitants is also transformed. The Indian woman present in the first drawing as a symbol of a collective, native identity but absent in the second, no longer has a place in the refurbished space; instead, we await the arrival of an acculturated housewife to take up residence there.

Those processes according to which subjectivities became reorganized acquired further legitimization during the 1960s by being conceptualized simultaneously in economic terms. As the schoolchildren learned the cleaning value of such utensils as the comb and toothbrush, they also discovered their economic value. For example, the lesson plans for the very first class on economics were organized around the children role-playing a "trip to the store" during which each was to inquire into the prices of soap and other cleaning items (*Guía didáctica de educación rural* 1963: 3). As the children ascertained the economic and cleaning value of different utensils, they also discovered the value of private property and why

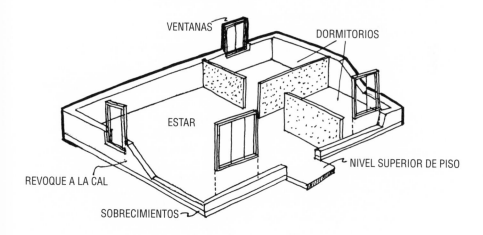

VIVIENDA MEJORADA

VENTANAS
DORMITORIOS
ESTAR
NIVEL SUPERIOR DE PISO
REVOQUE A LA CAL
SOBRECIMIENTOS

FIGURE 4.6.

Vivienda mejorada. *Architectural drawing courtesy of Jorge Saravia Valle.*

they should not share their comb or toothbrush with another (4). Individual property was therefore cast as capital through the consistent juxtaposition of hygiene and the practices of the market economy. Thus, lesson plans encouraged complementary activities: "Dramatizaciones de las actividades cumplidas: 'El Aseo,' 'En la tienda'" (5) [Dramatizations of the completed activities: "Cleanliness," "At the Store"]. Through hygiene, the subject was linked to the processes of privatization and domestication as well as to those organizing consumption. In other words, to be a cleaned-up, modern subject signified that one had already entered the monetary economy in the role of consumer. Consumption, like desire, according to the model proposed by Pierre Bourdieu and Jean Baudrillard, is founded on lack, a lack that cannot be satisfied (see Bocock 1993: 68–69).[20] By correlating the modern subject with consumption, the *Guía didáctica* ultimately reiterated the precarious situatedness of the Indian with respect to modernity, suggesting that only if indigenous peoples continued to engage in the practices of consumerism (buying soap, for example), could the tenuous relationship be sustained. In other words, hygiene, like desire, could never be satisfied; as a result, Indians, by definition, were always already lacking.

HYGIENE AND FASHION
IN URBAN GIRLS' SCHOOLS:
REGULATING THE PUBLIC-PRIVATE DIVIDE

The earliest debates surrounding the formulation of an appropriate curriculum for indigenous children coincided with an intensifying awareness of the need to develop a pedagogy for urban, upper-class girls and, later, for those of the urban working class. In his *Historia de la pedagogía boliviana* (1917), Enrique Finot reflects on why girls and Indians were denied access to an education during the colonial period: "Recordaremos . . . que los padres se negaban a dar instrucción a sus hijas, temerosos de que la escritura, por ejemplo, pudiera servirles para facilitarles relaciones galantes. Y en cuanto a los desgraciados indígenas, sometidos a mil gabelas y tributos, carecían del derecho de instruirse" (Finot 1917: 55–56) [We will remember . . . that parents refused to educate their daughters, fearful that writing, for example, would assist them by making flirtatious relations with men easier. And as for the wretched Indians, subjected to a thousand taxes and tributes, they lacked the right to be educated].[21]

In 1927, following her appointment as general inspector of girls' schools, educator Raquel Ichaso Vásquez undertook a seven-month inspection tour, visiting schools in La Paz, Oruro, Potosí, and Sucre. Based on her observations from this trip, she recommended in her written report that the government organize a uniform curriculum formulated specifically for girls. These recommendations, in conjunction with the document published the same year on the reorganization of the Normal School for Young Ladies, provide a detailed account of the role the education of girls was to have in the construction of the nation.

For Ichaso Vásquez, education should not distract young girls from their natural station in life. Rather, it should better prepare them for it. Sooner or later, she explains to the reader, the female student will inevitably assume her proper role as a wife and mother. To this end, she should be prepared to oversee the smooth functioning of the economic, social, and moral workings of the home. Ichaso Vásquez argues for two kinds of curriculum: one for the trade schools (Escuelas de Artes y Oficios) to train young girls who will seek employment as domestic workers; and another for preparation in vital subjects such as home economics, child care, and needlework in primary and secondary schools for *señoritas* (Ichaso Vásquez 1927: 58). The nascent interest in special schools that would ready girls to be good domestic help furthered the processes by which traditional communal ethnic identities were being reconfigured in favor of urban productive and reproductive class relations deemed appropriate to the elites. These new identities depended on the subordination of urban *cholas*' and indigenous women's labor as well as on their cultural and racial assimilation through a normalizing educational process.[22]

According to Ichaso Vásquez, the good school director, a graduate from the normal school in Sucre, should know how to bring her diverse student body together to create a harmonious family unit. Like a second mother, she must watch over every detail of the school's operations, acting as a moral guide to all: "ella con todas las ternuras maternales tiene que cuidar no sólo de la conducta y bienestar de su cuerpo docente, sino de las alumnas todas . . . haciendo en fin de su escuela el segundo hogar de las hijas que a ella concurren sin distinción de clases, sin odios y sin amores" (82) [with all maternal tenderness, she must look after not only the behavior and well-being of her teaching staff, but also of all the students . . . to make her school a second home for the daughters who attend it irrespective of class differences, without hatred and without favoritism].

The girls' school thus is "imagined" as a second home, where the director and the teachers assume the role of the mother. In this way, the school-as-home produces among the pupils a "legitimacy of filiation" (see Balibar 1991a: 56). Writing on racism and nationalism in the European context, Etienne Balibar explains, "the contemporary importance of schooling and the family unit does not derive solely from the functional place they take in the reproduction of labour power, but from the fact that they subordinate that reproduction to the constitution of a fictive ethnicity—that is, to the articulation of a linguistic community and a community of race implicit in population policies" (1991b: 102–103). By creating an illusory kinship among students of disparate racial, linguistic, and class backgrounds, the schools produce the image of the "nationalization of the family" (102) whereby "individual" family members "naturally" have different stations in life. Thus, returning to the Bolivian context, the girls' schools generate a fictive, shared ethnicity, "*as if* they formed a natural community, possessing of itself an identity of origins, culture and interests which transcends individuals and social conditions" (96; emphasis in original). Under the guise of producing and reproducing the "normal" and "customary" way of life, the paradoxical metaphor of the national family (one that assimilates and excludes) deployed by urban schools conceals the interlocking relations of race, gender, and class in the consolidation of political and economic power.[23]

In this context, body management emerges as a determining strategy in the educational process. Just as hygiene figures as a dominant ideologeme in the education of indigenous peoples, so too does it take on predominance in the curriculum for upper-class girls. Indeed, hygiene figures as one of several new subjects introduced into the national curriculum in 1905, along with physical education, the basics of natural sciences, needlework, shop, music, and drawing (Finot 1917: 73). If overseeing the hygiene of her own body and that of the family historically had been the purview of upper-class women, this responsibility is underscored in the new girls' schools established at the beginning of the twentieth century. For instance, the document published in 1927 following the reorganization of the Normal School for Young Ladies in Sucre also includes personal hygiene among the list of subjects that should be taught to girls.

In the section "Opiniones del profesorado," published as part of the Normal School's guidelines, professor of science R. Zamora Arrieta positions hygiene in opposition to fashion, to argue that young girls should be encouraged to avoid the more harmful dictates of fashion. They should follow instead the healthy, rational practices of personal hygiene. In contrast to hygiene, Zamora Arrieta maintains, fashion both sustains and intensifies female instability: "Se comprende: la higiene se dirije a la razón de la que existe poca dosis, salvo excepciones, en las adorables cabecitas de mujer; [. . .] mientras que la moda mueve los sentimientos más poderosos, el deseo de brillo, de notoriedad, la vanidad" (Escuela Normal de Señoritas 1927: 26) [It is understandable: hygiene is akin to reason, which, with some exception, exists only in small doses in the adorable little heads of women; [. . .] while fashion moves the most powerful feelings, the desire for splendor, for notoriety, for vanity]. By emphasizing woman's desire to aestheticize her body as a sign of the inherent irrationality of the feminine,[24] Zamora Arrieta's article signals a marked shift from the dominant values of the late nineteenth century, whereby social power and position were reflected in the conspicuous abundance of material wealth, the symbol par excellence of which was fashion.[25]

For example, in 1889, Carolina Freyre de Jaimes, the director of the women's journal *El Album* (Sucre) and mother of the well-known poet of Spanish American Modernism, Ricardo Jaimes Freyre, described fashion's crucial role in highlighting gender and social differences: "La moda, necesidad primordial e indispensable en toda sociedad culta [. . .] embellece cuanto toca. Realza los encantos femeniles [. . .] imprime elegancia y distinción en los objetos materiales y pone en relieve los esplendores de la fortuna"[26] [Fashion, the indispensable and fundamental necessity in every cultured society, [. . .] embellishes everything it touches. It enhances feminine charms [. . .] it imparts elegance and distinction to material objects, and it puts fortune's splendors in relief]. Fashion and social distinction, in other words, are correlates of progress. According to Freyre de Jaimes, ostentatious formal galas in particular epitomize the social and economic accomplishments of modernity:

En los países donde son frecuentes las grandes fiestas, la industria florece, el comercio prospera, el buen tono y la galantería llegan a su apogeo. Por eso se inventa cada día mayores novedades y se hace descripciones fantásticas y se crea modas nuevas y artículos de lujo y se eleva a obra de arte la vajilla y a maravillas de los cuentos de Las Mil y Una Noche, las joyas que adornan el tocado de las damas.[27]

[In those countries where grand parties are frequent, industry flourishes, commerce prospers, and prestige and gallantry reach their apogee. For this reason, greater novelties are invented each day and fantastic descriptions elaborated; new fashions and luxury items are created and china is elevated to an art form. The jewels that adorn the ladies' coiffures are marvels from the stories of *A Thousand and One Nights*.]

For Freyre de Jaimes, "mode" could not be separated from "modern" (see also Rossells 1988: 96).[28]

In contrast, by 1927, educators emphasized fashion's deleterious effects on the modern young woman. Zamora Arrieta's essay illustrates the hazards of fashion with two articles of clothing popular at the end of the nineteenth century, the corset and long, floor-length skirts, or *"levantadoras de tierrita,"* as they were sometimes called (Escuela Normal de Señoritas 1927: 28). He argues that long skirts frequently caused women to stumble or to fall and that they swept microbes and other filth from the streets into the house (Escuela Normal: 28–29).[29] Corsets subjected women to the physical torture of "una compresión asfixiante que desplazaba y deformaba las vísceras toráxicas y abdominales anulándolas en sus funciones" (28) [an asphyxiating compression that displaced and deformed the organs inside the thorax and abdomen, causing them to be unable to function]. While acknowledging that women's styles of the twenties emphasize simpler, less adorned models that do not physically constrain movement, Zamora Arrieta nevertheless signals his concern over fashion's new extremes; even as interest wanes in long, cumbersome skirts, the increasingly short (calf-length) "miniskirt" provokes a general sense of moral alarm (29).

The relationship between fashion and female irrationality that Zamora Arrieta's essay anxiously underscores suggests that clothing and subjectivity are inextricably connected. Kaja Silverman has argued that just as dress maps out and makes visible the body, it also expresses the psyche (Silverman 1994: 191). The relatively slight variation in men's fashion over time, for example, creates the impression that male sexuality likewise is unchanging. In contrast, female dress undergoes "frequent and often dramatic changes, accentuating the breasts at one moment, the waist at another, and the legs at another. These abrupt libidinal displacements, which constantly shift the center of erotic gravity, make the female body far less stable and localized than its male counterpart" (Silverman 1994: 191–192). Because of the many transformations in female fashion, the feminine is presumed to be unstable and disruptive of "gender and of the symbolic order, which is predicated upon continuity and coherence" (192). Taking this idea one step further, Silverman argues that if "clothing not only draws the body so that it can be seen, but also maps out the shape of the ego, then every transformation within a society's vestimentary code implies some kind of shift within its ways of articulating subjectivity" (193). Like fashion, the feminine is closely associated with volatility, instability, and transformation; therefore, the feminine becomes emblematic of changes in the social order. Zamora Arrieta's article on fashion and hygiene codifies the nexus of competing relations that converge in the feminine as that which at once destabilizes fixed boundaries and reinforces boundaries that appear to be eroding.

Zamora Arrieta warns of the dangers to the woman who becomes caught up in the libidinal economy of consumerism:

> Se aleja de los cuidados de la casa, de su dignidad de madre para satisfacer ansias de una vida febril en exceso que la apartan del hogar. No procura conciliar, lo que es posible, las obligaciones inherentes a su condición de mujer con las que encierra la existencia moderna. De aquí resulta que muchas veces no tenga en cuenta ningún sacrificio para ponerse a tono con los tiempos y siga ciegamente los dictados de la moda sin reparar que éstos pueden dañar su decoro,—las hay que desafían heroicamente el ridículo con tal de vestir a la última novedad,—o comprometer seriamente su salud. (Escuela Normal de Señoritas 1927: 29–30)

> [She moves away from household concerns, from her dignity as a mother in order to meet the anxieties of an excessively feverish life that separate her from the home. Although it's possible to do so, she doesn't attempt to reconcile the inherent obligations of her condition as woman with those that involve modern existence. Hence, many times she will sacrifice anything in order to be in tune with the times, blindly following fashion's dictates without noticing that these can harm her dignity—there are those women who heroically defy ridicule as long as they are dressed in the latest fad—or seriously jeopardize her health.]

The anxiety present in Zamora Arrieta's article suggests that he perceives a disintegration of the domestic sphere resulting from the excesses of modernity. This, in turn, points to an underlying concern about women neglecting their responsibility to produce babies. For Zamora Arrieta, women will only continue to exercise their natural role as mothers if they can be guided away from fashion's disturbing effects. Therefore, by encouraging young girls to follow the healthy mandate of hygiene over and against the irrational, unhealthy practices of fashion, Zamora Arrieta attempts to restore domestic stability, to eliminate psychosis, to shore up the boundaries of these segregated zones:

> Es necesario poner en guardia a la mujer contra las asechanzas de los que explotan su buena fé. Es preciso educarla en el conocimiento de las leyes

vitales de la economía humana, en la práctica de las leyes higiénicas y en el culto de la salud por sobre todas las cosas porque únicamente ella le permitirá llenar sus deberes familiares y sociales en forma completa. (31)

[It is necessary to put woman on her guard against the traps of those who exploit her good faith. It is imperative to educate her in the knowledge of the vital laws of human economy, in the practice of hygienic laws, and in the veneration of health above all else because only that will permit her to fulfill her familial and social duties.]

Zamora Arrieta's essay, important because of its impact on the curriculum for the nation's girls' schools, points suggestively to a crisis of modernity in Bolivia. According to Rita Felski, writing on turn-of-the-century Europe, the culture of consumerism, expressed most clearly through fashion, runs the risk of feminizing modernity because of its excesses: "No longer equated with a progressive development toward a more rational society, modernity now comes to exemplify the growth of irrationalism, the return of repressed nature in the form of inchoate desire" (Felski 1995: 62). Moreover, this irrationalism becomes psychosis once "[t]he culture of consumerism reaches into and disrupts the sanctity of the private sphere, encouraging women to indulge their own desires in defiance of their husbands and of traditional forms of moral and religious authority" (74). Zamora Arrieta's essay suggests that woman's return to the private sphere must necessarily be engineered by hygiene, which gently reminds her of her bodily and familial responsibilities that can only be carried out within the intimate, secure space of the home.

Fashion was likewise disavowed by the editors of the pioneer women's journal *Feminiflor*, inaugurated in 1921 in the city of Oruro.[30] In contrast to Zamora Arrieta, who feared that fashion would do away with home and motherhood as he knew it, however, the journal's staff appears to have discouraged a different interpretation of fashion's irrational effects: one that equates dress with success. According to journalist Lupe Cajías, only 25 percent of the journal's ads centered on fashion, accessories, perfume, and other similar items: "En la publicidad, también 'Feminiflor' se distingue de las tradicionales revistas femeninas. Les interesa informar al consumidor y no inducir la compra irracional y mucho menos hacer creer a las orureñas que con tal media nylon o que con tal perfume lograrán el éxito en la vida" (Cajías 1987: 66) [In its advertising, *Feminiflor* also stands out from traditional feminine magazines. The periodical is interested in informing the consumer and not in inducing irrational consumerism and even less in having Oruro women believe that with this stocking or with that perfume they will achieve success in life]. Cajías maintains that *Feminiflor* earnestly engaged the pressing social debates of the time as well as the problems concerning the citizenry, avoiding more frivolous topics such as fashion and recipes (66).

Compared to Zamora Arrieta's position, the editors of *Feminiflor* appear to have considered fashion not so much dangerous and disruptive as trivial. Reviews of feminist gatherings in the Americas, poems by Gabriela Mistral, and contests selecting the ugliest or most principled young man of Oruro take on greater significance in the magazine than the length of one's skirt line. Notwithstanding assertions to the contrary, however, fashion clearly played an important role in the upper-class woman's struggle for greater independence and freedom of movement. In one interview, the journal's chief editor, Betshabé Salmón de Beltrán remembers: "En ese tiempo el lujo de la mujer era el sombrero. Nadie que se apreciaba podía salir sin sombrero. Pero nosotras, Isabel [Barrenechea] y yo, íbamos con el sombrero en la mano, para decir 'tengo sombrero pero no me lo pongo.' Era otra rebeldía y tras de nosotras todas la mujeres se quitaron el sombrero y al final la gente dejó de molestar con tal detalle" (Vega and Flores Bedregal 1987: 88) [At that time, the hat was the sign of luxury for women. No self-respecting woman could go out without her hat. But Isabel [Barrenechea] and I, we would go out with our hats in our hands, to make the statement "I have a hat but I won't wear it." It was another form of rebellion. Following our lead all the women took their hats off and in the end that detail was no longer an issue]. The tactics employed by the young upper-class women who wrote for *Feminiflor* suggest that "[t]he resistance to fashion is not so much achieved as constantly staged," as Wigley has said in another context (Wigley 1994a: 155). The strategies of resistance employed by these women, many of whom went on to be writers and teachers, plainly indicate that their desire to refashion the social body could not be imagined without fashion itself.

THE BODY OF CONTAGION

Even though fashion did not warrant much direct attention in *Feminiflor,* sartorial practices certainly affected the daily lives of one group of women: the urban *cholas.* Throughout the 1920s, 1930s, and 1940s, the body of the *chola* came under increasing scrutiny and regulation. During this period, attempts were made to establish specific, legal boundaries that separated the upper class, categorized as clean and proper civilized society, from indigenous and *cholo* bodies, or the *"pueblo enfermo"* that continually resisted these limits. The upper class perceived native peoples to be disease-ridden pathological bodies boiling over their boundaries as contagion. The new emphasis on the hygiene/pollution of indigenous Andean bodies was bolstered by modern medical and biologistic paradigms on the rise at this time. Thus, the opposition between normalcy—marked by white bodies—and disorder—marked by indigenous bodies—had a crucial impact on racial politics, often affecting indigenous and *chola* women the most. The *pollera* became the visible emblem in which race and pathology intersected. For example, in 1935, upper-class *señoras* organized a campaign to keep *cholas* off the public streetcars. On July 31, a typical headline from the newspaper *El Diario* read: "Evitarse las infecciones en los tranvías" [Avoid Infections on the Streetcars] (cited in Wadsworth and Dibbits 1989: 67). To avoid infection, city officials announced:

> Queda terminantemente prohibido permitir la subida a los coches con cualquier bulto voluminoso que pueda entrar en contacto con los demás pasajeros, así como a las personas con muestras visibles de desaseo o cuyas ropas puedan contaminar a los demás pasajeros o despidan mal olor. Cualquier pasajero tendrá derecho de exigir que los cobradores hagan salir del coche a tales personas. (Wadsworth and Dibbits 1989: 67)

> [It is categorically forbidden to allow any large bundles or packages on the cars that might come into contact with other passengers; the same goes for people who are visibly dirty or whose clothing smells or might contaminate passengers. Any passenger has the right to demand that the conductor get these people off the streetcar.]

The women most adversely affected by this intended legislation were *cholas* who worked as domestics and cooks. One cook remembers this day vividly: "De repente, un día estaba yendo al mercado y no nos han dejado subir al tranvía; las señoras nos decían: '¡estas cholas con sus canastas nos rasgan las medias!'" (Wadsworth and Dibbits 1989: 66–67) [Suddenly, one day when I was on my way to the market they didn't let us onto the streetcar; the *señoras* told us: "these *cholas* tear our stockings with their baskets!"].

At the same time that efforts were made to prohibit *cholas'* access to public transportation, the Hygiene Police, the same authorities that examined prostitutes, began to insist that those women who worked in the homes of the upper class be routinely subjected to medical examinations.

They were to stand naked in front of the police, who looked their bodies over for any sign of infectious disease (Wadsworth and Dibbits 1989: 99). According to the *testimonio* of one cook affiliated with the anarchist Federación Obrera Femenina (FOF), any woman, young or old, "tenía que hacerse examinar toda pelada, si no tenía una enfermedad venérea u otra enfermedad contagiosa. Las amas de casa, las patronas exigían este carnet, con una fotito más, a las domésticas, las culinarias, las sirvientas, todo eso" (99) [had to be examined while she was buck-naked to see if she had a venereal disease or some other contagious illness. The housewives, the mistresses required this picture-ID card of domestics, cooks, servants, all of these]. Another cook protested: "El problema era que tenían que mirarnos nuestro cuerpo. Nosotras hemos dicho: '¿por qué nos van a ver?, ¿qué cosa?, ¿qué habíamos sido?, no somos enfermas.' Nos hemos enojado también esa vez" (100) [The problem was that they had to look at our body. We said: "why should they look at us?, what's going on?, what did they think we were?, we're not sick." We got very angry that time as well]. Far from being a neutral medical examination, the voyeuristic medical gaze of the Hygiene Police constructed the body of the *chola* as "legible" and, consequently, capable of being interpreted or diagnosed. The authoritarian gaze of the police, corroborated by the medical sciences, "reaffirmed" the working-class woman's body as a "sick" body, contaminated and contagious.

If the Hygiene Police's authority reaffirmed itself through the medical investigation, this same authority also required the conflicting confirmation/negation of the *chola*'s distinctiveness. Because dress constitutes the emblematic identity of the *chola* (Barragán 1992), the very act of having her undress for the inspection impugned the *chola*'s identity as a *chola*. As I discussed in Chapter 1, urban Andean cultural practices produced and reproduced most notably by the woman crystallize in the *pollera* and the *manta* of the *chola*. These hygienic inspections thus can be read as an explicit attempt first to erase the *chola*'s indigenous ethnicity by stripping her of her clothing. As Julia Emberley elaborates in an essay on the fashion apparatus and subjectivity, "Stripped naked and re-clothed, the heurmeneutic body uncovers its intimacy, secrecy and hidden meaning . . ." (Emberley 1987: 49). In the Bolivian context, through this process of stripping and inspection, the body of the *chola* can be re-dressed or re-contextualized (see Emberley 1987: 49) in terms of her pathology or contaminative essence.

The reaction to these new regulations on the part of unionized cooks and domestic workers was immediate. In November of 1935, an article of protest was published in *La República*. Culinary workers argued there

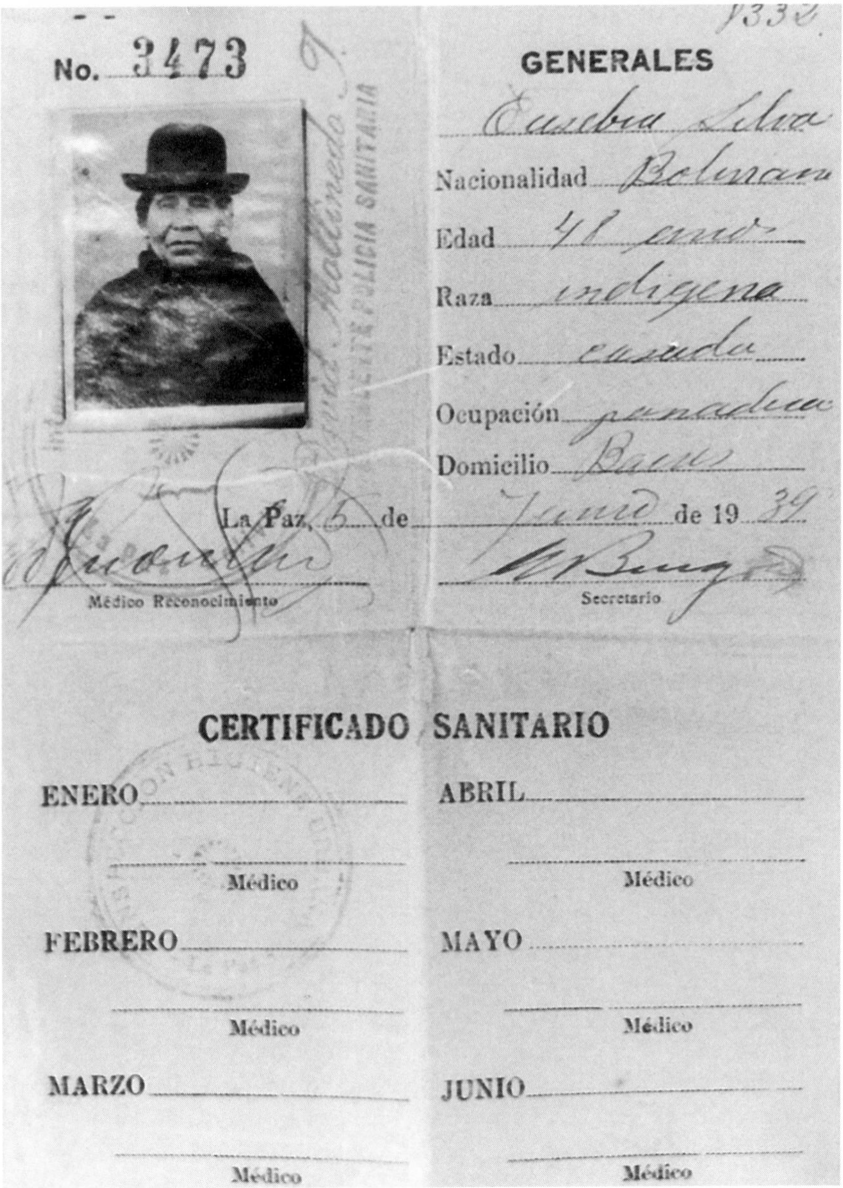

No. 3473

GENERALES

Eusebia Silva

Nacionalidad *Boliviana*

Edad *48 años*

Raza *indigena*

Estado *casada*

Ocupación *panadera*

Domicilio *Bajo*

La Paz, 5 de *Junio* de 19 39

Médico Reconocimiento   Secretario

CERTIFICADO SANITARIO

ENERO   ABRIL

Médico   Médico

FEBRERO   MAYO

Médico   Médico

MARZO   JUNIO

Médico   Médico

FIGURE 4.7.

Hygiene ID card, 1939. Photograph courtesy of Taller de Historia Oral Andina.

that the physical examination required in order to obtain the *carnet sanitario* constituted a personal indignity: "Por otra parte se reclama también que consideran lesivo y afrentoso a su moralidad, los reconocimientos que trata de efectuar la Policía de Higiene, una vez que las del gremio por las mismas necesidades de su servicio son personas sanas, aseadas y llevan una vida honorable" (cited in Wadsworth and Dibbits 1989: 99) [In addition they protest the inspections attempted by the Hygiene Police, considering them to be harmful and an affront to their morality; due to the necessities that their services call for, the union women are healthy, clean people who lead a decent life]. These women resoundingly rejected the examination in the Municiple Hygiene Office, suggesting instead: "Creen más bien, que trabajando en casas adineradas, son los patrones que deben, antes de recibir su servicio, hacer que sus respectivos médicos las sometan a exámen para tranquilizar a ambas partes" (cited in Wadsworth and Dibbits 1989: 100) [They believe, rather, that because they work in well-to-do homes that the employers, before taking on their services, should have their family doctors examine them [the *cholas*] to reassure both parties]. Such a strong statement cleverly brings up the hidden reference to problems of sexual harassment and rape that many domestic workers faced in the homes of the upper and middle classes. As they implicitly argue here, the *cholas,* too, needed to be reassured that their working environment would be safe, clean, and healthy.

The *cholas* organized a demonstration where they publicly protested the physical exam and the fact that they had to pay for these identification cards. The protest took a violent turn when the police confronted them in the streets. One cook, doña Natividad, remembers:

> A puñetes nos hemos agarrado con los agentes, con zapatos, de sus cabellos les hemos jalado. Pucha, grave nos hemos peleado. Les hemos ganado nosotras. "¿Por qué vamos a pagar? ¡No podemos pagar!" Ellos dicen: "¡van a pagar, van a pagar!" Y nosotras: "¡no y no y no!, nada de impuesto, nada de patente; la mujer no debe pagar, ¡no y no!" Hemos hecho correr a los agentes. Estábamos reclamando por bien de nosotras, cómo no me he de enojar. (cited in Wadsworth and Dibbits 1989: 97–98)

> [We went after those police with our fists, our shoes; we grabbed them by the hair. Goodness, we fought real hard. We women beat them: "Why do we have to pay? We can't pay!" They said: "you're going to pay, you're going to pay!" And we women: "no and no and no!, no tax, no permit fee; the woman shouldn't have to pay, no and no!" We made those agents run away. We were protesting for the good of us women; why shouldn't I get mad?]

The collective anger expressed in protests and clashes with the police reveal the *cholas'* rejection of the authority's attempts to strip them of their identity with the public examination. The insistence on the part of doña Natividad to repeat "nosotr*as*" [we women] further signals how the *cholas* reaffirmed themselves collectively as clean and healthy women who deserved the same treatment and respect as any *señora*.

In spite of public dissent, other efforts were made to restrict the *chola*'s freedom of movement. These included the implementation of a series of medical and health reforms that increasingly regulated her activities, such as where she could sell if she was a market vendor and where she should give birth (see *Polleras* 1986: 10–11; X. Medinaceli 1989: 72). In summary, then, the transformations in La Paz's racial makeup during the first half of this century reinforced criollo anxieties over the "impurities" that were increasingly erupting in the social body. This sense of vulnerability legitimized increasing regulation of *cholas'* bodies through medical and biologistic models as well as through the reorganization of a curriculum for urban working-class girls.

Even in the late twentieth century, the *pollera* continues to signify racial difference and disorder.[31] For example, in the collection of *testimonios* titled *60 años, ¿para qué?* (1987/1988?), members from one grassroots organization observe: "La discriminación viene de las señoras de vestido y de los caballeros, dicen: tanta pollera se ponen, por qué no ocupan un taxi, parecen huaca-huacas. . . . Otros dicen: Tu bulto me ensucia. . . . Porque tenemos polleras nos desprecian" (cited in *60 años* 1987/1988?: 95) [Discrimination comes from well-off ladies[32] and gentlemen who say: you wear so many *polleras*, why don't you take a taxi, you look like a large bundle. . . .[33] Others say: your carrying cloth gets me dirty. . . . Because we wear *polleras* they scorn us]. In effect, as a principal emblem of racial difference, particularly in an urban area such as La Paz, the *pollera* visibly manifests the failed criollo ideal of a racially homogeneous nation.

CULTURAL AND GENDER CROSS-DRESSING

The visibility of racial difference, encoded primarily through the signifier of clothing, is a central concern of writer and editor Elssa Paredes de Salazar's book, *Presencia de nuestro pueblo* (1976). Her first chapter, "La indumentaria como factor de integración nacional," aggressively argues in favor of *cholas* and indigenous peoples' changing their clothing so that they might be integrated more easily into the nation. Unlike the United States, she maintains, where racism results from the color of one's skin

(Paredes de Salazar 1976: 21), in Bolivia the source is one's form of dress (Paredes de Salazar 1976: 19–21). Although native Andean clothing appeals to tourists because of its color and exotic style, it creates an atmosphere of theater by portraying Indians as a grotesque spectacle and thus should be preserved solely for festivals and museums (19, 30). In particular, the clothing worn by the *chola* should be cast off, she asserts, because it is anything but indigenous to the Andean region. The *pollera* and *manta* are deformations resulting from the imitation of Spanish clothing worn by women during the colonial period (31). Paredes de Salazar thus presents the *chola* as someone who has been colonized through her clothing; in other words, the *chola*'s authentic or original self was displaced with the adoption of the *pollera*. According to the author, western attire promises to recuperate this original self, albeit in its modern form.

Paredes de Salazar insists that use of the *pollera* affects women negatively in many ways, including in their personal hygiene, physical health, and economic well-being:

lavar una pollera es muchísimo más difícil que un vestido. Es más, con una pastilla de jabón o con determinada cantidad de detergente se lava una sola pollera, mientras que con esa misma porción se lavan cinco o diez vestidos. El vestido por ser más ligero seca con mayor rapidez, en cambio la pollera puede tardar dos o más días para secar completamente. Los pliegues de la pollera acumulan polvo, bichos e insectos trasmisores de enfermedades que atentan contra la salud, y cuando los días son calurosos, el cuerpo debido a la transpiración de tanto abrigo, despide mal olor. (23)

[it is much more difficult to wash a *pollera* than a dress. Moreover, with a bar of soap or with a specific amount of detergent you can only wash one pollera, whereas with the same quantity of soap you can wash five to ten dresses. Because dresses are lighter in weight they dry out more quickly; in contrast, the *pollera* can take two or more days to dry completely. The pleats of the *pollera* accumulate dust, bugs, and disease-carrying insects that can harm one's health, and when the days are hot, the body gives off a bad odor due to sweating from being so heavily clad.]

In the name of modernity, Paredes de Salazar continues, the indigenous and *cholo* peoples must be freed of the cumbersome drag of this clothing that pulls them back into the ahistorical, disordered space of the barbarous other: "¿Qué papel juegan en el desarrollo nacional el poncho, la pollera, el rebozo, la manta y el aguayo en las espaldas de las campesinas? Acaso ante la presencia de uno de estos seres no fluye la pregunta inmediata de nuestra conciencia que nos dice: ¿hasta cuándo?" (25) [What role do the poncho, the *pollera*, the blanket, the shawl, and the carrying cloth on the backs of *campesina* women play in national development? In the presence of one of these beings doesn't the question "how much longer?" come immediately to mind?]. For Paredes de Salazar, Indians can be refashioned merely by exchanging their traditional, and therefore dirty, apparel for western dress, which, by definition, is fresh and clean.[34]

The image of the nation envisioned in the pages of *Presencia de nuestro pueblo* conveys the notion that fashion guarantees what Julia Emberley has described elsewhere as the "utopic experience," (52) one in which western clothing has the power to "cut across traditional barriers of limits of representation and efface, along the way, differences and historical specificities, thus producing, instead, a unitary effect of congenial pluralities that apparently 'hold-together' without contradictions" (Emberley 1987: 53). Thus Paredes de Salazar argues that a change of clothing and one language adopted by all will help obtain "transformaciones sociales y económicas; de modo que en el futuro, los indígenas o campesinos, los mestizos, los cholos y los blancos, formen una sola clase social, abriendo el camino que logre unificar la educación" (Paredes de Salazar 1976: 18) [social and economic transformations; such that, in the future, Indians or *campesinos*, mestizos, *cholos,* and whites will form a single social class, blazing the trail that will lead to educational unification]. Clearly, then, hegemonic discourses invest clothing with the power to undo the boundaries of race; in other words, cross-dressing seemingly enables cultural border crossings.

In light of the book's emphasis on the symbolic capital of clothing, the prologue to *Presencia de nuestro pueblo,* written by Vicente Terán Erquicia, takes on unexpected significance.[35] His opening remarks complicate the criollo/Indian binary by introducing another cultural anxiety: the gendered categories of "male" and "female." Terán Erquicia begins by addressing in general terms the challenges facing the intellectual who would undertake the written expression of elevated concepts and lofty ideas. This dauntless task can only be taken up by "espíritus selectos, de almas nobles y delicados temperamentos" (cited in Paredes de Salazar 1976: 9) [select minds with noble souls and delicate temperaments]. However, he continues, in a country of paradoxes, such as Bolivia, where the ability to write and publish a book represents a formidable ordeal, a quixotic enterprise, there is none more fit to the task than Elssa Paredes de Salazar, daughter of the renowned and authentic caballero don Manuel Rigoberto Paredes: "Consagrada a esa labor intelectual, en esta ocasión, no es un caballero que rompiendo lanzas, recorre el campo de las letras, es una dama, una distinguida señora, que se ha dado a la faena intelectual de escribir libros, como en otra hora lo hiciera su padre" (9) [On this occasion, the one dedicated to this intellectual effort is not a knight who, smashing lances, travels through the field of literature; it is a lady, a distinguished *señora*, who has devoted herself to the intellectual task of writing books, as her father did in the past]. The daughter now takes up her father's legacy with daring, "travestida de armadura, lanza y adarga, sale al campo intelectual de las letras con esta su tercera producción, desafiante, con una audaz, revolucionaria e iconoclasta tesis, para destruir prejuicios conservadores del traje típico regional; pero singularmente para acabar con la pollera de las cholitas" (9–10) [cross-dressed in armor, a lance, and shield, she goes out into the intellectual battlefield of literature with this her third production, defiant, with a bold, revolutionary, iconoclastic thesis, to destroy the conservative prejudices of traditional, regional clothing; but singularly to do away with the *cholitas' pollera*].

Given the power attributed to clothing throughout the book, these effusive remarks should not be dismissed too quickly. With a deft stroke of the pen, Terán Erquicia lays bare the unanticipated politics of representation. The white woman's precarious claim to authority is threatened with being divested of influence—hence the need to dress her in drag. While the image of the author cross-dressed as the Quijote, complete with her own lance and shield, is not one of her own making, it nonetheless signals a chain of ambivalences present throughout the book. On the most basic of levels, this image clearly delineates a fundamental principle of the dominant Symbolic as one organized around possession of the white phallus.[36] So that she may speak, the criolla, too, must change her clothes as it were and engage in masquerade. She takes up the armor and lance in a seemingly parodic yet ultimately serious hyperbolization of masculinity, an act that serves to align her identification with the selfsame (see Fuss 1995: 146). This move does not suggest that the criolla has suddenly occupied the same place as the Indian woman. The fact that her voice *is* present in the text clearly indicates that the process of othering is complex and multilayered and must be continually interrogated.

The precarious position of the white woman with respect to the Symbolic is likewise revealed in Ana María Condori's *testimonio, Nayan Uñatatawi: Mi despertar* (1988). Through her work as a domestic employee, Condori learns that even upper-class women are not always valorized. Because they are economically dependent on their husbands, many women dare not stand up for themselves during domestic quarrels for fear of being divorced or abandoned (Condori 1988: 88). Condori observes that their economic dependence is reinscribed through the fashion industry:

Si una ropa ya es moda antigua, tiene que venderla o tiene que cambiarla. Para esto el hombre debe disponer; si se pierde el hombre, la mujer ya no tiene pintura para sus labios. Yo me preguntaba: "¿Qué hará la señora toda una hora, pintándose?" Horas sabe tardar a ver qué ropa le queda o no le queda. Se ponen y sacan y lo botan a la cama; todo un montón dejan. La empleada después tiene que doblar, colgar, guardar otra vez. Eso pasa con la mujer burguesa. (88–89)

[If an article of clothing is out of style, she has to sell it or exchange it. The man should provide for that; if the man disappears, the woman no longer even has lipstick. I asked myself: "What can the *señora* be doing when she takes an hour to put on makeup?" She spends hours deciding which clothing fits, which doesn't. They put it on, take it off, and throw it onto the bed; they leave a huge pile. Afterwards, the maid has to fold it, hang it up, put it away again. This happens with the bourgeois woman.]

In this passage Condori returns the gaze to the dominant Symbolic, revealing the categories of differentiation within the household that configure criollo authority. Condori's countermove with which she unveils the ambiguous inner workings of the dominant domestic realm opens up a space for analysis of the relations of power encoded there: "En este sentido, esas mujeres [de clase media] son más sufridas que la trabajadora porque no tienen visión de lo que es la persona, sino que siempre están en miras del dinero, de no caer en la pobreza y tener que trabajar. Siempre están pensando en lo económico porque también de ello dependen" (88) [In this way, those (middle-class) women suffer more than the working woman because they don't have any notion of the value of a person; instead they always have their sights fixed on money, of not falling into poverty and having to work. They constantly think about their economic situation because they are dependent on it].

THE SARTORIAL PRACTICES OF RESISTANCE

From colonial times to the present, the racialized continuum between "visibility" and "invisibility" has endowed clothing, hairstyle, and language with crucial emblematic resonance. For example, as Rossana Barragán notes, during the colonial period many Indians passed as mestizos by deliberately changing their clothing as a strategy for resisting the onerous burden of tribute payments exacted from the indigenous peoples (Barragán 1992: 49–50). According to Karen Spalding, in 1663 representatives of the Spanish Crown lamented the fact that some native peoples were changing their clothing and speaking Spanish with the result that they were no longer recognizably Indian.[37] Olivia Harris observes as well that "It is not clear that the difference between Indians and mestizos was expressed systematically in cultural terms, although a precondition for 'passing' to mestizo status was the adoption of the Spanish language and dress" (Harris 1995: 359). In contrast, by the nineteenth century, while many Indians continued to adopt western apparel to escape payment of tribute, criollo authorities were more desirous of this "disappearance" because it facilitated the seizure of indigenous lands (Barragán 1992: 53).

In his oral *testimonio,* Leandro Condori Chura, an Aymara *escribano,* remembers how, at the end of the nineteenth century and the beginning of the twentieth, clothing concessions demanded by the oligarchy were continually negotiated by Indian caciques. According to Condori Chura, President Bautista Saavedra (1921–1925) disallowed the use of native clothing; anyone wearing indigenous dress would be prohibited from entering the center of La Paz:

> Esas vestimentas prohibió Saavedra: "Que desaparezca esa ropa; es fea, ya no sirve. Ya es el tiempo de la civilización; se tienen que civilizar. Las mujeres tienen que *acholarse* y tienen que saber leer," así. Así ocurrió, obligado. . . . Porque la noticia corría: "Ya no dejan entrar a chukiyawu, a la plaza principal." La Plaza principal era resguardada por los soldados; "Nos avergüenzan las naciones," decían. Saavedra impuso la civilización. (Condori Chura 1992: 62)

> [Saavedra prohibited that attire: "Let that clothing disappear; it's ugly, it no longer serves any purpose. It's time now for civilization; you have to become civilized. The women have to become *cholas* and they must learn to read," like that. Just like that it happened, by force. . . . Because the news spread: "They're no longer letting us into Chukiyawu [La Paz], into the main square." The main square was guarded by soldiers; "we are ashamed of the first nations," they used to say. Saavedra imposed civilization.]

Many Indians refused to change their clothing, or did so only temporarily if they had to travel to La Paz or another city. This slippage of identities, however, has tended to be more prevalent among the males, as the women were and continue to be more apt to preserve their traditional clothing or to take up the *pollera* of the urban *chola*. No matter what decision an individual or group adopts, the choice of clothing has always been a response to specific historical, political, and economic exigencies. As such, vestimentary choices figure predominantly in the ongoing practices of communal resistance, either as a point of negotiation or a visual sign of refusal, as in the instance of specific leaders like Santos Marka T'ula, the famous cacique of the Qallapa *ayllus.* According to Condori Chura, Santos Marka T'ula (1879?–1939) flatly rejected the use of western dress for many years. Condori Chura provides a detailed description of the clothing that the cacique wore. In the Spanish version, even the name for each item resists translation from the Aymara original:[38]

> [Santos Marka T'ula] usaba pantalón de bayeta como los indios de Oruro y Potosí: pantalones de oveja. No era civilizado como los *q'aras.* También usaba abarcas. Creo que era de cuero de llama, ya que recién después ha aparecido la goma. No sé si la abarca era de llama o de vaca, pero así era. Luego vestía con un ponchito de color plomo; no se lo quitaba nunca. Tenía su *ch'uspa.* Siempre estaba con la coca; masticaba de día y noche. Andaba preocupado, por eso no le faltaba nunca la coca y su *ch'uspita* estaba llena de coca y lejía; todo eso llevaba colgado al cuello. Tenía continuamente puesto un *lluch'u* tejido de lana de oveja o de llama. Usaba sombrero de lana de oveja. Recién después se ha civilizado. Solía decir: "Nosotros tenemos que vestir nuestra ropa, ya que tenemos vestimenta propia." (96)

> [(Santos Marka T'ula) used woolen pants like the Indians from Oruro and Potosí: lamb's wool pants. He wasn't civilized like the *q'aras* (whites).[39] He also used sandals. I think they were made from llama leather since rubber appeared later. I don't know if the sole was of llama or cow leather, but that's what it was like. Then he also wore a small, gray-colored poncho; he never took it off. He had his *ch'uspa* (coca bag). He always had coca; he chewed it day and night. He was continually worried, and so he was never without coca; his *ch'uspita* was filled with coca and lye; he wore all of that hanging from his neck. He always wore a *lluch'u* (Andean hat) knitted with sheep or llama wool. Over that he used a sheep's wool hat. Only later did he become civilized. He would say: "We have to wear our own clothing since it is ours."][40]

Notwithstanding the example of many indigenous leaders, clothing and resistance most notably converge in the feminine sign. Under the system of indentured labor known as *pongueaje,* rural Aymara women had to struggle with great personal sacrifice to make their family's clothing. *Testimonios* included in *La mujer andina en la historia* tell of women con-

——— FIGURE 4.8. ———

Leandro Condori Chura. Photograph courtesy of Taller de Historia Oral Andina.

gregating in one house to spin and weave their clothing until very late at night as that was their only "free" time. If they fell asleep the next day or could not work quickly as a result of their fatigue, they would be whipped by the overseer (THOA 1990: 24–26). In *Mujer y resistencia comunaria*, Aymara women similarly identify their persistence in making the family's clothing as an act of resistance:

> La tenacidad de este acto de resistencia, realizado a través de gestos silenciosos, pero cargados de significado, nos muestra a la mujer como un ser muy consciente de la simbología de la vestimenta y del tejido. Pensamos que esta sensibilidad se debe no sólo al hecho de ser la mujer la productora de la vestimenta familiar, sino también la generadora de un lenguaje de

significados muy elaborados, que encarna en las piezas textiles como en un texto silencioso, y permite a la comunidad expresar su identidad como diferencia. (THOA 1986: 42–44)

[The tenacity of this act of defiance, carried out in silent but meaningful gestures, illustrates that women were very conscious of the symbolism of their clothing and weaving. We consider that this sensitivity is due not only to the fact that women are the producers of the family's clothing but also because in the woven textiles, as in a silent text, they generate a language full of complex meanings that enables them to express the specific identity of the community.] (Rivera Cusicanqui with THOA 1990: 167)

Thus both the production and use of native clothing constituted acts of resistance carried out by women but which generated meaning and a sense of identity for the community as a whole.

During the period of *pongueaje,* the *pollera* was frequently targeted by the *patrón,* or boss-master, as a vehicle for the exercise of indiscriminate mastery over women. For instance, one Aymara woman describes a time when the *patrón* arbitrarily obliged the women to use *polleras* of a color other than the shade they normally wore:

En esa época nos vestíamos de color oscuro, con adornos de flores; *awayos* negros. Cuando nos poníamos ropa de color nos decían: "¡Trasero verde, trasero rojo!." De color azul oscuro siempre andábamos. Nos hemos puesto ropa de color porque el patrón nos reñía: "¡Hasta cuándo van a andar de negro, hasta cuándo no van a cambiar!" Los mayordomos iban de casa en casa y azotaban a las que usaban polleras azul oscuro; destruían las tinas en las que se teñía. Pero nosotros seguíamos andando con nuestra ropa. Ese patrón ya ha muerto ahora. El mayordomo sabía golpearnos y nos decía furioso: "¡Carajo! ¿acaso no tienen oídos?" Nosotros nos escapábamos a los rincones y a los ríos y ahí nos cambiábamos la ropa: la pollera negra, que estaba debajo, la poníamos encima, y la otra adentro. (THOA 1986: 42)

[In those days, we dressed in dark colours decorated with flowers, black *awayos.* When we wore coloured clothes they would call after us: "Green bottom, red bottom!" We always wore dark blue. But we had to put on coloured clothes because the landowner scolded us: "How long are you going to continue going around in black, when will you change?!" The foremen would go from house to house and whip those wearing dark blue skirts and destroy the tubs used for dyeing. But we carried on wearing our clothes. That landowner is dead now. The foreman would beat us up and say furiously: "Damn you, don't you have ears?" We would escape to some corners

or the river and change our clothes: the dark skirt that we had on underneath we put on top and the other underneath it.] (Rivera Cusicanqui
1990b: 167)

At a first reading, this account might be somewhat unexpected because
the stakes for the *patrón* are not western dress versus Andean dress. Instead, by obliging the women to exchange their dark *polleras* for more
brightly colored ones, he confirms his own authority and power by restag-
ing racial difference. Moreover, through his actions, the boss-master effectively fetishizes the *pollera* by disrupting the social and historical practices that intersect in the fashioning of the dark skirts.[41] The foremen are
ordered to destroy the pans in which the women dye their clothing the
customary color. Undaunted, the women actively resist this stratagem
when they hide their own skirts underneath the new ones. One of the
characteristics of the *pollera* is that its fullness permits the use of additional underskirts when extra warmth is desired. The new-colored clothing, therefore, ambiguously covers resistant layers which the women se-
cretly don as soon as the *patrón* turns away.

In urban areas the *pollera* of the *chola* also becomes a visible sign of
competing discourses. While hegemonic ideology charges the *chola* to
change her clothing, to discard the *pollera* for the dress, in the course of
everyday life this mandate becomes more ambiguous. Ana María Condori
recounts that on numerous occasions her employers did not pay her in
money but, instead, purchased her a new *pollera* and heavy slip (Condori
1988: 66). By keeping the domestic worker "in *polleras*," the criollo family could continue to construct her as "daughter/not daughter." In another instance, while working for a different family, Condori's employer
snipped off her braids in a fit of anger so that Condori was obliged to take
off her *pollera* and put on a dress, at least until her hair grew back: "Ellos
me decían: 'Sácate esa pollera, debes ponerte vestido.' Y ¡claro! si me han
cortado el pelo, no iba a estar andando con pollera, ¡chistoso sería!" (81)
[They told me: "Take off that *pollera*, you should wear a dress." Of
course, if they cut off my braids I couldn't go around in a *pollera*, it would
look funny!]. These accounts underscore how the domestic worker must
generally acquiesce to her employer's particular desire as to how she should
dress; the vested politics of the household, in turn, are overdetermined by
racism: "Hay patronas que prefieren 'empleadas de pollera nomás' porque
dicen que las de pollera son más sumisas y las de vestido son unas 'refi-
nadas y contestonas.' Otras prefieren de vestido porque dicen que son
más 'limpias'" (113) [There are mistresses who only prefer "maids who
wear the *pollera*" because they say the maids dressed in the *pollera* are

more submissive whereas the ones who have a dress are more "uppity and insolent." Others prefer maids who use dresses because they say they are "cleaner"]. Evaluating the *chola*'s situation, Condori draws the following conclusion:

> Lo que pasa es que no estamos permitidas. . . . En la ciudad una no vale lo que es. Sólo se fijan en la apariencia. Una mujer tiene que vestir elegante, con cintura delgadita, bien plantada. Ella sí puede conseguir fácilmente trabajo en una oficina o en una institución. Pero una mujer que "no tiene ni pinta," que tiene su "cuerpo cuadrado"—como dicen—no se la recibe pues. (113)

> [What happens is that we are not tolerated. . . . In the city one is not worth anything for who she is. People only pay attention to appearances. A woman has to dress elegantly, have a tiny waist, carry herself well. That woman can easily get a job in an office or in a business. But the woman who "has no looks," who has a "square-shaped body"—as they say—she won't be given the time of day.]

As Condori's analysis makes abundantly clear, use of the *pollera* does not necessarily signify a resistant position on the part of the woman wearing it. Lesley Gill has similarly shown that the *pollera* may not have been the woman's personal choice but many employers demand that the household workers wear them so that social distinctions are duplicated in the home. So, too, imitation, or use of western dress by a *chola* may not reflect identification with western cultural norms if she has been obliged to wear it at work: "Employers who themselves come from rural backgrounds may pressure their employees to use more typical Western dress. In doing so, they seek to distance themselves from their rural origins by attempting to display greater 'modernity' in the home, a goal that may affect the maid's appearance" (Gill 1990: 130). In the *pollera*, then, conflicting practices converge that both reinforce and place in question hegemonic discourses.

The heterogeneous relations that meet in the clothing of the *chola* point to the dynamic multilayering of urban identities that are rooted in Andean and criollo traditions. As I have claimed throughout this chapter, the complex ways in which pedagogical practices, fashion, and hygiene converge and reconverge throughout the twentieth century suggest that there is no simple way to generalize about the relation between modernity and identity in Bolivia. Rita Felski has convincingly argued that even though modernity is generally depicted in terms that highlight consistency and stability, in fact, the modern "acts as a mobile and shifting category of classification that serves to structure, legitimize, and valorize varied and often competing perspectives" (Felski 1995: 14–15). In Bolivia, these competing perspectives take shape through the ambiguous deployment of discourses on fashion and hygiene. Through sartorial practices we can read the inconsistencies of a hegemonic culture that calls for racial homogenization at the same time it implements strategies with which it protects its vested interests. The ambivalence of the paradoxical injunction to identify and to counteridentify constructs the very ground of racial and gender politics. For instance, the pedagogical manuals suggest that when Indian children and their families mimic hygienic practices the circuit of recognition and identification with the selfsame is set into motion. Yet, when the boundary between the Indian Other and the criollo begins to break down, as happens, for example, when Indians change their traditional clothing for western styles and migrate to urban areas, hegemonic discourses and actions become fraught with anxiety. The closer the Indian comes to the criollo the more imperative it becomes for the criollo to make visible the Indian's difference. Thus, from colonial times to the present, the racialized continuum between "visibility" and "invisibility" has endowed clothing, hairstyle, and language with crucial symbolic resonance. Importantly, however, these same terms have been continually redeployed by indigenous peoples in the ongoing struggle for self-determination and territorial autonomy.

✍
THE POLITICS OF HUNGER
✍

T he discourse of starvation and in-
gestion has resonated in Bolivian history from the colonial period to the
neocolonial present. European colonization set into motion new "nutritional regimes" that impacted on indigenous peoples throughout the
Andes, particularly as Indians and Spanish increasingly vied for control
over land and markets (Super 1985; see also Larson and Harris 1995).
During the twentieth century in (neo)liberal discourses of citizenship and
individual rights, hunger and eating are materially and metaphorically
linked to questions of modernity and development. The well-worn adage
"we are what we eat" suggestively points to the identificatory processes
bound up with dietary practices and privations. Moreover, it presumes a
fundamental relationship between subject formation and what might be
termed a politics of hunger. At a very basic level, hegemonic constructions of Bolivian modernity, deployed through discourses of national unification and racial homogenization, are organized through the interplay
of food and appetite or desire. Because prevailing discourses identify the
Indian woman-mother as the embodied sign of an Other Symbolic Order, she personifies a dissonant hunger that must be carefully disciplined.[1]
Indeed, hunger, like fashion, threatens boundaries of the (hegemonic) self
and of the (dominant) social body. Thus "consumption" and "incorporation," key expressions of neoliberal economic reform during the 1980s
and 1990s, figure predominantly in the reordering of civil society during
the harsh policies of worker relocation.

This chapter traces the political trajectory of hunger through four specific historical moments to examine the mutually consolidating themes of
incorporation, consumption, desire, and the body. It begins by examining the traumatic events of 1781, when Aymara leader Julián Apasa Tupak

Katari organized and directed an eight-month siege against the city of La Paz. The encirclement of La Paz by Aymara Indians eventually led to the death by starvation of more than a quarter of the city's Spanish and criollo inhabitants. The events surrounding these violent encounters triggered a dialectic of hunger defined by an ambivalent fear/desire of incorporation by/of the Other that continues to haunt Andean and white subjectivities to the present.

ZONES OF CONTESTATION, ZONES OF DESIRE: LA PAZ (WIRNITA)/CHUKIYAWU (KATARI)

The debates on the Andean insurrections of the late eighteenth century tend to locate their origin in the Bourbon taxation and mercantile reforms which benefited the rising commercial bourgeoisie of Lima at the expense of fragile Spanish-indigenous relations. Steve Stern suggests that these reforms, in conjunction with "a growing Indian population in need of more lands and productive resources," brought an end to "earlier quid pro quos, strategies of native resistance, and fragile colonial legitimacies" (Stern 1987: 75).[2] The heightened violence and exploitation of colonial rule that the indigenous peoples experienced on a daily basis confirmed their fears that the mutual respect for the laws and jurisdiction of the two distinct republics (one Spanish, one Indian) which had prevailed to this point was collapsing (Rivera Cusicanqui 1993: 43). With coexistence no longer a feasible alternative, the only solution for the native Andean peoples appeared to be the extermination or the expulsion of the Spanish (43–44).[3] According to Silvia Rivera Cusicanqui, the violence of the Aymara siege of La Paz, manifested most notably in the radical tactics employed by Tupak Katari, is best understood in light of this transformation of Indian–Spanish-criollo relations (44).

The prevailing accounts of the Aymara campaigns against La Paz that took place from March 14 to November 15, 1781, emphasize the terrible hunger the city's residents suffered when the indigenous encirclements effectively curtailed the flow of foodstuffs to the urban population. Although the Spanish and criollo diaries and histories of the blockades tell primarily of the numerous confrontations and battles fought between the white colonials and the Indians, the accounts unequivocally establish hunger as the most effective weapon used by the Aymaras. For instance, the criollo Captain Ledo remarked on June 22, "que hay más muertos de pura hambre que de balas en las acciones" (cited in del Valle de Siles 1980: 132) [that there are more casualties from sheer hunger than from bullets in action]. Ledo observed with great consternation how young children, mothers, and the elderly abandoned the city in ever-increasing numbers to give themselves up to the enemy because of the overwhelming desperation from starvation (132). Another witness, a Sr. Llanos, tells of the sickening stench of dead bodies that accumulated in piles throughout the city as there was neither place nor person to bury them (188–189). Llanos describes how the inhabitants were forced to eat leather trunks, skins, dogs, cats, mules, "y otros animales inmundos, pero concreta más todavía las cosas, hablando de antropofagía . . . y de la búsqueda de granos que quedaban sin digerir entre los escrementos de los muladares. Incluso, dice que los perros, cuando los hubo, eran muy apetecidos porque estaban gordos de comer cadáveres" (189) [and other filthy animals, but he specifies things even more, speaking of anthropophagy . . . and of the search for undigested grains in the excrement of the dungheaps. He says that even dogs, when they could be found, were greatly desired because they were so fat from eating cadavers]. One of the most sensational accounts described the lurid case of a woman who murdered and cooked one of her own children so that the surviving members of the family would have food to eat (169).

Well aware of the devastating effects hunger had on the residents of the interior, the Aymaras set up markets just outside the city walls as if they planned to sell foodstuffs and other necessities to their adversaries. When the Spanish-criollo residents saw that the slaves and maids sent to buy provisions returned unharmed, they too ventured beyond the walls to purchase food. As soon as they traversed the city gates, however, they were promptly taken hostage by the Indians (del Valle de Siles 1981: 48). Francisco Tadeo Diez de Medina, the Judge [*Oidor*] of the viceregal court and governing body [*Audiencia*], recounts the horrific events of one day when a group of sixty people, primarily women, were captured at these markets. The Indians reportedly separated the captives into two groups, only to return to the city the slaves, the domestic workers, the dark-skinned old, and those deemed ugly (48):

> las fueron entresacando y separando en dos clases. La una de toda mujer de cara blanca, de buen parecer, de buen ropaje, niña o vieja, casada, las que llevaron a las once y media del día, prisioneras, al campo enemigo de Munaipata. . . . La otra, de indias y las de mal pelaje, fue repudiada y las enviaron con libertad a la ciudad. (del Valle de Siles 1981: 49)

> [the women were selected and separated into two groups. One group consisted of all white women, young or old, or married, who were handsome

looking and wearing fine clothing; these were taken away at 11:30 in the morning as prisoners to the enemy camp at Munaipata. . . . The other group, consisting of Indian women and bad-looking women, was repudiated; they were sent back, free, to the city.]

Those whom the Indians returned, however, were not permitted to take with them any provisions from the markets.

The first-hand accounts of the Aymara encirclement of La Paz tell of the literal disintegration of criollo identity as both the city and its inhabitants wasted away, becoming mere remains of their former selves. For example, in his diary Diez de Medina wrote of the arrival in July of Commander Flores bringing reinforcements, and of the shock Flores and his troops experienced upon seeing the city in ruins and its population decimated:

la antes "opulenta y rica ciudad de La Paz," reducida en gran parte a cenizas, con la mitad de su población muerta. Les consternaba, a los recién llegados, ver el estado de flacura y desfallecimiento de la población, que trataba de subir al Alto en procura de los alimentos que llegaban en su socorro; muchos no eran capaces de resistir el esfuerzo y morían en el camino, mientras otra pobre gente "se arrojaba a la comida como verdaderos hambrientos, demostrando casi todos en su semblante, fisonomías de un puro esqueleto." (cited in del Valle de Siles 1980: 141)

[the once "opulent and wealthy city of La Paz," reduced in large measure to ashes with half of its population dead. The recent arrivals were dismayed to see the emaciated and weakened state of the inhabitants who tried to climb up to El Alto to procure the food that arrived to aid them; many were unable to withstand the effort and died en route, while other unfortunate individuals "fell on the food like true starving people, almost all of them looking like skeletons."]

The account of Sr. Llanos similarly indicates that the unrelenting onslaught of hunger, pestilence, and death undid criollo subjectivities to the extent that even language inside the walls of La Paz broke down, returning to a presymbolic indeterminacy of cries, laments, groans, and whimpers:

los llantos de los pocos muchachos que habían quedado de resultas del primer cerco, impelidos de la hambre, de ver a sus padres, madres, hermanos, etc. ya al morir o ya muertos o, por el contrario, éstos a aquellos hijos, las

más familias gimiendo su languidez, los hombres más robustos, unos ya
habían fallecido a manos de los rebeldes, otros que estaban heridos, otros
no tan de valor y ánimo valiente, sujetos a sólo el irse consumiendo . . .
(cited in del Valle de Siles 1990: 278)

[the weeping of the few boys who survived the first siege, (crying) from
hunger, from seeing their parents, mothers, brothers and sisters, etc. at the
point of death or already dead, or, on the contrary, the latter upon seeing
their children in the same state, the majority of families groaning at their
listlessness, the most robust of men, some of whom had already died at
the hands of the rebels, others who were wounded, others of less courage
and lacking a brave heart—all of these were subjected to simply wasting
away . . .]

In the *Diario de alzamiento de indios conjurados,* a study of the 1781
events based upon the diary of Diez de Medina, María Eugenia del Valle
de Siles emphasizes how the conflict unfolded literally at the boundary
formed by the city wall, which had been built for the sole purpose of dividing and keeping separate two racially distinct groups.[4] The Aymara
siege both reinforced and destabilized the borderline that separated the
Indian world from that of the Spanish-criollos. Before the rebellions began there existed the beginnings of a third space around La Paz occupied
by both whites and Indians as the city limits slowly encroached upon the
outlying indigenous communities. With the onset of the first rebellion
the criollo populations of this intermediate sector were moved back inside the city walls and housed in churches, convents, cemeteries, streets,
patios of private homes, and even in trenches (del Valle de Siles 1981:
29). The act of bringing all whites inside the city walls can be read as an
attempt to resecure the margins by shutting out, even eliminating this
third space and reincorporating the white populace that seemed to be
getting away from the colonial center.

The Spanish and criollo forces were compelled to seal off the interior
city space to protect the residents from the invading enemy. Describing
the wall and its gateways, historian José de Mesa writes: "La indicada
muralla tenía puertas que como es lógico, daban a las salidas y caminos
principales . . . cada una de estas puertas cerraba el acceso a la ciudad
controlando los puentes principales. Durante el cerco, estas puertas estaban defendidas por cañones" (Crespo-Rodas, Baptista Gumucio, and de
Mesa 1989: 414) [The indicated wall had gates which, as is logical,
opened onto the major outlets and roadways . . . each one of these gates

closed off access to the city, controlling the main bridges. During the siege, these gates were defended by cannons].

This bounded territory, fortified to prevent its penetration, evokes the image of a body. Mary Douglas has argued that "[t]he body is a model which can stand for any bounded system. Its boundaries can represent any boundaries which are threatened or precarious" (1992: 115). In the Bolivian instance, however, the body/city in question—that of Nuestra Señora de La Paz [Our Lady of La Paz]—is clearly designated as female. In her discussion of the sexualization of space, Sue Best maintains that "feminizing space seems to suggest, on the one hand, the production of a safe, familiar, clearly defined entity, which, because it is female, should be appropriately docile or able to be dominated. But, on the other hand, this very same production also underscores an anxiety about this 'entity' and the precariousness of its boundedness" (Best 1995: 183). As I pointed out in Chapter 3, in Bolivian hegemonic discourses the white female body frequently serves as a metaphor of the perfectly enclosed political entity, the openings of which are jealously guarded by the criollo male. In the case of the siege, the soldiers with their canons fought desperately to forestall the violation of the city by the indigenous rebels. The vulnerable and easily dominated white female body, metaphor of the familiar, clearly defined colonial center, had to be protected by the Spanish-criollo male, "understood as phallic and impenetrable, as a war-body simultaneously armed and armoured, equipped for victory."[5] The irony here, as the colonial accounts so graphically relate, is that the perfectly contained inside ultimately came undone due to the accumulation of its own filth and devastation. Immured within the city walls, the inhabitants of La Paz became their own abject.[6] Thus, although the Spanish fought to maintain the impermeability of the city's boundaries, the very act of doing so brought about the ruination of the interior space.

Even as the confrontation appeared to be a call, literally and symbolically, for the reinscription of identities and the reinforcement of the white/Indian binary, the accounts ultimately underscore the fragility of the boundary itself, thereby revealing the vulnerability of colonial unity and coherence. Although separated by a wall, the two groups were close enough so that they could call back and forth to each other during combat or when at rest, exchanging insults, threats, and jokes at the others' expense. Diez de Medina observes in his diary how the Indians "se mantuvieron vertiendo muchas crasedades, amenazas y desvergüenzas contra los españoles, sus mujeres y aún contra las monjas de los monasterios . . . y gritando insolencias contra nosotros, nos desafiaban y decían: Pies de gallinas, ¡salid fuera si sois hombres!" (del Valle de Siles 1981: 49) [continually called out vulgarities, threats, and shameless remarks against the Spanish, their wives, and even against the nuns of the convent. . . . and shouting insolence at us, they challenged us, saying: Chicken feet, come on out if you are real men!]. As these accounts suggest, the feelings of alarm and rage manifested by the colonial soldiers were clearly linked to fears of helplessness and impotence or loss of masculinity.[7] By challenging their enemies' manhood, the Aymara Indians impugned colonial subjectivity itself, calling into question its material and symbolic dominance.

This assault did not end with verbal insults. Criollo and Spanish witnesses told of the mutilation of prisoners taken by the Aymaras as well as of the dismemberment of soldiers' bodies who died outside the city walls. Diez de Medina graphically related the demise of one soldier in the following terms: "le rodearon y sacrificaron la cabeza, manos, piernas, genitales, y corazón que se llevaron con mucha algazara y sus bailes que en rueda acostumbraban" (cited in del Valle de Siles 1980: 94) [They surrounded him and cut off his head, hands, legs, genitals, and heart, all of which they carried away with great uproar, dancing in a circle as is their custom]. In other accounts of the siege the Indians were said to have drunk the Spaniards' blood or painted their faces with it, eaten the heart, pierced the eyes of the corpses, and cut off the tongue (Szeminski 1987: 169). Commanding officer don Sebastián Segurola wrote in his diary of the instance when the soldier Mariano Murillo was returned to the city on foot wearing only "shorts and shirt" and, "con los brazos cortados colgando al cuello y desangrándose" (del Valle de Siles 1980: 123) [with his cut arms hanging from his neck, bleeding to death]. On the occasion of another fierce encounter, Diez de Medina decried the Indians' violence against white corpses: "La matanza que causaron los indios la eleva el Oidor a la categoría de tragedia, hablando de 50 españoles muertos, flor y nata de la ciudad. Agrega que los indios se llevaron sables, fusiles, espadas, pistolas y la ropa de los muertos, a los que les cortaron la cabeza y otras partes ocultas" (107–108) [The *Oidor* distinguishes the slaughter caused by the Indians as a tragedy, speaking of fifty dead Spanish, the city's very best. He adds that the Indians carried off the dead men's sabres, rifles, swords, pistols, and clothing, after having cut off their heads and other hidden parts].

As I indicated in Chapter 4, clothing often constitutes a visible emblem of the spatial in/coherence of bounded zones. The soldier's body that is stripped naked and dismembered by the Indians becomes a public, material sign of the dismemberment of colonial power. Outright divestment of the colonial subject therefore became a useful strategy of the

Aymaras. For example, any Spanish or criollos who were at Indian camps, either as prisoners or guests, could be obliged to change their western clothing for indigenous attire. In one incident, the Aymara leader, Tupak Amaru, after having spent a considerable amount of time peaceably with the Spanish, returned to his encampment accompanied by two white soldiers only to send them back later wearing Indian clothes: "'Esta desvergüenza nos llenó de cólera e impaciencia, aunque nos mitigó el saber que los había tratado con mucha familiaridad'" (el Sargento Mayor, cited in del Valle de Siles 1980: 173) ["This insolent act filled us with anger and impatience, although we were somewhat relieved to learn that they had been treated with a great deal of familiarity"]. These accounts suggest that the destabilization of Spanish identity beyond the city walls paralleled the process of disintegration that was taking place within the city limits as the inhabitants gradually succumbed to the devastating effects of starvation.

At the heart of these colonial accounts of Indian rebellion, encirclement, and hunger, then, is an anxiety, one that results from the inability of Spanish-criollo society to sustain a coherent spatial-political-ontological unity in the face of prolonged onslaught. Even as the soldiers fought to defend the integrity of the wall separating the Andean aggressors from the Spanish and criollos, this boundary was continually transgressed as starving residents desperate for food crossed to the other side.[8] The challenge to stabilize the border was not just a military initiative, however. Colonial efforts also needed to be consolidated at the level of the social imaginary. Official records insistently portrayed the Aymaras as the abjected Other of the white Subject. For instance, the *Oidor* Diez de Medina likened the Aymaras to the Caribs in his diary on account of their supposed bestiality and depravation (del Valle de Siles 1981: 162–163). In the Spanish colonial imaginary the Carib was the cannibal, an "anthropophagus, a bestial man situated on the margins of civilization, who must be opposed to the very death" (Fernández Retamar 1989: 7). Diez de Medina quoted Dominican *fray* Tomás Ortiz's description of the Caribs that compared them to hares because of their cowardice and to pigs because of their filth. They embodied perversion because they ate "piojos, arañas y gusanos crudos donde quiera que los hallaban; no tenían arte ni maña de hombres y que se olvidan de las cosas de la fe que aprendían" (cited in del Valle de Siles 1981: 163) [lice, spiders, and raw worms wherever they found them; they had neither the skill nor cunningness of men, and they forget the articles of faith that they learned].

These analogies that equated the Aymaras with the Caribs heightened colonial fears of a monstrous Other lurking beyond the city wall, waiting to cannibalize them. At the same time, they constitute part of a consistent pattern of projection. Official accounts of the Aymara's "nature" inevitably begin to sound more like descriptions of the inhabitants within the city walls who, because of the terrible hunger they experienced, engaged in such extreme searches for food that even stories of cannibalism circulated among the residents. The walls could not keep the bestial Carib out, apparently, because it always already inhabited the inside. Moreover, del Valle de Siles's analysis suggests that the anxiety provoked by the indigenous Other was exacerbated further by ongoing conflicts and squabbles between Spanish and criollo authorities. These internal disputes eventually created a division of loyalties among the colonial soldiers made worse by a general lack of discipline (del Valle de Siles 1980: 108).

The corporeality and bestiality of the Indian attackers underscored in the colonial documents contrasted sharply with accounts of the dwindling flesh of the emaciated city residents. The Indians took on increasing bodily presence in the image of endless attacking hordes that appeared not to diminish in spite of the large numbers of casualties tallied by the Spanish. This phantasm progressively haunted the Spanish as the days of the blockade passed and more and more people languished from starvation. The idea of the expanding indigenous corporeal presence was fortified by the image of the Aymaras as providers of food and sustenance through their markets. Nevertheless, these markets became another source of native "gluttony" as the attackers "feasted" on the deserting soldiers and residents who were lured across the wall with the promise of acquiring food only to be taken hostage and carried off. In the colonial imaginary, indigenous bodies became engorged from the incorporation of Spanish bodies.

The Andean social imaginary was similarly haunted by an image of the Spaniard as a rapacious being. From as early as the sixteenth century, colonial documents describe the Andean vision of the Spaniard as that of a malignant being or kind of demon, someone not entirely human. *Lik'ichiri* in Quechua and *kharisiri* in Aymara are terms that literally mean one who kills by cutting or tearing out the fat [*untu*] of the body, "o sea el fluido vital más importante del cuerpo, de acuerdo a la visión indígena" (Rivera Cusicanqui 1993: 38; Szeminski 1987: 169–170) [in other words, the most important vital fluid of the body, according to the indigenous world view].[9] Certainly the accounts of the siege bear out that the Spanish wreaked havoc on the indigenous peoples, burning their homes and killing hundreds during any single offense. This construction of the Spanish as a demonic Other threatening indigenous subjectivities with engulfment constituted a fundamental element of the Andean understanding of colonial dominance, one that has continued to the present.[10]

These parallel accounts of incorporation that haunt both Andean and criollo imaginaries are founded on an appetitive relationship that unceasingly confounds the boundary separating the subject from its other. Each group attempts to annihilate the other (and fears annihilation by the other) through symbolic and/or literal incorporation. Hence, Spaniards captured by the Aymaras might be saved from slaughter if they were dressed as Indians when taken prisoner. So, too, Andean natives found wearing European clothing ran the risk of being executed by their indigenous captors (Szeminski 1987: 171).

Nevertheless, the colonial accounts suggest that the very act of incorporation by bringing the other inside the self can place the self's coherence in jeopardy. Critic Maud Ellmann observes:

> It is through the act of eating that the ego establishes its own domain, distinguishing its inside from its outside. But it is also in this act that the frontiers of subjectivity are most precarious. Food, like language, is originally vested in the other, and traces of that otherness remain in every mouthful that one speaks—or chews. From the beginning one eats for the other, from the other, with the other: and for this reason eating comes to represent the prototype of all transactions with the other, and food the prototype of every object of exchange. (Ellmann 1993: 53)

As this passage reveals, incorporation of the Other is also intimately linked to desire. For example, drawing from Freudian psychoanalytic theory, Ellmann stresses how the mouth, genitals, and anus, the orifices that "originally serve digestive needs . . . later function as the 'props' for sexuality" (38). Therefore, she continues, "[s]ince sexuality originates in eating, it is always haunted by the imagery of ingestion, having neither an object nor a territory proper to itself" (39). The orifices of the body, zones of exchange that enable the primal gifts of food and excrement to pass in and out, also constitute the "apertures through which the desire of the other is inscribed into the self" (39). Returning to the Bolivian context, then, one could say that the boundary of the wall separating whites from Andean natives becomes the paradoxical space where the subject and the object are at once disunited and unremittingly drawn to each other in an equivocal yet always reciprocal relationship of incorporation and desire.

One cultural negotiation of this ambivalent desire can be found in the oral Aymara myth that tells the story of Chuquil Qamir Wirnita. In the version recounted by Carlos Mamani Condori, Wirnita is the lovely daughter of the wealthiest Spanish family living in an unnamed city located somewhere in the intermediate zone between the high Andean cordillera and the Amazon tropics (Mamani Condori 1992: 10, 16 n. 7). Even though Wirnita can have any one of a number of attractive suitors, she wants only Katari [serpent]. Katari appears exclusively at night, taking the form of a handsome blond Spaniard who dresses with elegance. Although her parents attempt to put a stop to this relationship with the stranger, they fail, and Wirnita becomes pregnant, eventually giving birth to serpents. When Wirnita's parents try to burn these diabolic offspring and exorcize their daughter, the colonized space inhabited by the Spanish falls under an enchantment. *Kataris* invade and overrun the city as the day turns as dark as night (10–11).

Other versions of the story claim that Wirnita's children, the *kataris,* can still be found in the towers of some churches like the San Francisco cathedral in La Paz: "En el caso de la ciudad de La Paz, se tiene la idea— o la esperanza—de que el día menos pensado también ha de ser encantada por los *kataris,* o sea que la civilización ha de ser invadida y ocupada por la oscuridad y el salvajismo" (Mamani Condori 1992: 11) [In the case of the city of La Paz, people have the idea—or the hope—that on the day least expected it too will fall under the *kataris'* enchantment; in other words civilization will be invaded and occupied by darkness and savagery]. According to Aymara interpretation, the myth correlates darkness and Katari, the demonic serpent of Christianity, with liberation and the civilized city space with colonial domination such that "Salvaje = libertad y civilizado = sumisión colonial" (10) [Savage = freedom and civilized = colonial submission].

For Mamani Condori, the stories and myths transmitted orally from generation to generation constitute a form of resistant memory that enables a more profound and nuanced understanding of indigenous opposition to colonialism. The oral tale of the beautiful Chuquil Qamir Wirnita is particularly illustrative of the Aymara-Qhichwa struggle, personified in the image of Katari, to decolonize Andean memory and history and reclaim lost independence (1992: 17–23).[11] Therefore, Mamani Condori continues, it was especially appropriate that Julián Apasa assumed the name Tupak Katari in 1781 because of the sense of resistance and liberation that the word "*katari*" conveyed (23).[12]

The story of Wirnita and Katari, however, is unexpectedly haunted by desire as well as by resistance. Indigenous opposition endlessly circulates with desire, a dialectic set into motion through the metaphoric exchange

FIGURE 5.1.

Estoy aquí. *Original drawing by Eusebio Víctor Choque Quispe.*

of the invaded or penetrated colonial city space and the white female body. Moreover, in this erotic encounter, each subjectivity is refigured or transformed by the other (see Waldby 1995: 267). First of all, Katari appears to Wirnita as a Spaniard. Cross-dressing creates a permeable sense of self and subjectivity that enables him to pass as white. Passing facilitates his entrance into the space of the colonial-other because his body is no longer identifiable as Indian-other; racial fixity is lost here. Wirnita, on the other hand, can have any man she wants, but she actively chooses Katari even against her parents' wishes. Thus, the boundary line between white and Indian subjectivities is (temporarily) obliterated in "orgasmic dissolution."[13] Katari and Wirnita become the embodied symbols of di-

vision and union, of separation and re-creation or reproduction as inaugurated by colonialism.

Given this convergence of desire and resistance in the figure of Katari,
it was imperative for the Spanish to reassert colonial dominance precisely
at the site of the indigenous (male) body. If Wirnita's body personifies
the criollo colonial space, Katari's body can be read as a symbol of
Tawantinsuyu, the precolonial Andean empire. Only by physically tearing
Tupak Katari apart could Spanish colonial power appear to be reunified
and in possession of undisputed sovereignty. When they finally captured
Tupak Katari, the *Oidor* himself, Francisco Tadeo Diez de Medina, pronounced the sentence of execution: death by quartering. November 14th,
1781, the Aymara leader who had led two sieges against La Paz was taken
from his prison cell in the town of Peñas, lashed to a horse's tail, and
dragged to the central plaza. Following the horrific public spectacle of his
violent execution, the Spanish strategically displayed his severed limbs
and torso in Aymara communities as a lesson to the Indian rebels. María
Eugenia del Valle de Siles includes a description of the account as it was
recorded in one Spaniard's diary: "Todo lo que se ejecutó a presencia de
un crecido número de indios que quedaron asombrados de aquel castigo
aplicado a un indio que tanto habían respetado y que había tenido particular habilidad para reducirlos a sus malignidades" (1990: 322) [All of
this was carried out in the presence of a large number of Indians who
were astonished by the punishment applied to an Indian whom they had
highly respected and who had the special ability of bringing out their
malignant nature].

From the standpoint of the Aymaras, the fragmentation and circulation[14] of the body of Katari-Tawantinsuyu, initiated with the arrival of
the Spanish in the sixteenth century, is comprehended as setting into motion the process of rupture and revolution known as *pachakuti*. According to Rivera Cusicanqui, "*Pacha* = tiempo-espacio; *kuti* = vuelta, turno,
revolución. Como muchos conceptos andinos, *pachakuti* puede tener
dos sentidos divergentes y complementarios (aunque también antagónicos en ciertas circunstancias): el de catástrofe o el de renovación" (Rivera
Cusicanqui 1993: 37 n. 2) [*Pacha* = time-space; *kuti* = return, turn,
revolution. As with many Andean concepts, *pachakuti* can have two
divergent and complementary meanings (in some circumstances, these
meanings can also be antagonistic): that of cataclysm or renewal].[15]
Although rupture in the Aymara imaginary brings about upheaval, this
cataclysm eventually leads to renovation and the unification once again
of time, space, and society in community or *pacha* (Mamani Condori
1992: 9, 14). Therefore, even as the execution of Tupak Katari was sup-

posed to discourage further rebellions, the Aymaras interpreted his death as a catastrophe that would one day bring about the renovation and the restoration of Katari-Tawantinsuyu. Before the moment of his execution, Tupak Katari allegedly announced to the Aymaras present: "Nayaw jiwtxa nayxarusti, waranq waranqanakaw kut'anipxani"—"Yo muero hoy, pero volveré, convertido en miles de miles" (Santos Escóbar 1992: 42) [I die today, but I will return, transformed into thousands upon thousands]. According to Rivera Cusicanqui, even though the Indian soldiers recognized the message of defeat manifested in Tupak Katari's dismemberment, they also understood his execution as "uno de los movimientos pendulares en el curso cíclico y renovable de la historia. El cuerpo indígena despedazado volverá a unirse—lo hizo con Amaru y Katari—y habrá sonado entonces la hora del *pachakuti,* tiempo de la renovación/ revolución" (Rivera Cusicanqui 1993: 45) [one of the pendular movements in the cyclical and renewable course of history. The fragmented body will come together once again—as happened in the case of Amaru and Katari—and then the hour of *pachakuti* will have struck: the time of renovation/revolution].

The eighteenth-century sieges of La Paz that ended with the execution of Tupak Katari and the resurgence of colonial dominance bequeathed a double legacy. On the one hand, for the Aymara, it signaled the return of cataclysm and catastrophe consolidated in and through the violent moment of colonial usurpation that continues to the present. At the same time, however, for the Spanish and criollos, the panic and horror produced by the siege also figured as central elements in the politics of hegemonic memory, "y se convirtió en el hecho inaugural de las futuras relaciones coloniales entre la sociedad republicana y la población indígena sometida, con la cual se asociará cada vez más la idea ilustrada de *barbarie*" (Rivera Cusicanqui 1993: 44) [constituting the inaugural act of future colonial relations between republican society and the oppressed indigenous peoples; the latter will be increasingly associated with the Enlightenment notion of barbarity]. This fear of the Indian Other was relived in the 1899 siege of La Paz led by the Aymara cacique Pablo Zárate Willka and then again at various moments in the twentieth century. For example, Xavier Albó sees a parallel between the blockades and other actions of the militant Aymara *kataristas*[16] during the 1970s and 1980s and those of Tupak Katari: "A few years ago, in December of 1979, the *gente decente* ('respectable folk') of La Paz felt a panic which revived, perhaps unconsciously, the collective memory of that famous [1781] blockade. The peasantry—still *la indiada* ('the Indian mass') in the words of the gente decente—initiated a general blockade that isolated La Paz and other cities as part of a protest against certain economic measures" (Albó 1987: 379).

Throughout the twentieth century, this memory of hunger resurfaces in and through multiple and often conflicting configurations of incorporation, consumption, and desire in both hegemonic and resistant practices. For instance, the image of the engulfing, devouring indigenous peoples is increasingly associated with the barbarous impulse, an all-consuming desire which must be eradicated by the forces of modernization. Ironically, however, modernity's resolution to eliminate this barbarous desire also is gradually consolidated throughout the course of the twentieth century in cultural and institutional relations of consumerism and incorporation. Modernity enjoins the indigenous peoples to leave their ethnicity behind so that they may be incorporated into the socio-symbolic contract as acculturated (mestizo) citizens.

HUNGER AS DISCIPLINE IN TWENTIETH-CENTURY LA PAZ

If throughout the eighteenth and nineteenth centuries Katari emblematized the barbaric Other furtively lying in ambush at the outskirts of La Paz, in the twentieth century—because of the increasing presence of female domestic workers in the central neighborhoods of the city—this Other became concretized in the figure of the urban *chola* and the indigenous woman. As I noted in the Introduction, the changes in La Paz's spatial and racial formation during the first decades of the twentieth century reinforced the upper class's anxiety that the white social body was being encroached upon by the contaminated, racialized Other. The *chola,* whose ethnic and cultural ties were visibly differentiated from those of criollo society by her sartorial practices, constituted the inauspicious symptom of urban criollo instability.[17] The imminent danger embodied in the racialized female was depicted in hegemonic discourses as an alluring eroticism that threatened the criollo male with engulfment. Within this context, the regulation of food and appetite or hunger and desire emerged as a focal point. Official discourses in Bolivia during the decades spanning the first fifty years of this century utilized symbols of food and spectacle to facilitate the supervision of *chola* and indigenous female bodies. Testimonials and novels as well as other documents from this period reveal the increasing presence of hunger and appetite as fundamental organizing structures, both in urban working-class women's daily lives and in organized demonstrations, as well as in prominent institutional settings that addressed the problems of the larger social body. Moreover, if the white, upper-class male of the oligarchy saw himself as the public, rational agent of the modern nation, he perceived the *chola*, or urban working-class woman, as the personification of the material, hungering body that constituted an impasse to the realization of the modern state.[18]

The racialized working-class woman's body was rendered a barbarous spectacle in hegemonic texts through eroticized representations of appetite. Even in a contemporary study such as Antonio Paredes Candia's *La chola boliviana* (1992), the *chola* is defined by her appetite when the author portrays her as someone who delights in consuming heaping platefuls of highly spiced foods (Paredes Candia 1992: 239). According to Paredes Candia, the *chola*'s enjoyment of eating "naturally" leads her into the culinary profession, where she will undoubtedly achieve satisfaction and prosperity: "Es tan habilidosa para los quehaceres culinarios, que si no se emplea de cocinera, busca de ocupación el instalar una picantería, un restaurante o una pensión y con indudable éxito económico" (240) [She is so skillful at culinary tasks that if she isn't employed as a cook, she will find a job by establishing her own *picantería*, restaurant, or inn which will provide her with certain economic success].[19] The *chola*'s partiality for traditional Andean products and dishes, usually identified by their Aymara or Quechua names, prompts Paredes Candia to state categorically that the *chola* is "la creadora de la comida nacional" (239) [the creator of (Bolivian) national food].

Prevailing descriptions of unrestrained physical appetite—marked by the preference for native, spicy foods—and economic self-sufficiency converge in the image of the *chola* as a luscious, promiscuous woman. For Paredes Candia, the quintessential personification of the *chola* is the *ricuchico*, the beautiful young woman positioned in the doorway of the *chicherías* to attract clients. She serves patrons drink and food, collects their money, and then retires discreetly before the clients' (drunken) behavior gets out of hand (252–254). Paredes Candia cites Guillermo Lora, who notes the similar tradition of bringing *banderitas*, or attractive young women, to Llallagua, Uncía, and Andavilque from Cochabamba to stand in front of *chicherías*, enticing male customers to quench their thirst with a drink (254).

To cite a literary example, in Antonio Díaz Villamil's novel *La niña de sus ojos* (1948), the *chola* is depicted as a woman of insatiable appetite. Domy Perales's mother, the market vendor Doña Saturnina, whose name, of course, denotes excess, disorder, and lack of restraint, eats enormous quantities of traditional native dishes. To the obvious horror of the narrator, her noisy chewing and slurping is accompanied by a frequent licking of her fingers and smacking of her lips:

> Era de verla, tomar con una mano, por ejemplo, el colmado plato de "fritanga" y con la otra llevarse a la boca y saborear el trozo de carne de cerdo aliñado con una sabrosa salsa de ají amarillo, masticar ruidosamente el bocado, chuparse sonoramente los dedos y tomar en seguida un enorme chuño de Araca para engullirlo en sendos mordiscos; luego, llevándose el plato a la boca, sorber ruidosamente el líquido de la salsa, y, al terminar la vianda, limpiar concienzudamente los residuos del plato con el dedo índice para llevárselo a la boca y chuparlo con deleite; repetir en seguida la misma operación con otro plato de "ají de ulluco" o de "bogas fritas" y terminar el menú con el contenido de una infaltable "cervecita negra"; finalmente, limpiarse la boca y las manos en los pliegues de su pollera interior o "mankjancha," utilizada unas veces para servilleta y otras en lugar de pañuelo, y quedar lista para seguir atendiendo a sus clientes. (Díaz Villamil 1956: 30–31)

> [You had to see her pick up with one hand, for example, the overflowing plate of *fritanga* and, with the other, put into her mouth the piece of pork seasoned with a delicious sauce of yellow *ají* that she savored, chewing loudly, noisily licking her fingers, after which she gobbled down in a few bites an enormous *chuño* from Araca; then, bringing the plate up to her lips, she loudly slurped the liquid of the sauce and, once she finished the meal, she conscientiously cleaned any last bit with her forefinger, which she put in her mouth to suck on with pleasure; right away she repeated the same operation either with another plate of Ulluco *ají* or of "*bogas fritas*," finishing off the menu with the inevitable "glass of dark beer"; finally, she cleaned her hands and mouth on the folds of her underskirt or "*mankjancha*," utilized sometimes as a napkin and other times as a handkerchief; she was then ready to continue waiting on her clients.]

This passage serves to characterize Doña Saturnina according to her eating practices. The lengthy sentence enumerating the list of foods she consumes effortlessly reinforces an image of a "naturally" appetitive body that only finds (temporary) satisfaction after devouring prodigious amounts. By the end of the quotation, moreover, her unbridled appetite becomes permanently imprinted on and by her clothing. This description of Doña Saturnina underscores the fact that the *chola sells, prepares,* and therefore *is* food.[20]

The narrative's preoccupation with Doña Saturnina's appetite alludes to an underlying anxiety and even fear of the *chola*'s dietary practices.[21] Without question, her insatiable physical appetite is directly linked to an essential sexual craving. As I proposed in Chapter 2, the sexual and the economic converge in metaphors of consumption when Domy's mother calls out her wares to upper-class male clients. While displaying her fruits and vegetables she lures wealthy men with her tantalizing double entendres: "—¡Ay, caballero! Bien ricas siempre están mis paltas" (11) ["Oh!, gentleman!, My avocados are very delicious"]. This sentence, which I read earlier in terms of the maternal, can now be analyzed in light of food and appetite. The implicit reference to her breasts as fruit enables the *chola* to offer herself for consumption as her body becomes the enticing food that she sells. Thus, appetite, concretized in food, and the indigenous body merge into one as eating becomes a metaphor for the eroticized economic transaction.

A second example from literature of how prevailing discourses align the *chola* with the appetitive body can be found in Carlos Medinaceli's novel *La Chaskañawi* (1947). In this case the narrative construction of the *chola* links her with metaphors of service; she prepares the hot, spicy dishes [the *picantes*] for the *señoritos*, a meal that functions symbolically as foreplay to sexual intercourse. Exemplified by the figure of Petrona Rodríguez, the *chola* is portrayed as a dehumanized, emasculating woman who drags the upper-class man down to a state of physical and moral degradation. Or, alternately, like the heroine Claudina, she represents a sexual force, insatiable and voluptuous, that overflows the confines of her clothing just as the *picantes* she prepares spill over the edge of the plate. In the novel, when a woman aggressively initiates sexual relations, her desire is cast as appetite, one that will not be satisfied until the object desired (the male) is devoured.[22] Both *La Chaskañawi* and *La niña de sus ojos* exemplify female appetite constructed alternately as grotesque and sinister or seductive but disruptive. Moreover, if a specifically "feminine" appetite is perceived as threatening a "masculine" self, these novels suggest that the racialized female appetitive body threatens the social order, the rational, public realm which is the domain of the upper-class, white male.

The representation of the *chola* as at once seductive and threatening can be traced to the abject because of the way in which her appetitive body is culturally depicted by the dominant imaginary as eroticism incarnate. Revisiting the relationship between food and subjectivity, it becomes apparent that eating threatens the boundaries of the subject because, as Kelly Oliver, in her analysis of Julia Kristeva's work on the abject, explains, "food, what is taken into the body, along with excrement, what is expelled from the body, [is that which] calls into question the borders of the body" (Oliver 1992: 71). So, too, Maud Ellmann writes that the "notion of the self is founded on the regulation of the orifices. For it is at these thresholds that the other, in the form of food, is assumed into the body, and the body, in the form of waste, is expelled into the empery of otherness" (Ellmann 1993: 105). Oliver expands on the relationship between the abject and civilized society in Western culture to show how "Western Culture sustains itself by establishing borders between abject corporeal nature, which oozes and flows and defies categorization, on the one side, and civilized society composed of clean and proper individuals on the other" (Oliver 1992: 74). Thus, Oliver describes this abject corporeal nature as that which interrogates both the identity and unity of the social body because it problematizes the boundaries upon which both society and the subject are constructed: "The abject threat comes from what has been prohibited by culture, what has been prohibited so that the culture can be" (71).

In Andean Bolivia of the 1920s, 1930s, and 1940s, the abject threat to the unity of the dominant social body was indigenous feminine desire or agency, which took shape in the form of organized resistance. As I discussed in Chaper 1, these three decades were characterized by a flourishing of all-women labor unions. Formidable numbers of cooks, domestic employees, and market vendors, among others, repeatedly converged in the streets to demand labor reforms that included better working conditions, pay raises, child care facilities for working mothers, an eight-hour work day, and so on (see Wadsworth and Dibbits 1989: 101–102; *Polleras* 1986: 8–9). Therefore, indigenous feminine desire, made manifest in collective resistance, posed a clear threat to the social order and to the oligarchy's imagined nation-state. Within this historical context, the attempt to circumscribe the indigenous female body through food/hunger becomes of paramount importance. The need to curb feminine appetite (desire) arises from the perception that feminine desire or appetite will destabilize masculine order and threaten the "self" (the masculine, criollo hegemony).[23]

Social and economic practices converged in the withholding of food from the poor and working-class sectors of urban society through the systematic refusal to implement any of the labor reforms the women's unions sought. For instance, the working day for cooks and domestic employees extended anywhere from fourteen to seventeen hours. As I indicated in Chapter 1, upper-class women were fervently opposed to reforms implementing the eight-hour work day for domestic employees.

The long hours and minimal wages forced many working women to continually postpone their own needs. One cook, doña Graciela, tells of the contrast between working for Bolivian *señoras* and foreign *señoras:* "En una casa extranjera primero nos hacen tomar el desayuno; en cambio en casa boliviana se daba pues mal trato: una dentra a trabajar y el desayuno qué rato una va tomar . . . , nada, después que una termina" (Wadsworth and Dibbits 1989: 48) [In a foreigner's house first they let us have our breakfast; in contrast, in a Bolivian house they treated us poorly: a woman comes to work and there's no breakfast in sight . . . , nothing, not until she finishes work]. Furthermore, she notes that in the Bolivian home food was kept under lock and key: "Nuestros paisanos un queso bajo llave se están poniendo; el pan también, todo medidito" (48) [Our fellow countrymen even lock up the cheese; bread too, everything is carefully measured out].

The link between hunger, appetite, and desire that emerges in doña Graciela's description of her life when she worked for a Chilean *señora* demonstrates her awareness that, in contrast to dominant representations of the *chola*'s body as "naturally" appetitive, hunger and appetite (desire) are culturally and economically constructed. Upon first arrival at the Chilean woman's home, doña Graciela explains, she ate very little as was her custom because, since she was a child, her family had never had a lot of food: "Yo no quería [comer], poquito comía porque en la casa de mi madre, era pobre, poquito comía y me acuerdo que en mí decía: 'cuando sea grande, harto he de comer'" (Wadsworth and Dibbits 1989: 48) [I didn't want [to eat], I ate just a little bit because in my mother's house, I was poor, I would eat only a little, and I remember I used to think to myself: "when I grow up I'm going to eat a ton of food"]. In contrast, the Chilean señora trains her to eat and indulge her appetite: "Yo he sido bien comelona; cuando he trabajado en la casa chilena me han enseñado a comer tanto" (48) [I was a real big eater; when I worked in the Chileans' house they taught me to eat so much]. Doña Graciela perceives the Chilean woman's appetite, for its pleasure and unrestricted quantity, as exceeding normative femininity; therefore she associates it with a masculine economy: "Como hombre ella sabe estar tomando una taza de café con leche. '¿Más te daré, Graciela?' 'Bueno,' le decía. '¿Un poco más te daré?' 'Bueno . . .'" (48–49) [She always drinks a cup of coffee and milk like a man. "Can I give you some more, Graciela?" "Okay," I would say. "Can I give you a little bit more?" "Okay . . ."].

Doña Graciela's protestations that she did not normally eat this much, and therefore had to be "taught" to indulge a newly acquired appetite, draw attention to the ambivalence that results from the satisfaction of desire. Behind the pleasure is the recognition that she is surrendering to a forbidden appetite, one that the dominant culture has defined as both repugnant and offensive, and which, when unleashed, could successfully elude efforts to bring it back under control to the detriment of the social body. Susan Bordo has noted that both the curtailment of women's appetite and the corresponding idea that an unrestricted appetite is unfeminine are not only about women's relationship to food: "Rather, the social control of female hunger operates as a practical 'discipline' (to use Foucault's term) that trains female bodies in the knowledge of their limits and possibilities." Thus, for example, in anorexia, "[d]enying oneself food becomes the central micro-practice in the education of feminine self-restraint and containment of impulse" (Bordo 1993: 130). The illustration of doña Graciela's experience similarly suggests that the social control of indigenous female hunger functions as a practical discipline that educates *cholas* and indigenous women workers to their limitations and possibilities within dominant social, political, and economic structures. In this way, the widespread management of hunger/appetite is inextricably related to the dominant construction of indigenous feminine desire.

Because the female body has been defined sexually, in dominant Western culture, as a body that is acted upon, desire in women is coded as responsiveness (MacSween 1993: 248–249). Responsiveness is a taking in, an opening up. In eating disorders such as anorexia, "the experience of feminine bodily openness is centered on the mouth . . . Not eating deconstructs feminine responsiveness; it protects against the invasion which threatens to annihilate the self" (249). Similarly, Bordo has observed, "the practice of dieting—of saying no to hunger—contributes to the anorectic's increasing sense of hunger as a dangerous eruption from some alien part of the self, and to a growing intoxication with controlling that eruption" (Bordo 1993: 143). In Bolivia we can also see how during the first half of this century indigenous feminine desire was being recodified as an eruptive hunger, a threat that came from some alien part of the social self. This unsettling hunger was restrained not by facilitating equal access to food, but by clamping down on it, by denying its existence.

To take one example, in 1931, the anarchists organized a large demonstration to protest worker layoffs. A considerable number of women participated in the demonstration and many of them spoke out publicly against the harsh measures. *La Razón,* the newspaper published by the oligarchy, angrily denounced the demonstration. One article in particular targeted the participation of women as especially ludicrous, claiming that their allegations of hunger were hypocritical. The author of the article makes this claim by calling attention in detail to the supposed extravagance of one *chola*'s finery:

> El Señor Prefecto nos decía ayer que una de las oradoras más furiosas, mandada a detener, lucía unas polleras de raso, una manta de fina seda y unos faluchos de siquiera dos mil bolivianos de valor. Es posible hablar de hambre con tales atavíos? (. . .) Donde hay hambre es en la burguesía, en aquellos hogares donde el decoro impide pedir. (*La Razón*, October 7, 1931; cited in *Polleras* 1986: 4)

> [His Magistrate told us yesterday that one of the angriest (female) speakers, ordered detained, was decked out in satin *polleras*, a fine silk shawl, and some gold earrings worth at least two thousand *bolivianos*. Is it possible to speak of hunger with such a getup? (. . .) Where there is hunger is among the bourgeoisie, in those homes where dignity keeps people from begging.]

The article continues, arguing that needy families from the upper classes can neither perform manual labor nor beg. Yet their position in society obliges them to maintain a facade of success and prosperity in public: "Allí hay hambre, junto a las exigencias de una vida social, o semi social, con el imperativo de vestirse y guardar apariencias. Allí hay hambre. No en la chiquillada alborotera ni la indiada aprovechadora" (4) [Hunger is there, with the exigencies of a social or semi-social life where the imperative of dressing well and keeping up appearances prevails. That's where there is hunger. Not in the childish (female) rabble-rouser nor in the opportunistic Indian hordes]. These images deployed by the article's author evoke the memory of Tupak Katari's sieges of La Paz to underscore the upper class's fear of starvation at the hand of the indigenous insurgents. This memory of hunger resonated in the dominant imaginary and effectively denied other hungers. Indeed, this memory provoked a misrecognition of the *chola*'s hunger as evidenced by the article's claim that hunger circulated only among the white upper classes and not among the indigenous multitudes.

The author's choice of such words as "*furiosa*" [angry], "*chiquillada*" [childish], "*alborotera*" [(female) rabble-rouser], and "*aprovechadora*" [opportunistic] to describe the principal speaker and the crowd emphasizes her/their inanity by casting them as absurd spectacles. The article suggests that if they would only stop talking they could eat because their claims to hunger are disingenuous. Discussing the "phantasmatics of ingestion," Maud Ellmann writes that "the fact that language issues from the same orifice in which nutrition is imbibed means that words and food are locked in an eternal rivalry. . . . Since language must compete with food to gain the sole possession of the mouth, we must either speak and go hungry, or shut up and eat" (Ellmann 1993: 46). The anonymous author's response to the woman's speech, and, for that matter, to the entire demonstration, dismisses their hunger or inanition, relegating it to the realm of the senseless, the inane. These two words, "inanition" and "inane," share the same root, one meaning "starved of sustenance" and the other "starved of sense" (Ellmann 1993: 19). The denial of the protesters' hunger can be read as a deliberate attempt to delegitimize any further claims the workers might have. Furthermore, the negation of their hunger by rendering it "senseless" is tantamount to denying their desire. The political ramifications of this act are clear: if desireless, the self can neither contain nor claim anything (see MacSween 1993: 252). Thus, the overall effect of the letter portrays the workers assembled as figures of extreme instability, without sense or reason, whose mere presence threatens to disrupt the social order without the slightest provocation.[24] Moreover, the detention of the speaker takes on important symbolic value because the act establishes a "normative" model according to which subaltern desire is disciplined within the dominant social body.

The unionized women of the FOF were neither passive victims nor rendered powerless by the many abuses they suffered on a daily basis. Instead, the all-women's labor unions transformed the private, bodily experience of hunger into a public, collective resistance. This resistance took shape in the form of massive demonstrations in public arenas, such as markets, the main square of La Paz, and the streets, and often ended in violent confrontations with the police. Records of the FOF document rallies and demonstrations where numbers of women attending ranged from two thousand to five thousand (*Polleras* 1986: 24). The impressive participation by women led one male anarchist, don Lisandro Rodas, to comment that: "eran multitudes pues. Ellas iban por delante y nosotros por detrás" (cited in Lehm and Rivera Cusicanqui 1988: 80) [well, there were multitudes of them. The women walked ahead and we men followed behind]. The majority of these women were of Aymara origin, and they continued using the Aymara language and the *pollera*. Unlike their male companions and partners, the women of the FOF were less inclined to be divided by doctrinal differences: "la sindicalización de las mujeres obedecía a motivaciones más concretas y estaba animada por experiencias cotidianamente sentidas en los puestos de trabajo, donde la confrontación con la casta dominante y con los representantes del estado estaba a la orden del día" (Lehm and Rivera Cusicanqui 1988: 69) [the unionization of women was a response to more concrete motives, and it was encouraged by daily experiences lived out at their workplace, where the confrontation with the dominant caste and state representatives was the order of the day].

If at first the women became organized as a means of countering the abuses confronted each day through their work and directed at them by police and other authorities, the FOF soon came to play other important roles in the lives of its membership. Through the experiences gained as members, women learned how to organize, how to talk to the authorities, how to network with other groups, and, finally, how to act at work. For example, the leader doña Petronila Infantes repeatedly recommended that the women who worked as cooks never steal food from their employers: "Que nadie saque, que nadie lleve, para que no nos digan que somos ladronas. 'Las cocineras roban,' decían. Pero la cocinera no roba si lleva alguna vez su ración. Porque de tanto servir uno no tiene deseo de comer, ya está hartada. Entonces su ración puede llevárselo, pero sacar ya no" (cited in *Polleras* 1986: 21) [Let no one take anything or carry anything away so they can't say that we are thieves. "The cooks steal," they would say. But it's not stealing if the cook sometimes takes her portion with her. Because from serving and waiting on them so much sometimes she doesn't feel like eating, she's fed up. So she can take her portion with her, but to take more than that, no]. In this way, doña Petronila established the cook's right to take what was due her; she also made it clear that domestic workers were not "by nature" subservient. Instead, serving was, in large part, an exhausting performance that they enacted daily. For these reasons, many women considered the FOF to be like a school. The valuable lessons they learned, however, did not "domesticate" them in the sense of the newly formed trade schools [Escuelas de Artes y Oficios] which instructed children of the working class, preparing them to better serve the upper classes.

Contrary to the anorectic, who, by engaging in an isolated "hunger strike," is unable to adopt a conscious political stance grounded in a broader social and political understanding of her protest (Bordo 1993: 159), the women of the FOF were well aware of the double and triple burdens of oppression that they faced as *chola* and indigenous working-class women. Through the collective experience of hunger, the women concretely understood the relations of power and were acutely aware of the need for broadscale social, economic, and political changes.

THE HUNGER STRIKE: A TESTIMONIAL
OF RESISTANCE IN THE MINING CENTERS

In contrast to the social and cultural practice of withholding food from urban domestic workers, a practice that varied somewhat from household to household, the repressive measures adopted by the military dictatorships during the 1960s and 1970s expose the government's systematic and deliberate method of utilizing food to control the miners and their families.[25] From beginning to end, the question of hunger pervades all of the testimonials, reports, and other documents published by and about the Housewives Committees. For example, Domitila Barrios de Chungara's initial descriptions of the worker's life in the mines call attention to the institutionally sanctioned inanition the miner must regularly endure because of very low salaries, few benefits, and poor working conditions. He begins the long day by consuming before the 6 A.M. shift a meager breakfast prepared for him by his wife or *compañera*. Unlike the white-collar worker, who has access to on-site food service, he has no opportunity to eat again until he returns home after 3 P.M. One way miners typically ward off hunger is by chewing coca leaves while they work (Barrios de Chungara 1987: 26). According to the prevailing imaginary, however, the miner who chews coca does not really require much food because the coca leaf supposedly enables him to endure strenuous exertion without the need of replenishment. Presumably, the constant working of the jaw and the visible bulge of the coca in the cheek suggest a satiety so extreme that there is no room inside to swallow the final bite.[26]

Other practices, such as the implementation of a politics of scarcity through the calculated withholding of supplies from the mining encampment company stores, attest to the government's use of food to suppress the workers and their families. In her first testimonial, Domitila Barrios de Chungara acknowledges that hunger can be a powerful weapon deployed by the government to make the miners docile: "Claro, el gobierno tiene sus aliados bastante fuertes y tiene la posibilidad de tomar otras medidas en contra de los trabajadores en el futuro. Por ejemplo, como no tenemos fondos, puede ser que nos someta por el hambre" (Barrios de Chungara 1987: 201) [Of course, the government has pretty strong allies and has the possibility of taking other measures against the workers in the future. For example, since we don't have funds, they might beat us through hunger] (Barrios de Chungara 1978: 181–182).

Nevertheless, when the miners' housewives counter government-sponsored hunger with a hunger strike, they effectively thwart those efforts that would reduce them to a state of helplessness and victimization. Hunger mobilizes the women who refuse to be made submissive by need. Moreover, by making public the limit situation they suffer individually and collectively on a daily basis, the hunger strikers oblige spectators to read their own complicity in the text of the emaciated flesh.[27] Thus even as hunger constitutes one of the primary tactics of hegemonic oppression, it also structures the anatomy of resistance. A close reading of the well-known hunger strike initiated in 1977 by four miners' housewives helps to clarify how this complex dynamic develops.

At the time of the hunger strike, the president of Bolivia was General Hugo Bánzer Suárez. Bánzer Suárez headed a repressive military regime responsible for numerous assassinations of men and women and for the detention and torture of hundreds. Many more had been forced into exile. On December 28, 1977, four women from Siglo XX—wives of miners, one of them pregnant—took their fourteen children to the archbishop's residence in La Paz and initiated a hunger strike. Two of the women's husbands had been arrested and later fired from their jobs; the third woman's husband was in hiding, and the fourth woman's remained in jail. The housewives presented four demands to the press: amnesty for all political exiles, the reestablishment of labor unions, the rehiring of those workers who had been fired for their covert participation in organizing labor, and the removal of the military troops occupying the mining districts.

The hunger strike, a testimonial of resistance that began with four women and their children, grew during the course of twenty-three days to include more than twelve hundred hunger strikers congregated throughout the major cities of the country. Various groups around the world also demonstrated their solidarity with Bolivia by joining in on the strike. By publicly refusing to eat, the hunger strikers dramatically threw the spotlight onto the desperate conditions and privations, including unremitting malnutrition and starvation, which the working classes, the miners, and the poor experienced each day. Through their actions they effectively challenged the utterly bankrupt social contract that would have them passively and silently starve.

The individual testimonials of the participants in this hunger strike provide dramatic examples of the people [el pueblo] as agents of their own history. One of the most compelling accounts is the essay authored by the Jesuit priest Luis Espinal.[28] Espinal participated in the dramatic events alongside Domitila Barrios de Chungara and many others.

Describing his experience of hunger, Espinal acknowledges the paradox inherent for those like himself who joined the strike out of solidarity even though they did not genuinely know what it is like to feel hunger every day:

> Caí en la cuenta de que nunca había tenido la experiencia del hambre. Esta experiencia el pueblo la sufre con frecuencia; nosotros la hemos sufrido como en un laboratorio. El hambre se nos ha convertido también en un medio de comunicación; en una manera de comprender mejor al pueblo que hambrea siempre y no solamente en una circunstancia excepcional. El hambre es una experiencia violenta que nos hace comprender la valentía y la ira del pueblo. Cuando se tiene hambre se comprende mejor la urgencia de trabajar para que haya justicia en el mundo. Los pobres hambrean todo el año; pero ellos no están en vitrina, como estábamos nosotros y su hambre es tan crónica que ya ha dejado de ser noticia. Este pensamiento me hacía sentir un hambriento muy especial, muy alharaco, muy burgués. (Espinal 1991: 11)

> [I realized that I had never undergone hunger. That experience which the *pueblo* frequently suffers, we endured it as if we were in a laboratory. Hunger became a means of communication for us as well; a way of better understanding the *pueblo* that always hungers and not just in exceptional circumstances. Hunger is a violent experience that makes us understand the courage and wrath of the *pueblo*. When you are hungry you understand better the urgency of working for justice in the world. The poor are hungry all year round; but they aren't on display in a showcase like we were and their hunger is so chronic that it has ceased being news. This realization made me feel like a very special kind of hungry person, one who is making a big deal out of a mundane experience, very bourgeois.]

For Espinal, the strike should be understood as a critical performance because it elicited the complicity of the upper and middle classes in the hunger experienced daily by the poor.[29] Maud Ellmann has similarly contended that self-starvation constitutes a form of performance, one in which the spectators must be made to recognize that "they are implicated in the spectacle that they behold" (Ellmann 1993: 17). As a performance or means of communication, hunger loses its numbing and immobilizing familiarity to become news, once again. Javier Sanjinés claims that the hunger strike transformed individual resistance into social resistance whereby the individual body metaphorically represented the larger social group. Thus the hunger strike came to represent both life and the nation, as the collective act of starving was transformed into an authentic means of social communication, a speech act rooted in the long history of the Bolivian people (Javier Sanjinés 1992a.: 165–167).

Drawing from David Herlihy's definition of the family as those individuals who sit down to eat together, Maud Ellmann posits the dinner table as a symbol of the social contract (Ellmann 1993: 80). Taking this idea one step further, we can say that the Bolivian hunger strike drew the public's attention to the disastrous breakdown of the social contract, underscoring its exclusion of the miners and their families. One of the original four women, Aurora de Lora, declared the Christmas holidays as an especially opportune time for their strike: "Que sepan, pues, que mientras ellos están comiendo sus pavos, nosotros estamos muriendo de hambre. Que les golpee su conciencia" (Barrios de Chungara 1985: 41) [Well, let them know that while they are eating their turkey, we are dying of hunger. Let their consciences haunt them]. According to Barrios de Chungara's *testimonio,* this strategy proved effective because members of the Unión de Mujeres de Bolivia [Union of Bolivian Women] joined in the strike, declaring "que estaban de acuerdo en apoyar la huelga, que no era correcto que en las fiestas de fin de año hayan tantos niños muriendo de hambre" (51) [that they were in agreement about supporting the strike, that it wasn't right that during the end-of-the-year festivities there were so many children dying of hunger]. Similarly, Luis Espinal remembers that the strikers told the mediators not to rush the negotiations on their account. After all, they maintained, "[l]a huelga de hambre debe ser más angustiosa para el que la contempla que para el que la sufre" (Espinal 1991: 12) [the hunger strike must be much more distressing for those who are watching than for those who are participating in it].

Crucial to this process, then, is the struggle for representation. Luis Espinal observes: "La huelga de hambre vale políticamente en la medida que es una experiencia publicitada. . . . Por supuesto, entiendo por publicitario que ha de ser público y publicitado; no que deba ser falso y ficticio. Esto nos separa totalmente de la moral individual puramente privada y personal" (Espinal 1991: 13) [The hunger strike is of political use insofar as it is a publicized experience. . . . Of course, by publicity I mean that it must be public and publicized; it should not be false or fictitious. That is what distinguishes us from an individual ethic that is purely private and personal]. With the help of the press the strikers were able to communicate their hunger beyond national boundaries so that groups around the world might collaborate, offering their support and solidarity. Consequently, because the hunger strike was joined by so many

Bolivians of all classes, at home and abroad, it triggered the downfall of General Bánzer Suárez's military dictatorship.

A feminist reading of the hunger strike shifts the focus somewhat to call attention to the centrality of working-class motherhood as a powerful symbol of convocation and resistance. When the original group of four women initiated the hunger strike, they deliberately called attention to themselves as mothers and wives by including their children. Indeed, at the beginning of the hunger strike, what most shocked horrified onlookers was the participation of the children and the disclosure that one of the four women was also pregnant. These desperate measures created a scandal because they violated the fundamental tenets of dominant womanhood that emphasizes self-sacrifice and the privileging of the child's needs above all else.

As late as 1980, Emma Aranzaes v. de Butrón, a teacher of philosophy and literature, argued that even if a mother does not have food for her children she has the obligation to teach them that love rather than hate can conquer all adversity and bring lasting happiness:

A una madre de verdad no le importará que alguna vez pueda faltar el pan, pero que jamás falte el cariño, la ternura, el buen trato para sus hijos, que nunca se sientan abandonados, porque el amor construye, por el se vencen los más grandes obstáculos, se enfrentan los reveces de la vida, por ese amor se lucha hasta lograr la felicidad. En cambio el odio destruye, y para evitarlo, es preferible sembrar en el corazón de nuestros hijos amor, ternura y comprensión. (Aranzaes v. de Butrón 1980: 19)

[For a real and true mother it will not be important if at times there is no food; but never should there be a lack of affection, tenderness, and good treatment of her children; let them never feel abandoned, because love edifies; with it, it is possible to conquer the greatest of obstacles, to confront the misfortunes of life; for this love a mother fights until happiness has been achieved. In contrast, hate destroys, and so, to avoid it, it is preferable to sow love, tenderness, and compassion in the hearts of our children.]

The four women's decision to bring along their children unquestionably flew in the face of "normal" maternal behavior and practices. Nevertheless, their actions foregrounded the limit situation in which the miners and their families lived each day, underscoring how the government's politics of hunger spared neither mothers nor children.

After eight days Aurora de Lora, the hunger striker who was pregnant, had to receive medical treatment because of her state of severe weakness. In spite of her deteriorating condition, she refused to end her participation in the strike, declaring to the press on January 5, "con todo el dolor de madre estoy decidida a perder al hijo que está en camino, y a perder yo también la vida por alcanzar la justicia" (cited in Mansilla T. 1978: 43) [with all of a mother's pain, I would even lose the baby which is on its way and my own life as well in order to achieve justice].

Public outcry over the children's involvement compelled Monsignor Manrique to rebuke Domitila Barrios de Chungara, the representative and spokesperson of the striking mothers: "—Ustedes son unas herejes, unas bestias. ¿Cómo se les ocurre meter a los niños a la huelga de hambre? Por eso es que vienen tantas maldiciones contra ustedes— me dijo monseñor" (Barrios de Chungara 1985: 53) ["You women are a bunch of heretics, animals. How could you think of bringing those children along on the hunger strike? That's why so many curses are coming down onto you," the Monsignor told me]. Refusing to interview the strikers themselves, Bolivia's state-run television spoke instead with women onlookers who neither knew any of the strikers nor had ever experienced hunger themselves. According to Barrios de Chungara, they knew nothing of the circumstances in which the poor lived. The news media seized the opportunity to use these women's statements "en contra nuestra, criticando el hecho de estar en la huelga junto a nuestros hijos. Nos mostraban como madres desnaturalizadas, sin conciencia" (1985: 60) [against us, criticizing us for going on strike with our children. They depicted us as perverse mothers, without a conscience]. And yet, Barrios de Chungara countered, those women who put their own lives on the line as well as their children's were the ones most politically conscious of themselves as mothers: "Pero nosotros pensábamos que esas madres que fueron con sus hijos eran las más conscientes. Porque al luchar por la libertad de sus compañeros, estaban luchando por el pan que no tenían sus hijos, por el futuro de esos y otros niños. Ellas sí eran madres" (60–61) [But we believed that those mothers who participated in the strike with their children were the most aware. Because, by fighting for their partners' freedom they were fighting for the food that their children didn't have, for the future of these and other children. Those women truly were mothers]. By defamiliarizing the maternal body through the public display of their hunger, the four miners' housewives could reappropriate motherhood as a powerful symbol of agency and resistance.

SUBJECT TO RELOCATION: REPRESENTATIVE
DEMOCRACY AND THE NEW ECONOMIC POLICY

If, in 1977, the miners' housewives were able to utilize the hunger strike to keep onlookers riveted in the zone of estrangement, the dialectic of hunger shifted once again following the political and economic reforms of the mid 1980s. Between the years 1982 and 1985, Bolivia came into the international limelight because hyperinflation was reaching annual rates ranging from 8,000 to 22,000 percent (Toranzo 1989a: 10). These same years of runaway inflation marked the inauguration of a new period of representative democracy, characterized by the implementation of the New Economic Policy (NEP), under which hyperinflation was brought to a screeching halt.[30] The NEP introduced a series of austerity measures designated as a "free-market 'shock treatment,'" which included the "deregulation of prices, exchange rates and trade; elimination of subsidies and price supports; and the dismantling of the state enterprises dominant since the revolution of 1952" (North American Congress on Latin America [NACLA] 1991: 9). Although celebrated as an economic miracle (see Farthing with Villegas 1991: 24) and as a model that should be exported to other countries experiencing hyperinflation (Toranzo 1989a: 12), the NEP engineered enormous economic and political upheaval in Bolivia, radically redefining social structures in the process.

According to economist Carlos Toranzo, one specific goal of this economic shock treatment was the deproletarianization and subsequent depoliticization of Bolivian society (Toranzo 1989b: 235–236). The formidable political power unionized labor had exercised since the 1952 Revolution was systematically dismantled by the layoff and relocation of thousands of miners, factory workers, and public employees. For example, between the years 1985 and 1989 the state-owned mining corporation, COMIBOL, reduced its workforce from twenty-seven thousand workers to six thousand. Private mining companies laid off similar percentages of their employees (Toranzo 1989a: 17).[31] Linda Farthing gives a figure of some forty-five thousand jobs eliminated in both the state-owned mining industry and public administration (Farthing 1991: 18); factory closures resulted in thirty-five thousand additional layoffs (18). As a consequence of this "white massacre," (Davila 1991: 12) more than 60 percent of the urban population was suddenly forced to support itself in the informal sectors of the economy (Farthing 1991: 18). In the mining districts, the process of relocation began somewhat gradually with the retirement of older workers, followed by voluntary departure and, eventually, by massive layoffs (*Por la vida* 1986: 13). According to one miner, the workers were forced to leave the mines in droves: "los compañeros relocalizados han salido de nuestros distritos en caravanas, han salido de diez en diez, así sucesivamente" (cited in *Por la vida* 1986: 13) [the relocated *compañeros* have left our districts in caravans, ten by ten, one group after the other]. The newly unemployed converged on the outskirts of La Paz literally by the busload when they had nowhere else to go.

This unprecedented migration to El Alto, the satellite city situated on the rim of the canyon that looks down into La Paz proper, strikingly depicts how relocated peoples were positioned once again outside the sociosymbolic contract.[32] The language used in the testimonials of the newly unemployed alludes repeatedly to spatial images that reflect this disenfranchisement. For example, one miner's housewife from Siglo XX points out how the official policy of "relocation" adds up to the dismissal, abandonment, and casting out of the workforce: "Nosotros hemos entendido relocalización sacar de un trabajo y poner a otro, pero yo pienso que el gobierno no ha leído el diccionario, no entiende de esa forma, entonces, relocalizar quiere decir botar afuera" (cited in *Por la vida* 1986: 12) [We understood relocation to mean to be removed from one job and placed in another, but I think that the government hasn't read the dictionary, and so doesn't understand it in that way; thus, relocation means to be thrown out]. If citizenship has always been structured by market relations, the accumulation of capital, and the ability to consume, the fact that those who moved to the city were forced to sell most of their meager belongings in order to obtain money for food points to further evidence of their marginalization by the social contract. One housewife observed: "yo he estado en la ciudad de La Paz hace un mes, yo he visto, me he encontrado con algunos compañeros vendiendo sus cositas, sus radios, sus frazadas y eso es una cosa triste" (cited in *Por la vida* 1986: 14) [I was in the city of La Paz a month ago, and I saw with my own eyes; I ran into some *compañeros* selling their few little belongings, their radios, their blankets, and that is a sad thing].

The overwhelming numbers of homeless people unveiled the violent underpinnings of a relocation grounded literally in processes of defamiliarization. For elderly and retired miners, relocation was especially traumatic because they had no place to go, nor any home where they might stay as the mining companies began dismantling their houses to coerce them into leaving:

aquellos compañeros trabajadores antiguos, viejos, que no tienen casa, que han trabajado 35 años, desde antes de la nacionalización de las minas aún están en los campamentos mineros, no saben donde ir, inclusive sus beneficios sociales están gastándolos con el transcurso de este tiempo. Desde enero a la fecha no tienen dinero ni donde ir, entonces se encuentran todavía dentro del campamento, pese a que la empresa está haciendo destechar las casas de los campamentos, están recogiendo las calaminas y puertas, entonces, al hacer eso, a la fuerza están queriendo desalojar . . . (*Por la vida* 1986: 15–16)

[those fellow workers who have been at their jobs a long time, the old ones, who have no home, who have been working for 35 years since before the nationalization of the mines, they're still in the mining camps because they don't know where to go; they're even spending their social benefits in the space of this time. Since January they have neither money nor place to go, so they're still in the mining district in spite of the fact that the company is having the roofs removed from the camp houses; they're taking down the roofing and the doors, forcibly trying to evict (the old ones) . . .]

By unhousing the working class, including the elderly retired miners, the state made it clear that there was no longer any secure space for these sectors of the population. These official actions unquestionably had devastating repercussions. As I pointed out in Chapter 3, the miners continually affirmed their identity as men and as members of the working class within the space of the mineshaft. Their dismissal resulted in the undoing of these identities and, as a consequence, in the dissolution of the political effectiveness of the working class. Many poor women's lives underwent similar transformation as a result of their husbands' unemployment. They became doubly and triply burdened by having to work long hours in the informal economy as vendors, washerwomen, cooks, artisans, and so on, in addition to their normal domestic chores that could take up as much time as five hours each day (Farthing 1991: 21–22). While hunger and necessity affect men, women, and children, it is primarily the women who continue to bear the brunt of its discipline. For example, one miner's wife whose husband had been laid off remarked: "It's we women who have to worry about keeping our homes running. The men have no idea where the food comes from. They just demand a meal, without thinking what we're going to have to do to produce it" (cited in Davila 1991: 15–16). Furthermore, those women who were now unhoused had even fewer claims to the rights and privileges of dominant womanhood that defined Woman/Mother in terms of spatial metaphors of enclosure and interiority. In summary, the high number of families becoming homeless literally overnight pointed to the further fragmentation of the body politic and the opening up of new pathological spaces.[33]

Linda Farthing notes that just as there was a shift to the family unit as the economic mainstay, so, too, was there a shift from the workplace, where labor's demands were generated and around which they were usually centered, to the neighborhood as the new locus of organization. Moreover, as the workplace became eclipsed in importance by neighborhood associations, pressure to bring about structural changes increasingly gave way to a greater emphasis on single issues (Farthing 1991: 21). What's more, large numbers of unemployed people led to an increasingly conservative labor force: "No hay duda que los obreros ocupados, por temor a perder su puesto de trabajo, asumen actitudes muy tímidas en la política, fenómeno que no siempre es captado con claridad por sus direcciones" (Toranzo 1989b: 244) [There's no doubt that the employed workers, for fear of losing their jobs, adopt a very timid attitude toward politics, a phenomenon that is not always understood clearly by the union leadership].

In response to the new government's harsh measures, which resulted in untold numbers of unemployed or underemployed, many characterized its policies as comprising a deliberate politics of hunger.[34] Attempting to find some solution to these desperate circumstances, in January 1986 the miners' housewives convened their first national meeting. The report of this historic gathering is striking for the testimonies of hunger and necessity that fill its pages as each delegate spoke with great emotion about the terrible conditions those still living in the mining centers were forced to endure. Lidia de Mendieta, delegate from Siete Suyos, told of the lack of supplies in their company stores and of how they had to travel to nearby cities to obtain meager quantites of high-priced goods such as rice, sugar, pasta, and oil. Neither meat nor produce was shipped to their district. The miners and their families had found themselves shut off from the rest of the population, enclosed in a space deliberately emptied of sustenance. In Mendieta's words, it was as if they were being deliberately excluded from civilization, which had turned a deaf ear to their plight: "Prácticamente nosotros nos encontramos en un aislamiento. Estamos quizás fuera de esta civilización, por el hecho mismo que nos encontramos alejados de las ciudades, nos encontramos rezagadas, no nos escuchan, compañeras" (Federación Sindical de Trabajadores Mineros de Bolivia 1986: 54) [We are more or less in isolation. We're outside of this civilization perhaps, for the very reason that we are a long way from the cities; we find ourselves left behind, they don't listen to us, *compañeras*].

This exclusion was graphically illustrated in August 1986, when the miners began a historic five-day march "Por la vida y la paz" [For Life and Peace] in protest over the closing of the mines, the dismissal of workers, and, in some instances, obligatory cooperativization of mines. According to the Centro de Promoción Minera's (CEPROMIN) *testimonio*/report on the march, the trekkers planned to walk from Oruro to La Paz in order to present their demands, which included: "pedir, exigir de parte del gobierno la atención a sus primeros y fundamentales necesidades, pan, herramientas de trabajo, educación y vestimenta para poder desarrollar sus actividades con el mínimo de requerimientos que se quiere para un ser humano" (CEPROMIN n.d.: 3) [asking, demanding from the government attention to their basic and fundamental needs: bread, work tools, education, and clothing so that they can carry out their activities with the minimum requirements needed by a human being]. A second *testimonio* published as *Por la vida y por la paz: Testimonio de la marcha minera* claims that some five thousand workers, housewives, and students began the arduous 230-kilometer walk. Along the way they were joined by increasing numbers of miners as well as by other workers and *campesinos* who wanted to demonstrate their solidarity. By the end, estimates suggest that more than ten thousand people had participated in the march (*Por la vida* 1986: 22–27).[35]

The trek was long and painful as many of the people had inadequate footwear and clothing. One man from San José, Benito Brañez, refused to stop walking in spite of the fact that his feet were covered with blisters and his legs were swollen and sore: "[Brañez] indicó que nada le dolía más que sus heridas que el haber dejado a su esposa e hijos sin un peso con que conseguir comida" (CEPROMIN n.d.: 10) [(Brañez) said that the only thing that pained him more than his injuries was that he had left his wife and children without a cent for food]. One miner remarked that all along the way the indigenous peoples demonstrated remarkable solidarity with the miners, offering them shelter and food whenever possible. In contrast to government policies which caused people to hunger, these collective shows of support sustained the marchers: "Nos han ofrecido en todo pueblito, grande o pequeño, alojamiento y comida, y eso creo que es muy significativo. Yo creo que ningún trabajador minero se va a quejar que ha pasado hambre en esta marcha; al principio podíamos haber pensado que íbamos a tener algún padecimiento en este sentido pero no ha ocurrido" (cited in *Por la vida* 1986: 27) [In every community, large or small, we were offered food and a place to stay, and I think that that is very significant. I believe that no miner will be able to complain that he was hungry on this march; at first we might have thought that we would experience some hardships of this nature but it just wasn't so].

Throughout the march the government reiterated that it would not intervene in any way and that it would permit the miners to enter La Paz as long as they remained peaceful. Nevertheless, when the procession reached Calamarca, the government sent out a thousand troops with planes, tanks, assault vehicles, and helicopters to encircle the marchers, prohibiting their advance. Fernando Barthelemy, the minister of the interior, argued that this action was necessary because the march was being manipulated by political parties anxious to bring about the overthrow of the Paz Estenssoro government (*Por la vida* 1986: 46). Troops completely surrounded the exhausted participants, refusing to allow them to continue their trek; in addition, the soldiers prohibited the ingress of food, water, and needed medical supplies for those weakened by the effort of walking so far. If the image of thousands of miners converging on La Paz could be read by the government as the returning metaphor of the colonial phantasm of "barbarous" Others about to erupt into the city limits, military actions which blockaded the miners' advance confirmed that they no longer had any legitimate claim to a voice or place in the new social contract. Prevented from entering La Paz, the marchers were ultimately forced to return to the mining centers, where they initiated work stoppages and a large-scale hunger strike. Only with the mediation of the Church were the two groups eventually able to reach a compromise according to which the government ostensibly agreed to find jobs for relocalized workers, release jailed political leaders, and allow for the free affiliation of the workers rather than require obligatory cooperativization of mines (from the newspaper *Presencia,* August 14, 1986; cited in *Por la vida* 1986: 57; see also 58).

In spite of the short-term successes of the march, the government did not substantially alter its program of economic reform. Neither the image of more than ten thousand destitute miners and their families marching to La Paz nor—three years later on April 20, 1989—the horrifying spectacle of twenty-two relocated miners who crucified themselves on the grillwork of the San Andrés University in La Paz swayed the relentless advance of the NEP. Javier Sanjinés chronicled the events of the crucifixion, describing it as an act of communication that attempted to reclaim a political space and voice by visibly depicting the government's violation and subsequent abandonment of the popular sectors (Sanjinés 1992c: 353). The protest ultimately was ineffectual, Sanjinés explains, because the NEP had irrevocably disrupted the power of the working class. "Podríamos entonces hablar del acto como una 'escritura' de la desproletarización y de la 'informalización,' escritura ésta que, a su vez, va conectada a la pérdida de peso de la clase obrera sobre la sociedad civil" (1992c: 357) [Thus we could speak of the act as a kind of "writing" of deproletarianization and "informalization"; a writing which, in turn, is connected to the loss of the working class's weight over civil society]. The working class's "loss of weight" in the political arena, evident literally in the emaciated bodies of the relocated miners and their families, signified that the futile act of crucifixion had deteriorated into the realm of the abject, constituting an anorectic moment of self-destruction:

> En efecto, cuando estos mineros desempleados se crucifican, sus cuerpos humanos ya no simbolizan la posibilidad solidaria y vivificante de la clase obrera, sino, por el contrario, la defensa neurótica y anorética que congela la comunicación. Hay en esta situación una cierta regresión de lo simbólico, donde los cuerpos humanos retroceden a lo imaginario, a la metáfora lacaniana de lo pre-verbal, con lo cual quedamos confrontados(as) con la pérdida de la significación. Así la crucifixión, de modo muy similar a la represión del lenguaje, es ahora la humillada "no-representatividad" de la clase obrera que ha perdido su norte. (Sanjinés 1992c: 362)

> [In effect, when those unemployed miners crucify themselves, their human bodies symbolize the neurotic and anorectic defense that immobilizes communication in contrast to the solidarity and life-giving possibility of the working class. In this situation there is a certain regression of the symbolic, where human bodies move back to the Imaginary, to the Lacanian metaphor of the preverbal, such that we [men and women] are confronted with the loss of signification. Thus, in a way similar to the repression of language, the crucifixion is now the humiliated "non-representative" character of the working class which has lost its bearings.]

These bleak representations of starving relocalized workers and their families stand in stark contrast to the capital-logic of the newly democratic government's policies of consumption. Silvia Rivera Cusicanqui argues that the NEP's aggressive promotion of consumerism, the epitome of "economic democracy," functions within a larger discourse of citizenship and the promotion of individual rights to complete the disciplinary processes of cultural and racial homogenization that were begun in the nineteenth century (Rivera Cusicanqui 1993: 90–91). In addition to the successful dismantling of the working class, the New Economic Policy broadened the measures that encourage citizens' rights over and against communal indigenous identities, in part, through its emphasis on consumption.[36] Imported agricultural products undersell locally grown staples which simply cannot compete in the market. In other words, Rivera Cusicanqui explains, the ultimate goal of the NEP is not to improve the nation's capacity to bring about economic prosperity for all,

FIGURE 5.2.

Untitled. *Photograph courtesy of Eusebio Víctor Choque Quispe.*

but rather to substitute imported, processed carbohydrates for native proteins and an unstable salary or commercial activity in the informal sector for the communal indigenous tradition of exchange and reciprocity (1993: 91–92).[37]

Paradoxically, however, due to the increased emphasis on consumption, the New Economic Policy continues to be a polarizing force in society by segregating the population into different strata according to each one's ability to consume. Even as the policies officially promote a smoothing out of the social striation through the attempt to create a racially neutral consumer, analysts nevertheless identify an even greater hypersegmentation of the social space than has ever existed before.[38] For the urban consumer whose level of poverty is rapidly escalating, the abundance and variety of products on the market is meaningless when she cannot manage a basic subsistence for either herself or her family (Rivera Cusicanqui 1993: 92). As I suggested in Chapter 4, it becomes possible to see how the relationship between consumption and incorporation into the market of the indigenous peoples necessitates the creation of insatiable appetites, a hunger for "modern" goods and products. According to this paradigm, methods of modernization and development do not eliminate hunger; rather, they require it.

In her *testimonio,* Ana María Condori recalls that she dreamed of being the perfect housewife and of preparing the many dishes for her own family that she had learned how to make while working for the upper classes. These pipe dreams have vanished with the knowledge that she cannot afford to replicate those models learned among the wealthy: "Pero ahora, que ya tengo que ver mi casa, el dinero no alcanza. Ni un postre de gelatina puedo hacerme y eso que es tan sencillo. Leche tampoco puedo comprar. Yo pensaba hacerme *chantilly* . . . , tantas cosas ricas. Pero desde que me he casado hasta ahora ningún *chantilly*" (Condori 1988: 109) [But now that I have to look after my own house, there is not sufficient money. I can't even make a simple gelatin dessert. I can't buy milk either. I always intended to make *chantilly* cream . . . , so many delicious things. But since I got married, no *chantilly*].

Following the reforms of the 1980s, women from poor urban neighborhoods and from the families of relocated workers were newly interpellated by the wide-scale organization of mothers' clubs funded, primarily, by nongovernmental organizations (NGOs). NGOs became a crucial form of mediation between the state and the popular sectors in the areas of nutrition, education, health, housing, economic development, and the basic rights of the citizenry (G. Sandoval 1993: 10). Carlos Toranzo argues that NGOs evolved into a major force behind the constitution of a new clientelist politics of the left (Toranzo 1989b: 236). As the traditional safety nets of the union and workplace were eroded and an already deteriorating economic situation grew even worse, NGOs targeted women in particular and began to form nuclei of assistance usually in the form of mothers' clubs which were qualified to receive and distribute food obtained through Public Law 480. To give an idea of the growing importance mothers' clubs were beginning to exercise, studies indicate in 1983 a total of 1,309 mothers' centers throughout the country comprising a total membership of 151,211 women (Jiménez, Sillerico, and Freitas 1989: 9). By 1990, the number of centers had climbed to more than 10,000, distributing food to almost a million people, or one sixth of the population (*Mujer, participación y donación* 1990: 24). Thus, as the manual *Mujer, participación y donación de alimentos* explains, food, a right of all citizens, had become a service for which massive numbers of urban women had to join mothers' centers (23).[39]

By the late 1980s, poor women who had been members for a while began to argue that the mothers' clubs deliberately create and perpetuate dependency since a woman receives flour, oil, and milk merely for showing up at a meeting (*Mujer, participación y donación* 1990: 16).[40] They argued persuasively that the centers reinforce passive behavior in the population. Not only does the growing need for donated food subordinate poor women to the centers that distribute basic essentials, it also fosters a parallel dependency of the national economy on the United States and other donor countries. The associates stressed that although the donated food might alleviate the immediate problems of unemployment by sustaining a population that has very little to begin with, nevertheless, these minimum subsistence levels keep people submissive and lethargic in the face of severe national socioeconomic problems (35). According to the associates, the Bolivian government was mitigating the effects of the economic crisis by accepting donated food rather than aggressively looking for solutions to its chronic unemployment (35). Other members ironized on the term "donated food" because many organizations have "food for work" programs where women labor seven to eight hours a day on the construction of streets, buildings, and other public works in order to receive their allotment (37; see also *60 años* 1987/1988?: 51–59; Farthing 1991: 20–21).

As a result of these kinds of sustained critique, over the last ten years many of the mothers' clubs have undergone a transition from being "assistance"-oriented to becoming grassroots centers that promote more activist participation among the urban mothers. Members play a greater part in shaping the role they want the center to assume in their lives. The successful centers have combined practical needs such as nutrition and the acquisition of favorable credit with leadership training programs. According to Nancy Ventiades Rivero, Etelvina Marconi Ojeda, and Luis Antonio Cabrerizo Barrientos from the Centro Boliviano de Investigación y Acción Educativa, when the educational processes are directly linked to economic projects formulated by the women themselves and based on the material reality of their everyday lives, theory and practice are more likely to form a cohesive logic that better enables the group to achieve its goals (see *60 años* 1987/1988?: 106–107). These centers, therefore, have proposed alternative forms of education for women that meet the pressing needs of the moment. With the increase of educational seminars on the relationship between dependency and food donations, mothers' centers have begun to look for alternative sources of food. Moreover, women have begun to form cooperative day care programs for working mothers and to generate new proposals for the acquisition of credit (*Mujer, participación y donación* 1990: 40).[41]

While many women have seen real improvements in their lives and neighborhoods through their participation in mothers' clubs, including greater access to food and the betterment of some local municipal services, NGOs also have their limitations. Godofredo Sandoval cautions that projects implemented by NGOs tend to be diffuse, with little coordination or networking between agencies, often resulting in the duplication of projects and higher expenses than might be necessary. Moreover, NGOs can take on new activities in areas in which their personnel have little experience or expertise, creating problems in the formulation and comprehension of priorities. It is still the norm that communities targeted by NGOs have little say in the creation of projects; there are even fewer mechanisms designed to turn the control of the project over to the constituents. Other times, NGOs experience obstacles to systematizing the information they have gathered after operating over a period of a few years; thus it can be difficult to determine their efficacy and value. Finally, technical staff might be unable to update their skills and knowledge, thereby running the risk of implementing outdated methodologies (G. Sandoval 1993: 67–69).

It is perhaps too early to tell whether mothers' centers in Bolivia are forming organic intellectuals or if they are instead contributing to the normalization and homogenization of certain sectors of the population under the rubric of promoting citizens' rights: the right to vote, the right to participate as individuals in political parties, the right to receive credit, and so on. The Fundación San Gabriel alone has generated numerous publications on the participation of women in the electoral process.[42] It remains necessary to ask what kinds of social, cultural, and political transformations these centers initiate. Certainly, mothers' centers continue to utilize an evolutionary rhetoric of "development," "education," "formation," and "capacitation" when describing their methodology of organization. Writing on the "instrument-effects" of development, Arturo Escobar observes: "Like the prison in Foucault's case—which fails in terms of its explicit objective of reforming the criminal and yet succeeds in producing a normalized, disciplined society—the development apparatus shows remarkable productivity: not only does it contribute to the further entrenchment of the state, it also depoliticizes the problems of poverty that it is supposed to solve" (Escobar 1995: 143). It is possible that, by targeting women, mothers' centers constitute a kind of socio-racial threshold that works to discipline (acculturate) the large numbers of relocated workers and their families as well as the growing numbers of rural indigenous peoples migrating to urban areas.

In the case of the rural peoples, Rivera Cusicanqui similarly argues that NGOs have tended to mediate indigenous demands only to redirect them toward new, reformist "mestizo" projects (1993: 107; 1990). For example, in the *ayllus* of northern Potosí the indigenous communities historically have maintained "'theatrically courteous' relations" with the state according to which they were willing to make certain concessions in exchange for the right to maintain their land tenure and the traditional system of tribute. With the influx of NGOs into the countryside, this re-lationship of negotiation can be disrupted or adversely affected; for ex-ample, *ayllus* might be obliged to exchange votes for NGO resources (Rivera Cusicanqui 1990: 111–112).

According to Rivera Cusicanqui, the *ayllus* have adopted new strate-gies of resistance to NGOs and other organizations not native to the communities. The 1980s witnessed the resurgence of the myth of the *lik'ichiri*, who wanders the countryside and extracts the fat from its victim. No longer dressed as a priest or Spanish soldier, the *lik'ichiri* re-portedly was appearing as a gringo or foreigner prepared to extract the fat not just from individuals but from entire communities: "Their meth-ods were also more modern: they no longer extracted fat with knives, but with special 'machines' that could be operated at a distance. They trav-elled about the region in jeeps and had modern laboratories and facilities where they would process the fat into commercial ointments such as pe-troleum jelly" (Rivera Cusicanqui 1990: 113).[43] In response to the return of this threatening Other, indigenous communities strategically opposed the NGOs by various means, including road blockades, frequent denun-ciations both on the radio and through alternative communication net-works, use of dynamite, and threats on their rural centers.

The rearticulation of the foreigner as a *lik'ichiri* is a contemporary manifestation of the "dynamic of mutual exclusion" that has its roots in the colonial period, exemplified compellingly by Katari in the eighteenth-century siege of La Paz. As Rivera Cusicanqui notes, "The perception of mestizo/creole institutions as a non-human space is but the mirror image of the centuries-old threat that has been closing in on the *ayllus*, the threat of being excluded from society, confined to the dark and amor-phous world of nature, a threat implicit in all of the 'civilising' work carried out by the dominant society, which considers the Indians to be sub-human so long as they adhere to their distinct outlook, their cultural and religious practices, and their own forms of organization and collective life" (114). Thus the returning metaphorization of the foreigner-outsider as *lik'ichiri* foregrounds the rapacious relations of incorporation underpinning the neocolonial socio-symbolic contract.

THE *LIK'ICHIRI* AS A METAPHOR OF WESTERN MODERNITY

The resurgence of the figure of the *lik'ichiri*/foreigner raises important questions regarding the dialectic of hunger and incorporation that haunts First World–Third World relations. As the crystallization of culturally dominant ideological discourses and political practices, hunger (resulting from multiple forms of repression, such as methods of food distribution as well as eating disorders) continues to be fundamental to contingent relations of power that interpellate and manage individual and collective bodies within and across national boundaries.[44] In the United States, mass media representations of the hungry focus on bodies as the principal site of struggle over which political and ideological battles are waged.[45] These culturally specific symbols result in simplistic and asymmetric assessments of the First World (satiated bodies) and the Third World (starving bodies). Moreover, these contrasting images of well-being and necessity play a key role in the legitimization of the North's political and economic hegemony over the South. Writing on the interplay between representations of hunger and relations of power, Arturo Escobar observes: "To be blunt, one could say that the body of the malnourished—the starving 'African' portrayed on so many covers of Western magazines, or the lethargic South American child to be 'adopted' for $16.00 a month portrayed in the advertisements of the same magazines—is the most striking symbol of the power of the First World over the Third. A whole economy of discourse and unequal power relations is encoded in that body" (Escobar 1995: 103).

The emaciated, malnourished body of the Third World is depicted as a body in need of development and modernization. Vandana Shiva argues, "It is useful to separate a cultural conception of subsistence living as poverty from the material experience of poverty that is a result of dispossession and deprivation" (Shiva 1992: 342). Understood as a culturally constructed perception, poverty may not necessarily mean that people experience actual physical hardship. "Yet the ideology of development declares them [poor] because they do not participate overwhelmingly in the market economy, and do not consume commodities produced for and distributed through the market *even though they might be satisfying those needs through self-provisioning mechanisms.* People are perceived as poor if they eat millets (grown by women) rather than commercially produced and distributed processed foods sold by global agri-business" (Shiva 1992: 342–343; emphasis in original).

As Shiva suggests, this dominant model depicting the well-fed First World body and the starving Third World body both foregrounds and privileges particular models of consumption. For example, the First World unloads its surplus (modern) commodities on the (backward) Third World ostensibly in order to alleviate the latter's (insatiable) appetites, thereby establishing a predictable flow of consumption that seemingly begins in one place and ends in another.[46] To provide further nuancing of this model, it is worthwhile to turn again briefly to the 1977 Bolivian hunger strike. Curiously enough, in the United States there was little public resonance from the strike. Although representatives from the World Council of Churches, the National Council of Churches, and the United Nations traveled to Bolivia in the role of observers, there was not a single reference to the strike in the *New York Times.* George Yúdice's words ring depressingly true when he writes that "[s]tories of solidarity overcoming oppression do not sell in our market" (Yúdice 1988: 234 n. 26). Following up Yúdice's remarks in light of the discussion at hand, we might say that these stories do not sell because we don't want to consume them. The flow of consumption, particularly of stories of solidarity overcoming oppression, is supposed to be North–South and not vice versa.

And yet, the resurgence of the *lik'ichiri* in Bolivia suggests that patterns of appetite/consumption cannot be understood with such unitary directionality. The image of the *lik'ichiri* as a gringo come to extract the fat of entire indigenous communities transposes hegemonic narratives to portray the foreigner as the one who is all-devouring. In the adopt-a-child advertisements mentioned by Escobar, the actress Sally Struthers has come to occupy increasingly more of the foreground of the picture over the years.[47] It would seem that even as her body looms larger, the figure of the child recedes. Projecting into the future, one could imagine the day that the First World body occupies the entire space of the photograph. The alarming statistics on the declining population of rural areas of the Third World following the implementation of development projects suggest that peasants/Indians are indeed being gradually eliminated as a group—"as if the alleviation of the peasants' suffering, malnutrition, and hunger had required not the improvement of living standards in the countryside, as most [development] programs avowedly purported, but the peasants' elimination as a cultural, social, and producing group" (Escobar 1995: 106). Perhaps the return of the *lik'ichiri* asks us to reevaluate the complicity rather than the exclusivity of the appetitive relations that unremittingly draw the North and the South together.

"'ALTERNATIVE' INSTITUTIONS"

In the attempt to understand the conveyance of western modernity in the Bolivian Andes, this book project engaged rhetorical strategies created by hegemonic literary and cultural discourses throughout the twentieth century to create a racially and economically integrated body politic. By focusing on the intersections of race and gender, it sought to examine the powerful ideology of the self-same underlying the criollo nationalist agenda. The analysis of prevailing notions of womanhood expressed through discourses of desire, the house, hygiene, fashion, and hunger brought to light ways in which disciplinary practices of modernity interpellate individual bodies, continually measuring them against a culturally dominant ideal, with the result that crucial questions, such as indigenous self-determination and the right to territory, can be dismissed as irrelevant. History reveals long-standing indigenous agency and resistance to (neo)colonial forms of domination that have coexisted alongside the criollo logic of the selfsame and its contradictions and fissures. Indeed, the renewed efforts of indigenous organization and mobilization during the last two decades and the growing presence of indigenous peoples in political and social sectors of urban life have caused some to remark that *criollaje* has finally failed,[1] a recurrent leitmotiv well expressed by René Zavaleta Mercado when he said that in Bolivia: "Las ideas de la clase dominante no han logrado aquí convertirse en las ideas de toda la sociedad sino de un modo trasvestido aunque perseverante" (Zavaleta Mercado 1986: 130) [The ideas of the dominant class have only become the ideas held by all of society by means of their persevering cross-dressed guise].[2] Of course, the increased prominence of racial and cultural differences does not mean that the prevailing socioeconomic and political structures have undergone the fundamental reordering that they should.

Writing on the relation between the state and civil society in Latin America at the close of the twentieth century, anthropologist Guillermo Delgado observes how even as popular movements and the traditional Left have challenged dominant notions of centrist politics and criticized the limitations of the arenas in which public debate can take place, these groups continue to be taken aback by gender and ethnic demands. According to Delgado, "a total process of decolonization is necessary before new political entities can appreciate the force of ethnic, gender, and class demands as they become the new generators of Latin American political life" (Delgado P. 1994: 77). In Bolivia, the emergent debates on governability led Aymara intellectual Víctor Hugo Cárdenas to declare that the current principles and institutions of "western" democracy reflect exclusively the vision of a colonial minority (ILDIS 1992: 55) and impede the participation of traditionally marginalized majorities (40-41). Speaking in 1991 on behalf of *katarismo*, a pro-indigenous cultural and political movement which embraces more inclusive forms of democracy,[3] Cárdenas called for an "intercultural dialogue" that would foster the genuine participation of rural and urban First Nation peoples (ILDIS 1992: 57). Forging such a vital exchange is indispensable, he argued, because "hoy se requiere entender que la historia de la modernización del Estado no debe ser un acto de la modernización de la dominación colonial" (58) [today we need to understand that the history of the modernization of the state should not be an act of modernizing colonial domination].

The kind of transformation Cárdenas and others have called for is fraught with many difficulties. The Andean term *Pachakuti* [the world turned on its head] has been used to designate both the catastrophic processes of colonization of native peoples and the environment, and the aspirations for renewal emerging from sustained movements for decolonization. What proponents of change frequently overlook, Delgado emphasizes, is that "[i]ndigenous histories are not just about exclusion; above all they are about land" (Delgado P. 1994: 82). The indigenous peoples' call for "territory and dignity" encapsulates the ongoing struggle for autonomy and self-determination taking place throughout the Americas, a struggle neglected to date by the Left, political parties, and other social or popular movements (Delgado P. 1994: 77–81).[4]

The indigenous struggle for the right to land and dignity historically has come up against many obstacles. For example, Delgado reminds us that "capitalistic encroachment on indigenous territories founded a strange legal formula: Indigenous peoples were entitled to sell but not to buy lands" (81). In the Bolivian Andes, the Aymara word *mayt'ata* [on loan or borrowed] describes the precarious territorial position of the indigenous *ayllu* with regard to the state (Choque Quispe 1998: 19). According to THOA member María Eugenia Choque Quispe, "[t]his means that the law is unable to recognize the indigenous community as the proprietor of its own needs and aspirations" (1998: 19). Native Andean peoples are subject to the state rather than subjects in their own right. For this reason, autonomy and the right to self-determination constitute fundamental demands of indigenous peoples (Choque Quispe 1998:19).

The First Nations' movement for territory and dignity can be linked to the indigenous woman's passage to subjectivity as Choque Quispe's seminal essay "Colonial Domination and the Subordination of the Indigenous Woman in Bolivia" demonstrates. Choque Quispe traces this relationship through the analysis of the terms *mayt'ata* and *sullka* [a minor or adolescent]. *Sullka cancaña* describes the condition of the Indian woman's "natural" subordination to the husband's authority in marriage. The term *mayt'ata* expresses the idea that "the woman is a being who does not belong to herself, thus implying that she does not belong to her family: *imill wawaxa jaqitak uywañakiwa* [literally, 'a daughter is raised for other people']" (Choque Quispe 1998: 19). There is a saying, "a woman is only borrowed." If any problems develop in the marriage "the groom or his family can return the bride to her family and even demand compensation," according to Choque Quispe. Her discussion pinpoints the parallel between forms of gender subordination within the Andean community and the dynamics of racial subordination that subject the *ayllu* to the state. Like the *ayllu,* which has access primarily to borrowed lands and therefore cannot guarantee its future survival, the indigenous woman may occupy an equally tenuous position within her own family as well as within her husband's family.

In recent years, as Aymara women like Choque Quispe have gained leadership experience, they have taken on more influential positions of authority generally reserved for men. Historical precedent can be found in the period of the Chaco War, when women had to take charge of the *ayllu*'s governance and defense as the men were drafted and sent to the front lines (Choque Quispe and THOA n.d.: 1). Through her work with THOA, Choque Quispe has organized a leadership program for indigenous women entitled *"P'iqi Aptañani:* Formación de liderazgo femenino con capacidad de participación y gestión propia" [*"P'iqi Aptañani:* The Formation of Feminine Leadership with the Know-How for Participation and Self-Governance"]. Choque Quispe argues that the movement to reconstitute the *ayllu* which advocates indigenous autonomy and self-determination must go hand in hand with the guarantee of equality for women regardless of their marital status (Choque Quispe and THOA n.d.: 3). Ultimately, the Andean goal of *suma jakaña* ["living well"] based on respect and the practice of indigenous communal rights can only be achieved with the full and equal participation of women (4). To date, Choque Quispe's move to introduce gender in discussions of Andean self-determination has not been pursued by many of her male cohorts. Her insistence on the centrality of gender for these debates thus resonates with Chela Sandoval's call for "a new subjectivity, a political revision that denies any one ideology as the final answer, while instead positing a *tactical subjectivity* with the capacity to recenter depending upon the kinds of oppression to be confronted" (Sandoval 1991: 14; emphasis in original).

Expanding on this idea of a "tactical subjectivity," Norma Alarcón has observed with insight: "A bi- or multiethnicized, raced, and gendered subject-in-process may be called upon to take up diverse subject positions that cannot be unified without double binds and contradictions. Indeed, what binds the subject positions together may be precisely the difference from the perceived hegemony and the identity with a specific auto-history. The paradoxes and contradictions between subject positions move the subject to recognize, reorganize, reconstruct, and exploit difference through political resistance and cultural productions in order to reflect the subject-in-process" (Alarcón 1996: 138). In Bolivia, the urban Aymara woman in particular confronts on a daily basis the paradoxes, contradictions, and double binds that result from the diverse subject positions she must assume. When circumstances oblige the indigenous woman to relocate to metropolitan areas such as La Paz, she becomes subject to urban forms of (neo)colonial racism and sexism.[5]

The Aymara woman generally undergoes a dual transition as she learns to cope with a new lifestyle. She must negotiate, recontextualize, and even expand native Andean cultural traditions at the same time as she confronts western forms of modernity (Choque Quispe 1998: 20–22; see Ströbele-Gregor 1996: 80–83). It is not uncommon for her to come under fire for abandoning certain traditional ways of life as she assumes a more prominent, even public, role in the family's decision-making process and economic well-being. As she forges a new, more independent path, the indigenous woman's negotiation of Andean and western cultural and economic norms can be a very painful as well as liberating experience. The political and cultural forms of agency underpinning this tactical subjectivity point to an alterNative, resistant modernity emerging from the experiences of racial and gender domination.[6]

NOTES

INTRODUCTION

1. In their introduction to *On Edge: The Crisis of Contemporary Latin American Culture,* George Yúdice, Jean Franco, and Juan Flores make a similar claim about the neutralizing effects of neoliberalism's ideology of pluralism: "The current 'integration' of Latin American economies into the 'new world order,' with its emphasis on phasing out the welfare state, privatizing national enterprises, and placing the management of political matters in the hands of technocrats, has provoked new thinking on questions of modernization, modernity, and postmodernity, and particularly on the meaning of pluralism as the ideology of contemporary neoliberalism. Pluralism camouflages itself behind an egalitarian mask, whereas it in fact neutralizes class conflict and the claims of the new social movements" (Yúdice, Franco, and Flores 1992: ix).

2. Appearing as a noun and as an adjective throughout this study, "criollo" is used interchangeably with the terms "white," "oligarchy," "elite," "upper class," "hegemonic," and "dominant."

3. This study maintains a clear distinction between the *chola* and the westernized, acculturated mestiza.

4. My reading of desire here draws on Nancy Armstrong's study of the rise of the novel in eighteenth- and nineteenth-century England (1987).

5. In the context of Chicana identity, Norma Alarcón has similarly brought attention to the issue of rupture and dismemberment that results from colonial, racist, and sexist practices: "It is worthwhile to remember that the historical founding moment of the construction of mestiza(o) subjectivity entails the rejection and denial of the dark Indian Mother as Indian which have compelled women to often collude in silence against themselves, and to actually deny the Indian position even as that position is visually stylized and represented in the making of the fatherland. Within these blatant contradictions the overvaluation of Europeanness is constantly at work. Thus, Mexico constructs its own ideological version of the notorious Anglo-American 'melting pot,' under the sign of

mestizo(a). The unmasking, however, becomes possible for Chicanas as they are put through the crisis of the Anglo-American experience where ('melting pot') whiteness not *mestizaje* has been constructed as the Absolute Idea of Goodness and Value. In the Americas, then, the native woman as ultimate sign of the potential reproduction of *barbarie* (savagery) has served as the sign of consensus for most others, men and women" (1990a: 252).

6. In following this approach, the project acknowledges its debt to earlier studies of consequence such as Ileana Rodríguez's *House/Garden/Nation: Space, Gender, and Ethnicity in Post-Colonial Latin American Literatures by Women* (1994); Jean Franco's *Plotting Women: Gender and Representation in Mexico* (1989); and Doris Sommer's *Foundational Fictions: The National Romances of Latin America* (1991).

7. The *pollera* is a full skirt worn by the *chola*. In Bolivia urban women are distinguished as being "de vestido" [wearing a (western) dress] or "de pollera" [wearing a *pollera*].

8. In her important study of nineteenth-century La Paz, Rossana Barragán describes the strategic location of the city. Referring to Thierry Saignes's essay "De los ayllus a las parroquias de indios: Chuquiago y La Paz," she writes: "la elección del sitio de La Paz no se debió de ninguna manera al azar ni al capricho y comodidades del sitio, sino más bien a su emplazamiento como frontera de diferentes jurisdicciones étnicas, área intersticial, confluencia multi-étnica que le permitía crear su propio espacio" (1990: 19) [the choice of the site for La Paz was not based on chance, caprice, or convenience. Rather, it was selected because of its position as a border zone between different ethnic jurisdictions, as an interstitial area, and as a multiethnic intersection that allowed [the city] to create its own space].

9. The *ayllu* is the basic Andean social unit, comprised of kinship groups and communal landholdings which include multiple lots located in a variety of ecosystems.

10. I borrow this phrase from Tristan Platt, who has argued that this political positioning by indigenous peoples in Bolivia has a long history and tradition in the struggle against (neo)colonial domination. See Platt 1984, especially p. 7.

CHAPTER 1

1. From *Mujer/Fempress*. 1990. Special issue "La mujer y el humor," no. 2: 43. The cartoon drawing, by the artist "Alfredo," was originally published in *Mujer y Sociedad*, n.d., Peru.

2. My discussion on the ideologies of womanhood is influenced by Barbara Welter's seminal, early essay "The Cult of True Womanhood" (1966) and Hazel Carby's important work on the dynamics of womanhood and race in the U.S. South (1987).

3. For more detailed discussion of the origins and historical circumstances of women's organizations in Bolivia, see the following excellent studies: Ardaya

(1992); Lehm and Rivera Cusicanqui (1988); X. Medinaceli (1989); *Polleras* (1986); and Wadsworth and Dibbits (1989).

4. Josefa Salmón's analysis has demonstrated similarly that Medinaceli's novel is deeply embedded in a discourse that establishes "la unidad con el ambiente, la naturaleza, y los deseos sexuales [como] el punto de partida para el discurso de la autenticidad nacional" (1986: 134) ["unity with the environment, nature, and sexual desire [as] the point of departure for the discourse on national authenticity"].

5. Two important critical studies were also published which include detailed attention to this period of anarchist organization: Ardaya (1992); Lehm and Rivera Cusicanqui (1988). In addition see the video production *Voces de libertad* (1989).

6. More recently, Nancy Fraser has also argued that "[t]he rhetoric of domestic privacy seeks to exclude some issues and interests from public debate by personalizing and/or familializing them; it casts these as private-domestic or personal-familial matters in contradistinction to public, political matters. The rhetoric of economic privacy, in contrast, seeks to exclude some issues and interests from public debate by economizing them; the issues in question here are cast as impersonal market imperatives or as 'private' ownership prerogatives or as technical problems for managers and planners, all in contradistinction to public, political matters. In both cases, the result is to enclave certain matters in specialized discursive arenas and thereby to shield them from general public debate and contestation" (1990: 73).

7. Gillian Rose (1993) provides a fruitful discussion of the ways in which hegemonic discourses conflate women with Woman.

8. *Pongueaje* constituted an oppressive practice of forced labor within the hacienda system whereby Indians (*pongos*) had to provide free labor and pay tribute in exchange for the right to cultivate a small parcel of land. Women (*mitanis*) and even children could be compelled to work inside the oligarch's house.

9. There is no simple translation of the word "*patrona*" in English when describing the *criolla/mitani* relationship. The *criollas* were neither "employers" nor female "bosses" because the *mitanis* did not receive reimbursement for their labor. The closest equivalent might be that of the mistress/slave relationship from the Southern plantation system. Therefore, I have elected to render "*patrona*" as "mistress of the house."

10. For example, Rowe and Schelling observe that "Gramsci's great contribution to the study of culture is the understanding that culture is inseparable from relationships of power. One way of developing his insights is to take popular culture not as a given view of the world but as a space or series of spaces where popular subjects, as distinct from members of ruling groups, are formed. The stress in this case would be democratic rather than utopian, in the sense of recognizing actual differences between the subjectivity of different classes, rather than creating ideal models which assume that there is—or should be—a single popular identity" (1991: 10).

11. The video *Voces de libertad* (1989), a testimonial-dramatization of the Federación Obrera Femenina, suggests that the *cholas* were forcibly removed

from the gathering because their very physical presence, as well as their vehement declamations against the conditions under which they worked, provoked a general disruption.

12. For example, describing the inauguration's seating arrangement, the newspaper *La Razón* observed: "La ocupación de asientos para las señoras y señoritas asistentes, se sujetará a la antigüedad de las instituciones adheridas a que pertenecen" (cited in *Polleras* 1986: 35) [The seating for the *señoritas* and *señoras* in attendance will abide by the seniority of the institutions with which they are affiliated"].

13. I use Alarcón's phrases here to discuss the Bolivian context (see Alarcón 1990b).

14. Judith Rollins's work (1985) was very useful for the elaboration of my discussion on the relations between *señoras* and domestic workers. See also Lesley Gill's excellent studies (1990, 1994) and Grace Esther Young's important essay (1987) that describes similar issues in Peru.

15. This is another instance when "daughter" is used as a condescending term to designate the domestic workers, to underscore their inferior social and economic status.

16. Norma Alarcón's discussion on the creation of the female subject of color (1990b) was particularly useful for the theoretical elaboration of this section. See especially p. 359.

CHAPTER 2

1. Thanks are due Aparajita Sagar for her fine essay "Indian Modernity: 1913-1953," which helped me to formulate many of the ideas worked out in this chapter, and for reminding me of the relevance of Rey Chow's work to this discussion.

2. Antonio Díaz Villamil (1897-1948) was a prolific writer of novels, short stories, and historical drama as well as textbooks. A graduate of the Instituto Nacional Superior with a speciality in history and geography, he dedicated his life to the teaching profession. He was made director of La Paz's Colegio Bolívar, and he formed part of the Consejo Nacional de Educación. In addition to his busy career as a writer and teacher, Díaz Villamil promoted the development of a number of intellectual institutions in La Paz, including the Ateneo de la Juventud and the Sociedad de Autores Teatrales. A partial list of his works includes: *Khantutas* 1922; *La hoguera* 1924, 1974; *Curso de geografía física de Bolivia* 1929, 1943; *Leyendas de mi tierra* 1929; *La niña de sus ojos* 1948, 5th ed. 1971. He was also named coordinating director of the monograph project *La Paz en su IV centenario* 1948 (Guzmán 1982: 190-192).

3. See, for example, Luis Felipe Vilela's "Apéndice" to Enrique Finot's *Historia de la literatura boliviana* (1955: 566); Fernando Diez de Medina's *Literatura boliviana* (1954: 307); and Augusto Guzmán's *Biografías de la literatura boliviana: 1520-1925* (1982: 191-192). Susan Tritten's article, "Los cholos y la búsqueda de una nueva sociedad" is one exception in that she reads the novel not

as a portrait of society but rather as a vindication of the *mestizo* character (Tritten 1986).

4. Rafael Reyeros estimated in 1949 that some 64 percent of the Bolivian population did not participate in the national economy, either because they did not receive monetary remuneration for their work or because they were unemployed (Reyeros 1949: 129).

5. Aymara historian Roberto Choque Canqui also argues that criollo interest in the education of Indians, from the government of President Melgarejo (1864–1870) through the Chaco War (1932–1935), focused on subduing ongoing native rebellions (Choque Canqui 1986b: 57).

6. My paradigm of "motherhood as nation, motherhood as anti-nation" is derived from Anita Levy's work on nineteenth-century Britain (1991). In particular, see p. 68.

7. Throughout my study I speak of the Symbolic in the Lacanian sense to designate the order of subjectivity characterized by language, meaning, desire, and cultural structuration. See Kaja Silverman 1983: 149–193. For the indigenous peoples of Bolivia, the Symbolic has been a site of contestation and conflict precisely because from the conquest to the present, acquisition of both the Spanish language and western culture has become the measure of an individual or group's access to "civilization" or "meaning."

8. My discussion on the redefinition of the desirable woman draws from Nancy Armstrong's introductory chapter to her book *Desire and Domestic Fiction: A Political History of the Novel* (1987), as well as from Barbara Welter's article "The Cult of True Womanhood" (1966).

9. Kaja Silverman, cited by Teresa de Lauretis (1984: 149).

10. See Renato Rosaldo's *Culture and Truth: The Remaking of Social Analysis* (1989) for an analysis of "imperialist nostalgia," especially pp. 68–87.

11. See p. 9 in Armstrong (1987) for a similar situation in England.

12. See Carby (1987, especially p. 25) for in-depth discussion of the racialized external indicators of ideal womanhood. Anne McClintock similarly has shown how hands, as a recurring image in Victorian (male) memoirs, "visibly expressed the overdeterminations of sex, money and work." Moreover, "[h]ands expressed one's class by expressing one's relation to labor. Dainty hands were hands that were unstained by work. The language of gloves spoke of 'good breeding,' leisure and money, while smooth white hands revealed that one could afford to buy the labor of others" (McClintock 1995: 99).

13. The novel's repudiation of the French (foreign) woman can be traced back to Franz Tamayo's *Creación de una pedagogía nacional* (1910) and the criollo school of thought that rejected Arguedas's call for more foreign economic intervention. See Salmón (1986) for her insightful critique of elite *indigenista* discourse.

14. For a discussion on the acquisition of race, see Diana Fuss, *Essentially Speaking: Feminism, Nature and Difference* (1989: 74–96).

15. My discussion of mothers who "fail" draws from Patricia Hill Collins (1990: 70–82).

16. Luis H. Antezana's introduction to *Oprimidos pero no vencidos* outlines

the meaning of agency as collective resistance and recuperation (Rivera Cusican-qui 1984: 12).

CHAPTER 3

1. Only since the 1980s has work been published exploring the cultural con-struction of gender in Bolivia. Publications by nongovernmental organizations such as the Taller de Historia Oral Andina (THOA), Centro de Información y Desarrollo de la Mujer (CIDEM), and Taller de Historia y Participación de la Mujer (TAHIPAMU) as well as other women's organizations interrogate tradi-tionally held views of womanhood and motherhood. While by no means a com-plete bibliography, see for example, THOA (1986, 1990); for an English ver-sion of the 1986 monograph, see Rivera Cusicanqui with THOA (1990); León (1990); Criales Burgos (1994); X. Medinaceli (1989); Rossells (1988); Paredes and Galindo (1992); Barragán (1990, 1992); *Polleras* (1986); and Wadsworth and Dibbits (1989).

2. This description fits what Doreen Massey considers to be the predomi-nant understanding of space, one that "attempts to fix the meaning of places, to enclose and defend them." Such views, she continues, "construct singular, fixed and static identities for places, and they interpret places as bounded en-closed spaces defined through counterposition against the Other who is out-side" (Massey 1994: 168). Criollo depictions of space in Bolivia have tended to emphasize a similar formulation as the texts referred to demonstrate. Never-theless, in her analysis of the relationship between identity and place, Massey argues that place has to be interrogated in the same way as personal identity (167–168).

3. As Wigley explains, "The subject, like the surface, does not simply occupy space. Rather, the image of occupiable space wraps itself around the subject po-sition. It is a kind of clothing" (Wigley 1992: 387). As will be apparent, Wigley's critical work on architecture has impacted greatly on this chapter. Although his essay "Untitled: The Housing of Gender" (1992) focuses primarily on founda-tional works such as those by Leon Battista Alberti (15th c.), I have taken the lib-erty of extending many of his ideas to the Bolivian context.

4. Toward the beginning of *La niña de sus ojos*, the reader learns that Domy Perales's real name is Domitila. Domy's best friend from boarding school, Rosario, does not know anything about her chum's background until she is cornered by her two cousins and classmates, Celia and Hercilia, who are only too willing to fill her in on the gossip. At first Rosario does not want to hear anything about Domy from her cousins, but she listens reluctantly to them after they shock her with the statement that she has been running around with the daughter of a mar-ket vendor. Celia says, "¿No te lo dice su apellido plebeyo: Perales, y aún más, su mismo nombre? Porque has de saber que no se llama Domy sino Domitila" (Díaz Villamil 1956: 29) ["Doesn't her plebeian last name, Perales, tell you something? And, what about her first name? Because you should know that her name is Domitila, not Domy"]. Hercilia continues triumphantly, "Eso es . . . porque, la

muy astuta de la Perales, para dar cierto acento de aristocracia a su nombre tan vulgar como para una chola lo ha abreviado de acuerdo a la moda. ¿Te das cuenta, prima?" (29) ["That's right . . . because Perales is so shrewd that, to give a more aristocratic ring to her name that's so ungenteel it could belong to a *chola*, she fashionably shortened it. Do you realize that, cousin?"].

5. This same cluster of signifiers has been deconstructed by French feminists. See for example, Luce Irigaray (1985) and Hélène Cixous and Catherine Clément (1986). In the Bolivian context, this cluster of signifiers is not only about the construction of gender; race and class or economic issues as well as spatial considerations are similarly implicated in representations of "order," the "proper," the "improper," and similar concepts.

6. Betsy Wing, the translator of *The Newly Born Woman*, writes that she rendered the French "*propre*" as "Selfsame: ownself. It has overtones of property and appropriation. It also means 'proper,' appropriate,' and 'clean'" (Cixous and Clément 1986: 167). For an analysis of Cixous's reading of the "*propre*," see also Brian Duren's article (1981).

7. From the Cochabamba newspaper *Los Tiempos*, November 22, 1949. Cited in Terán de Pohl 1950: 17–18.

8. Writing on the relationship between architecture and the construction of the proper, Catherine Ingraham notes: "I refer to the two exemplary stories [Vitruvius] recites, the first about the marble statues of the Caryatides that take the place of columns, and the second about the Lacedaemonians and their victory over the Persian armies that results in statues of prisoners who hold up the Persian porch. These stories interest me not as historical narratives, but as instances of how architecture defines its sphere of propriety as the fixing of what is, at any given moment, the authoritative interpretation of an event. This localized interpretation is then elevated to a transcendental level and made to appear as an enduring system of meaning" (Ingraham 1988: 8).

9. Terán de Pohl's essay was originally published August 14, 1935, in Oruro's newspaper *La Patria* and reprinted fifteen years later in *Anticomunismo*.

10. One could argue that René Zavaleta Mercado's description of social structures from the late nineteenth century is useful for understanding the pre-1952 oligarchic state:

La razón señorial en todo caso no era una razón burguesa y, en cualquier forma, no era racionalista; es una racionalidad interior a supuestos irracionalistas de la existencia de una casta. Lo de 'mentalidad' feudal, por tanto, aunque es sin duda una explicación un tanto socorrida, no deja de tener su profundo sentido objetivo. Aun lo que se obtenía de un modo capitalista, se desperdiciaba de un modo señorial. La causa de ello no era sino la inexistencia ni aun como proyecto remoto de la reforma intelectual. Es fácil de otro lado percibir hasta qué punto el poder político, la ideología, la vida jurídica y la vida cotidiana no se parecían en nada a sus paradigmas capitalistas. Después de todo los indios estaban obligados a la capitación o contribución indigenal por el mero hecho de ser indios, es decir, por su condición. Este era un impuesto nacional a los indios. No se puede pedir un ejemplo más estructurado de desigualdad legal. (Zavaleta Mercado 1986: 111)

[At any rate, seigneurial reason was neither bourgeois reason nor was it rationalist; it was a rationality internal to presumed irrationalists for the existence of a caste. As for a feudal "mentality," therefore, although it is somewhat of a handy explanation, it still has an effective usefulness. What one obtained by capitalist means was still squandered by seigneurial means. The reason for this was that a project for intellectual reform still did not even remotely exist. It's easy, on the other hand, to perceive how distant political power, ideology, juridical and daily life were from capitalist paradigms. After all, Indians were required to pay an Indian tax simply because they were Indians; that is to say, because of their nature. This was a national tax imposed on Indians. You can't ask for a more structural example of legal inequality.]

11. Here I am indebted in part to Wigley's analysis of the relationship between deconstruction and architecture (1993: see especially 29–33; 131–138).

12. The implicit meaning of this statement could be summarized as: "Aren't you simply a *cholita* wearing a dress instead of a pollera?" The man wants her to understand that he "recognizes" her "true" identity in spite of her attempts to pass as white.

13. Albó, Liberman, Godínez, and Pifarré (1990) describe the typical Andean living space as one that has been adapted according to the distinct climatic variations of the *puna*, valley, and *yungas:* "[La vivienda] es mucho más pequeña, sin (o con poquísimas) ventanas y puertas diminutas en el frío altiplano. En cambio en los valles y yungas tiene mayor tamaño y ventilación, con más ventanas, escalera externa y a veces incluso porches. En lugares fríos es más probable que todos duerman en el mismo cuarto y que allí mismo se cocine para mantener más caliente el ambiente" (101) ["[The house] is much smaller, without (or with only a very few) windows and tiny doors on the cold, high plain. In contrast, in the valleys and *yungas* the house is larger and more ventilated, with more windows, an external stairway and sometimes even porches. In cold areas it is more probable that everyone sleeps in the same room and that cooking is done there as well to keep the room warmer"]. See also Teresa Gisbert's two volumes on the history of Bolivian houses and settlements: *Historia de la vivienda y los asentamientos humanos en Bolivia* (1988); and *Historia de la vivienda y los conjuntos urbanos en Bolivia* (1991).

14. Platt recounts how the first *Revisita de Exvinculación* [Expropriation Commission] took place in 1882, under the direction of Narciso de la Riva, who resigned three years later, exhausted "physically and morally" because of indigenous uprisings protesting the law and the government's seeming inability to "someter a obediencia a la indiada" (cited in Platt 1982: 95) ["force the Indian hordes into obedience"].

15. The use of "originary" in the English rendering of "tierras de orijen" derives from Andean terminology that defines *"originario"* or *"originarios"* as

"ayllu Indians still living among original kin groups descended from common ancestor-gods" (Stern 1995: 87).

16. See Arze (1988); THOA (1986, 1990).

17. I am grateful to Josefa Salmón, who reminded me of Arnold's work.

18. For more on the relationship between drinking and Andean cultural and political practices, see Saignes (1993).

19. In her noteworthy study (1992), Debra A. Castillo employs the concept of talking back as a trope for Latin American feminist practices which critically engage and dialogue with other feminisms.

20. I borrow the title "The Tyranny of Home" from Barbara Harlow's book *Barred: Women, Writing, and Political Detention* (1992). In her chapter "The Tyranny of Home versus 'Safe Houses'" she elaborates arguments that are similar to my own, calling attention to the relationship between home, nation, and border crossings.

21. Zavaleta designates 1941, the year of the massacre of miners and their families in Catavi, as the time of symbolic rupture.

22. For example, during the 1950s, 1960s, and 1970s, unions held much more power and currency than the traditional political parties (Zavaleta 1987a: 232–233).

23. For a similar situation in the United States, see Nast and Wilson's analysis of two housing projects in Lexington, Kentucky (1994).

24. No matter how many children the miner's family had, their home was uniformly limited to one- and two-room units. In contrast, Barrios de Chungara noted while living in political exile in Sweden that housing for refugees was distributed according to the size of the family in residence (1985: 193–194).

25. According to Nash, with the harsh economic measures adopted during the 1970s that resulted in the depopulation of the mining areas, the doubling up of more than one family in a unit became less frequent (1979: 93, n. 3).

26. Denise Arnold's study on the Aymara house of Qaqachaka also suggests that there exists a correspondance between the house and the body: during the *ch'allas* the straw roof is affectionately referred to as the hair on the head (of the house's body) (1992: 57); the end beams of the roof are called "ribs," "sugiriendo que el techo es un armazón animado que respira" (63) ["suggesting that the roof is an animate skeleton that breathes"]. Other references to the house associate it with the womblike center of reproduction (69–70, 74–77).

27. Francine Masiello has observed how novels by women authors from feminist modernism similarly depict the domestic space as literally disintegrating before the eyes of the female protagonists. The effects of this disintegration on the literary personages are, of course, quite different: "In novels of this kind, the domestic sphere is never left intact; in fact, the space of the home is subject to constant erosion. This is apparent, for example, in Bombal's *La última niebla*, which begins with a description of the invasive rain that leaks through the roof of the protagonist's country estate" (Masiello 1990: 41). Masiello argues that for these authors and their protagonists, the gap or fissure in the wall enables flight (real or fantasized) from the oppressive domestic sphere (41).

28. According to the 1976 National Census figures, three quarters of the na-

tion's population were living in dwellings that contained zero to one bedroom. The report of the *Instituto Nacional de Estadística* takes note of the high percentage of peoples occupying such close quarters: "Si tomamos en cuenta que el número promedio de personas por vivienda particular es de 4,5, es fácil darse cuenta de que es muy elevado el alto grado de hacinamiento [*sic*] que existe en el país. Es interesante observar que esta situación prevalece en todo el país, puesto que las variaciones departamentales alrededor del promedio nacional son relativamente pequeñas" (Instituto Nacional de Estadística 1980: 2) ["If we take into account that the average number of people per individual house is 4.5, it is easy to realize that there exists a very high degree of crowding in this country. It is interesting to observe that this situation prevails throughout the country, since the departmental variations around the national average are relatively small"]. Nash notes that in 1970, some of the old one-room row houses of the mining camps were being either repaired or replaced with new dwellings that had more, albeit smaller, rooms. Again, these were distributed among the hardworking miners and, apparently, to those with larger families (Nash 1979: 92–93).

29. While it is not infrequent that rural and semirural Bolivian houses in warmer climates have kitchens located outside the main living quarters, in the case of the mining encampment houses of Siglo XX, there was a small space designated for the kitchen inside that sometimes had to be adapted for a sleeping area. I would like to thank Josefa Salmón for emphasizing this distinction.

30. Although Wigley is writing about architectural ornamentation, I find it useful to extend his discussion of ornament to include interior decoration, furnishings, and the arrangement of commodities.

31. For more on the role of oppositional radio broadcasting, especially in the mining areas, see Preiswerk (1988); Slaughter (1989); Montes (1987); Gumucio Dagrón (1983); and Gumucio Dagrón and Cajías (1989).

32. Guillermo Delgado, e-mail message to author, October 19, 1995.

33. See Chela Sandoval's fundamental essay on oppositional consciousness (1991); the essays, pamphlets, and books published by THOA provide detailed histories and critical analyses of indigenous resistance in Bolivia.

34. See also Jean Franco, who observed:

Todo el mundo recuerda la intervención de Domitila en las reuniones del año internacional de la mujer, en 1976, cuando niega la soridad de la mujer y se dirige a las mujeres latinas de la clase media como a Betty Friedan cuando pregunta: "¿de qué igualdad vamos a hablar entre nosotras? Si usted y yo no nos parecemos, si usted y yo somos tan diferentes. Nosotros no podemos, en este momento, ser iguales, aún como mujeres . . ." La interrupción de Domitila evidentemente marca la destrucción de una falsa universalidad, pero no afecta la importancia del concepto género sexual que en el mismo libro Domitila tiene que introducir para hablar del día doble de trabajo. (Franco 1988: 89)

[Everyone remembers Domitila's intervention at the meetings of the International Year of the Woman, in 1976, when she denies the shared consciousness of women and she addresses middle-class Latina women and Betty Friedan when she asks: "So what equality are we going to speak of between the two of us? If you and I aren't alike, if you and I are so different? We can't, at this moment, be equal, even as women . . ." Domitila's interruption evidently marks the destruction of a false universality, but it doesn't affect the importance of the concept of gender, which in the same book Domitila has to introduce in order to speak about the double work day.]

35. The most notable exception was the *khoyas locas,* or women who worked in the mines during the Chaco War when even the miners were drafted to fight in the front lines.

36. Sanjinés's discussion of the *Tío* emphasizes his ambivalence; the *Tío* both divides and unifies the space of the *interior mina* and the space of the *exterior mina:* "Entre el mundo precapitalista campesino y el capitalista proletario, el Tío es un modelo aculturado que incluye la disyunción y la conjunción. Es como el borde de un vaso que, separando el interior del exterior, también los une y da sentido. Por ello el Tío, morador de los parajes más oscuros de la mina, puede estar a la entrada de ella, dividiendo y uniendo el exterior de su interior. Es entonces el Tío, lo Otro, una *différance* mediadora que al propio tiempo en que divide, une" (Sanjinés 1992a: 145) ["Between the precapitalist *campesino* world and the capitalist proletariat, the *Tío* is an acculturated model that encompasses both disjunction and conjunction. It's like the edge of a glass that, separating the interior from the exterior, also unifies them and gives them meaning. For that reason, the *Tío,* dweller of the darkest regions of the mine, can be at the mine entrance, dividing and unifying the exterior from its interior. The *Tío,* therefore, is the Other, a mediating *différance* which, at the same time it divides, unifies"]. As a figure of mediation, the *"Tío"* represents both the precapitalist system of reciprocity and exchange rooted in indigenous communal practices and the asymmetrical relations of power and domination that arise with capitalism (Sanjinés 1992a: 145).

37. See Rose (1993: 137–160) for a discussion of the notion of paradoxical space and feminism.

38. Judith Butler has written: "In what senses, then, is gender an act? As in other ritual social dramas, the action of gender requires a performance that is *repeated.* This repetition is at once a reenactment and reexperiencing of a set of meanings already socially established; and it is the mundane and ritualized form of their legitimation. Although there are individual bodies that enact these significations by becoming stylized into gendered modes, this 'action' is a public action. There are temporal and collective dimensions to these actions, and their public character is not inconsequential; indeed, the performance is effected with the strategic aim of maintaining gender within its binary frame—an aim that cannot be attributed to a subject, but, rather, must be understood to found and consolidate the subject" (1990: 140).

39. Jean Franco has similarly noted, in the instance of the Mothers of the Plaza de Mayo, how the military authorities dismissed the women as "locas"

["crazy women"], thereby positioning them "outside the family of the nation" (1992: 67).

40. bell hooks has made a similar argument with regard to black women: "Contemporary equation of black liberation struggle with the subordination of black women has damaged collective black solidarity. It has served the interests of white supremacy to promote the assumption that the wounds of racist domination would be less severe were black women conforming to sexist role patterns" (1990: 48).

41. The Centro de Promoción Minera has published several texts about the Housewives Committees, including: Federación Sindical de Trabajadores Mineros de Bolivia (1986); CEPROMIN (1988, 1987); and a subset within the series *Cuadernos populares* on "La mujer minera."

42. Javier Medina, in his introduction to Filemón Escóbar's *Testimonio de un militante obrero*, writes the following about the housewives: "De la profundidad de esos socavones habla una Bolivia andina, un proletariado de todavía frescas raíces campesinas, unas amas de casa que, sin los circunloquios feministas de las metrópolis, articulan lo que podríamos llamar 'socialismo y feminismo' en un solo hálito a través de una silenciosa práctica que la voz de Domitila ha roto" (F. Escóbar 1984: 6) [From the depth of those mineshafts speaks an Andean Bolivia, a proletariat with fresh *campesino* roots; housewives who, without the feminist circumlocutions of the metropolises, articulate in a single breath what we could call "socialism and feminism" through a silent practice that Domitila's voice has broken.]

CHAPTER 4

1. David Arnold has similarly observed that the plague in India positioned the body of the Indian subaltern "as a site of conflict between colonial power and indigenous politics. During the early phase of the epidemic the body had a specific medical, administrative, and social significance: much of the interventionist thrust of the state was directed towards its apprehension and control, just as much of the resistance to plague measures revolved around bodily evasion or concealment. The body, however, was also profoundly symbolic of a wider and more enduring field of contention between indigenous and colonial perceptions, practices and concerns. The exercise of British power touched in many ways upon the issue of the Indian body. Moreover, as the early plague years demonstrated, the problematic was not only one of a colonial divide. It also deeply involved the growing assertion of a middle-class hegemony over the mass of the population and the equivocal responses—part resistance, part emulation—which such hegemonic aspirations evoked among the subaltern classes" (1988: 392–393).

2. I have borrowed the idea of hygiene as an ideologeme of the modern nation from Kristin Ross's study of postwar France (1994).

3. My discussion in this chapter of clothing as a salient ethnic signifier was influenced by Kobena Mercer's work on black cultural studies (1994).

4. A salient example of rupture leading to ontological transformation is that of the Bolivian vice president Víctor Hugo Cárdenas. In an article on Cárdenas the *New York Times* foregrounds this process of changeover: "There are many things that Víctor Hugo Cárdenas laments about his youth—the poverty of his Aymara village on the windy banks of Lake Titicaca, his father's inability to get a state-approved teaching job because he was an Indian, being forbidden to speak his native language in school and that his name really should not be Cárdenas. 'My father's name was Chokewanka,' Mr. Cárdenas said. 'But he gave his two sons a Spanish name—the name of my maternal grandmother—so that we would not have to suffer the discrimination that he did.'" September 19, 1993, n.p.

In the testimonial of his life as an *escribano* (an Indian scribe who could read and write Spanish), Leandro Condori Chura similarly acknowledges the impact that race and the politics of identity will have on his formation. Condori Chura begins by recalling an anecdote from his childhood about his surname. When he first attended school, he explains, the teachers instructed him to change the Aymara "Condori" to the Spanish "Conde": "'Condori es feo; es como si fueras come burro; lleva Conde,' diciendo. Por eso les dije: 'Está bien.' Pero fue por poco tiempo. Después mi padre obtuvo mi certificado de nacimiento y me sujeté a eso. No es bueno negar su apellido: soy Condori desde mi bautizo" (Condori Chura and Ticona Alejo 1992: 22) ["Condori is ugly; it's as if you were a donkey eater; change it to Conde," they said. That's why I said: "All right." But it was only for a short time. Afterward, my father got my birth certificate and I abided by that. It isn't good to deny your last name: I've been Condori since my baptism]. Condori Chura's narrative establishes some of the evolutionist ideologies of the dominant pedagogic that call for the modernization of Andean native peoples. Modernity is depicted here as a matter of a simple choice: the young schoolboy can begin to remake himself merely by replacing the bestial (Condori) with the man (Conde).

Condori Chura's story, however, is also a narrative of refusal. He resists the school's efforts to commute his Andean genealogy, culture, and history (Condori) for a new, fictitious heritage (Conde). Ironically, his rejection of the terms of modernity is ingeniously legitimated by modern (i.e., western) institutions: the official record (birth certificate) and the Catholic Church (baptism).

5. Important studies on this period of Bolivian history are Condarco Morales (1965), and Zavaleta Mercado (1986: 96–179).

6. For detailed accounts of the history of indigenous education, including the evolution of both hegemonic indigenous discourse and indigenous resistance, see Salmón (1986); Claure (1989); Rivera Cusicanqui (1984; 1993); Choque Canqui (1986a; 1986b); Choque Canqui and Soria, et al. (1992); Mamani Condori (1991); THOA (1988); and Condori Chura and Ticona Alejo (1992).

7. Drawing from the work of Gustave Le Bon, Guillén Pinto hastened to clarify that even though the Indian could be educated, he would never reach the level of either whites or mestizos. Nor, however, should he be confused with the "negro," who was the epitome of an underdeveloped race (Guillén Pinto 1919: 97–98).

8. Writing generally on the Third World, Etienne Balibar similarly identifies

this legacy of colonialism as a "fluctuating combination of continued exteriorization and 'internal exclusion'" (Balibar 1991a: 43).

9. See Claure (1989); Rivera Cusicanqui (1984); THOA (1988); Mamani Condori (1991); Choque Canqui (1986a).

10. According to Mamani Capchiri, the *cuartel* [military quarters and barracks] generally supported the move to educate the Indians because it was easier to train recruits if they already spoke Spanish (Mamani Capchiri 1992: 85). The *ayllu* Indians, or *comunarios*, sought support for and protection of schools from the army even though, not surprisingly, the armed forces backed the *criollos* and the *vecinos de pueblos* [mestizo town residents] without fail when conflicts arose (86). "Por un lado, los patrones y las autoridades locales en principio vieron al cuartel como un efectivo centro disciplinario, para que de ahí regresen indios sumisos y obedientes. Sin embargo, al aprender a leer y escribir, retornaban cumpliendo una función dentro del movimiento reivindicativo de la época, y resultaban más rebeldes aún" (86) [On the one hand, the boss-masters and local authorities at first saw the *cuartel* as an effective disciplinary center, so that Indians would return submissive and obedient. Nevertheless, upon learning to read and write, they came back fulfilling a function within the resistance movement of that time and they wound up even more rebellious"].

11. On curriculum as a form of cultural politics, see McLaren (1995: 29–57).

12. As Salmón's analysis demonstrates, the predominant image of Indians as teluric beings affirmed evolutionist discourses of the 1940s which cast them as less evolved than the white urban populations and in need of technical assistance to expedite their development (Salmón 1986: 222).

13. See also Donald (1992: 45–47) and McLaren (1995: 37–41), who both discuss the vital symbolic and cultural currency of the curriculum.

14. Such as how to use silverware, drink from a glass, and so on.

15. According to Georges Vigarello, hygiene began to be constructed as a scientific, medical term in nineteenth-century Europe. As a result, "[i]ts status also changed. Medicine, at the end of the eighteenth century, had entered politics. It had played a role in the planning of towns and other public places" (Vigarello 1988: 168; see also 207–212). The relationship among modern science, medicine, hygiene, and politics clearly was at the forefront of Bolivian pedagogic concerns, as is evident from the education manuals. For instance, Enrique Finot includes two books in his bibliography on hygiene: (1) Juan Montero Jiménez, *Nociones de anatomía e higiene,* "para uso de las escuelas de Santa Cruz, con sujeción a las modernas orientaciones pedagógicas. Edición de Santa Cruz, 1914" ["for the use of Santa Cruz schools that are employing modern pedagogical methods. Santa Cruz Edition, 1914"]; and (2) Corsino Rodríguez Q., *Nociones de higiene científica.* Potosí, 1913 (Finot 1917: 113).

16. On identification and desire, see Fuss (1995: 120–129) and Silverman (1988: 101–140).

17. For an intriguing discussion on schools, sexuality, and contagion, see Fuss (1995: 107–140).

18. See Salmón for an analysis of the transformational power attributed to education during the 1940s and 1950s (1986: especially 196–228).

19. María Eugenia Choque Quispe cautions against overly idealizing the Andean concept of *chacha-warmi*, arguing that even in the *ayllu* the indigenous woman traditionally has occupied a subordinate role to the man:

> Se ha escrito mucho acerca de la condición de *jaq'i*, como productor de cultura, que el individuo andino alcanza sólo después del matrimonio, sin embargo se debe entender que *jaq'i*, es un concepto masculino de humanidad, el varón que adquiere esta categoría deja en ese momento su condición de subordinado *sullka* [condición de menor o inferioridad], pero como condición necesita subordinar a otra persona, de otro grupo familiar, para alcanzar su condición de mayoridad *jaq'i*; el matrimonio *marido y mujer* se vuelve una sola persona *jaq'i*, y la persona es el marido; con ello éste adquiere control absoluto sobre su propiedad personal y la de su mujer. (1995: 13)

["A lot has been written about the condition of *jaq'i*, a producer of culture, that the Andean individual only reaches after marriage. Nevertheless, it is important to understand that *jaq'i* is a masculine concept of humanity; the man who acquires this category leaves behind at that point his subordinate condition *sullka* [inferior status as a minor], but as a necessary prerequisite he needs to subordinate another person, from another family group, in order to achieve his adult age *jaq'i*; the married couple, *husband and wife*, becomes unified into one person *jaq'i*, and that person is the husband; with that he acquires absolute control over his personal property and that of his wife.]

20. Drawing from the work of Pierre Bourdieu, Robert Bocock describes the role of consumption in the following terms: "Consumption . . . can be seen as a set of social and cultural practices which serve as a way of *establishing* differences between social groups, not merely as a way of *expressing* differences which are already in place as a result of an autonomous set of economic factors" (Bocock 1993: 64; emphasis in the original). For Jean Baudrillard, however, "consumption is always the consumption of symbolic signs"; therefore, "[c]onsumption is to be conceptualised as a process in which a purchaser of an item is actively engaged in trying to create and maintain a *sense of identity* through the display of purchased goods" (67; emphasis in the original).

21. At the end of the nineteenth century, La Paz remained largely an "illiterate" city. Although the population figures vary substantially from one source to another, it is estimated that there were approximately seventy-two thousand inhabitants at the turn of the century. Some 62 percent of the population had no instruction, 24 percent had received a primary education, 13 percent reached middle school, and only 10 percent had had university training (Barragán 1990: 205). For the most part, the amount of education people received corresponded with where they lived in the city; the higher the education level reached, the more centrally located the population. In addition to reflecting the amount of education attained, the spatial layout of the city also reflected people's work. The more traditionally indigenous the occupation, the more peripheral the area in which the

person lived. Thus, women who worked as spinners, *chicha* makers and vendors, weavers, and hagglers lived almost exclusively in the peripheral neighborhoods (225), whereas those who worked as cooks, washwomen, small shopkeepers, cigar makers and vendors, and seamstresses lived in peripheral areas too, but they could also be found in central neighborhoods in important percentages (220-225).

22. For a similar situation in Canada, see Roxana Ng (1993: 54). According to Ichaso Vásquez, education must be suited to the specific needs of girls, but that should not prevent the proper training from improving someone's general lot in life. She contends that in spite of the different gender, class, and race relations inherent in a "natural" social and economic hierarchy, even the most insurmountable circumstances can be ameliorated with education: "Dentro de nuestra encantadora democracia, existe naturalmente la diferencia de clases determinadas, unas veces por la situación económica, otras por la tradicional ocupación y otras en fin que podríamos llamarlas por costumbre o tradición, sin que tales diferencias sean inalterables o permanentes, pues ha sucedido y sucede que de las clases más humildes, han surgido las grandes entidades, todo por el estudio y quizás una autoeducación desfavorecida por el propio medio" (Ichaso Vásquez 1927: 67) [Within our charming democracy, different classes exist naturally, sometimes for economic reasons, or because of traditional forms of work; other times, well, they exist because of what we could call reasons of custom or tradition. These differences are neither unchangeable nor permanent, since in the past and present some of the great entities have emerged from the most humble classes, all as a result of study and perhaps a self-taught education disadvantaged by the same environment].

23. Not surprisingly, there was also rapidly growing support for the training of female teachers. The document of the reorganization of the Normal School for Young Ladies declares, "Para concluir, hacemos constar una vez más, que la Nación necesita *maestras* . . . para renovar el ambiente y formar hombres de bien, pero quiere, no maestras en número, sino en calidad" (Escuela Normal de Señoritas 1927: 12; emphasis in the original) [In conclusion, we state one more time that the Nation needs [*female*] *teachers* . . . to renew the environment and to form good citizens, but it calls for quality of teachers and not quantity].

24. Kim Sawchuk, for example, observes: "A woman's concern for the aestheticization of her body was seen as a sign of her unreasonableness, her potential weakness in contrast to the rationality of men. The argument for austerity in dress and the return to more neutral forms not only valorizes what is seen as characteristic of men (their rationality), but there is the possibility that an anti-fashion sentiment feeds into an already existing discourse of woman's superficiality, duplicity, and the threat that her sexuality poses to men" (1987: 68).

25. Indeed, as Marjorie Garber reminds us, sumptuary and consumption are etymologically related words (Garber 1993: 21).

26. From "Algo sobre modas," published in the journal *El Álbum* 2 (May 10, 1889): 5. Cited in Rossells (1988: 68). According to Freyre de Jaimes, the wife of the President of the Republic, Amalia de Arce, known for her beauty, social distinction, and first-hand knowledge of European culture, symbolized the "centro de la sociedad más distinguida y de los placeres más delicados [. . .] acostumbrada [. . .] a las grandes fiestas de las cortes europeas, habiendo asimilado con

arte y con talento, todo lo bello que ha visto, todo lo suntuoso que ha admirado, todo lo grande de los homenajes que ella misma ha recibido" ("Revista de la semana," *El Album*, 1 (May 3, 1889): 7. Cited in Rossells 1988: 65) ["the center of the most distinguished society and of the most exquisite pleasures [. . .] she customarily attends the grandest parties of the European courts, having assimilated with skill and talent all the beautiful and noble things that she has seen, all the sumptuous objects that she has admired, all the greatness of the tributes that she herself has received"]. For more on nineteenth-century fashion in Bolivia, see Rossells 1988: 55–73.

27. From "Revista de la semana," *El Album* 6 (June 7, 1889): 7; cited in Rossells 1988: 65.

28. My discussion here on the relationship between fashion and modernity borrows from Wigley, who, writing on the dress-reform movement of the latter half of the nineteenth century, observes that "this influential alliance of clothing reformers did not merely transform modern dress. It produced the very sense that dress could be modern, as in timely, a form of its time, one consistent with the realities of a new epoch instead of a means of covering up these realities: the sense, that is, that one could, and should, move from 'mode' to 'modern'" (1994b: 10).

29. For a similar situation in colonial Latin America, see Meléndez (1995).

30. The journal was published regularly for the next three years. For more details on the journal and the young women who spearheaded the project, see Beltrán (1987).

31. This is not to suggest that the clothing of the *chola* has not changed over time. Indeed, popular studies such as Lic. M. Lissette Canavesi de Sahonero's *El traje de la chola paceña* (1987), and Antonio Paredes Candia's *La chola boliviana* (1992) call attention to the wide variety of styles and fashions of the *pollera*, the *manta*, underclothing, shoes, and earrings and other jewelry that have evolved during the course of the twentieth century. As Jennifer Craik maintains: "Symptomatically, the term fashion is rarely used in reference to non-western cultures. The two are defined in opposition to each other: western dress is fashion because it changes regularly, is superficial and mundane, and projects individual identity; non-western dress is costume because it is unchanging, encodes deep meanings, and projects group identity and membership. In either case, dress is taken out of its 'lived' resonances and theorised in structural or functionalist terms to account for beliefs located elsewhere" (Craik 1994: 18).

32. In Bolivia, people distinguish between *señoras de vestido*, literally "ladies wearing a dress," and *mujeres de polleras*, or "women wearing *polleras*." Clothing is thus a primary characteristic in the distinction between a "lady" and a "*chola*."

33. There is no direct translation of "*huaca-huacas*," which is linguistically derived from "*vaca-vacas*" [cow-cows]. The "Dance of the *Huaca-Huacas*" is a popular dance satirizing the bullfight. The women dancers wear numerous *polleras*, which give their bodies a large, bulky shape.

34. Paredes de Salazar's controversial position appears to have been seconded by many criollos, both individuals and affiliations. For example, in the acknowledgements to her book, Paredes de Salazar thanks a number of people and organizations that supported her project, including Radio Progreso and the Grupo

Integracionista. In particular, she expresses gratitude to the president of the Asociación de Amigos de la Moda, Víctor Omonte, who, she affirms, was an ardent supporter of the integration project from the beginning. Omonte's convictions regarding the *pollera* clearly mirror her own. Making reference to a conversation they had, she cites him directly on the first page of her text: "la pollera es un resabio colonial que atomiza la personalidad de las mujeres con su secuela de complejos discriminatorios" [the *pollera* is a bad habit left over from colonial times that pulverizes the women's personality, resulting in discriminatory complexes]. He emphasizes that "sexual, racial y socialmente, es un cepo opresivo y humillante y que es de necesidad perentoria descolonizar la moda boliviana de nuestras mayorías" (7–8) [sexually, racially, and socially, it is an oppressive and humiliating fetter and it is of urgent necessity to decolonize the Bolivian style of dress of our majority populations].

35. Vicente Terán Erquicia was a prominent educator and lawyer who taught at the Normal School in Sucre as well as at the Instituto Normal Superior in La Paz. Following his efforts at university reform, he taught philosophy of law at the universities in Potosí and Sucre; later he held the prestigious position of District Judge in La Paz.

36. The inability to accept the woman who writes has a long tradition in Bolivia. Raquel Ichaso Vásquez opens her study of *La enseñanza nacional femenina* (1927) with a defense of taking up the pen and a general lamentation of the prevailing attitudes that declare women incapable of authorship (5). Importantly, however, even though Ichaso Vásquez believes that a good education is the only way women will learn to adapt to modern life (189), it should not lead to an exaggerated feminism (53).

37. Karen Spalding, *De indio a campesino: Cambios en la estructura social del Perú colonial* (Lima: Instituto de Estudios Peruanos, 1974), p. 181. Cited in Barragán (1992: 51). Mariselle Meléndez (1995) similarly examines the role of clothing in the cultural production of identities in the colonial period.

38. Condori Chura's *testimonio,* originally collected in Aymara, is published as a bilingual Spanish-Aymara text. The Spanish translation retains these Aymara terms although a glossary is provided at the end of the book.

39. "*Q'ara,*" literally a shorn or skinned animal, designates the Spanish, whites, or acculturated *mestizos.* As the glossary at the back of Condori Chura's *testimonio* explains, "*q'ara*" is a term denoting "abuse, oppression, and exploitation" (Condori Chura 1992: 145–146).

40. For more information on the life of Santos Marka T'ula, see THOA (1988).

41. For a cogent discussion of racial fetishism, see Mercer (1994: 171–219).

CHAPTER 5

1. On the relationship between hunger and discipline, see Bordo's prominent collection of essays *Unbearable Weight: Feminism, Western Culture, and the Body* (1993). Bordo's work has been influential to the writing of this chapter.

2. For detailed analysis of eighteenth-century Andean relations, see Stern (1987).

3. For a discussion comparing the strategies and tactics used by Tupak Amaru and Tupak Katari, see Rivera Cusicanqui 1993: 41–44.

4. Del Valle de Siles writes: "hay que pensar que los acontecimientos se desarrollaron en una villa defendida por una muralla que separaba a dos mundos; por un lado estaban los sitiados, por el otro lado los sitiadores; dentro estaban los grupos de gente blanca, fuera, los indígenas. Existía, por tanto, una ciudad, un muro que la protegía y un espacio que, rodeando tal muro, servía de contorno a la villa" (del Valle de Siles 1981: 29) [we have to consider that the events took place in a town defended by a wall that separated the two worlds: on one side were the people under siege, on the other side were the besiegers; inside were groups of white people, outside, the Indians. There existed, therefore, a city, a wall that protected it, and a surrounding space that served as outskirts to the town].

5. I borrow this description from Catherine Waldby, who is writing on subjectivity, gender, erotic practice and how "boundary difference [between male and female imagos] is displaced outward from (imaginary) genital difference" (Waldby 1995: 268).

6. Writing about the precarious boundaries of the body, Judith Butler observes: "The boundary between the inner and outer is confounded by those excremental passages in which the inner effectively becomes outer, and this excreting function becomes, as it were, the model by which other forms of identity-differentiation are accomplished. In effect, this is the mode by which Others become shit. For inner and outer worlds to remain utterly distinct, the entire surface of the body would have to achieve an impossible impermeability. This sealing of its surfaces would constitute the seamless boundary of the subject; but this enclosure would invariably be exploded by precisely that excremental filth that it fears" (Butler 1990: 133–134).

7. Anne McClintock's discussion of the scene of discovery of America similarly charts out the anxious relationship between boundaries and (masculine) subjectivity: "This anxious vision marks one aspect, I suggest, of a recurrent doubling in male imperial discourse. This may be seen as the simultaneous dread of catastrophic boundary *loss* (implosion), associated with fears of impotence and infantilization and attended by an *excess* of boundary order and fantasies of unlimited power. In this way, the augural scene of discovery becomes a scene of ambivalence, suspended between an imperial megalomania, with its fantasy of unstoppable rapine—and a contradictory fear of engulfment, with its fantasy of dismemberment and emasculation. The scene, like many imperial scenes, is a document both of paranoia and of megalomania" (1995: 26–27; emphasis in the original).

8. Judith Butler has observed in the case of the consolidation of identities that "'Inner' and 'outer' make sense only with reference to a mediating boundary that strives for stability. And this stability, this coherence, is determined in large part by cultural orders that sanction the subject and compel its differentiation from the abject. Hence, 'inner' and 'outer' constitute a binary distinction that stabilizes and consolidates the coherent subject. When that subject is challenged, the meaning and necessity of the terms are subject to displacement" (1990: 134).

9. For more information on the conceptualization of the Spanish from the Andean point of view, see Szeminski (1987).

10. For more on the construction of the Spanish or white outsider as a *"lik'ichiri"* or *"kharisiri,"* see Szeminski (1987); Crandon-Malamud (1991); Payne (1995); Wachtel (1994); and Portocarrero Maisch, Valentín, and Irigoyen (1991).

11. Other variations of the story of Wirnita can be found in the following volumes: Aranzaes v. de Butrón (1980: 114–116); Albó and Layme (1992: 78–79); Condori Chura and Ticona Alejo (1992: 36).

12. Mamani Condori underscores the present-day relevance of *katari* for the Aymara as well: "Muchas veces hemos tenido una sensación de 'espera,' como si supiéramos que las ciudades, los espacios que habitan nuestros dominadores, están por ser encantadas. ¿Acaso no nos dicen que los cerros que rodean a la ciudad de La Paz están llenos de kataris? ¿No seremos nosotros los kataris?" (1992: 23) [Many times we have had the sensation of "waiting," as if we knew that the cities, those spaces inhabited by our oppressors, were on the verge of falling under enchantment. Haven't we been told that the hills surrounding the city of La Paz are full of *kataris*? Aren't we those *kataris?*"].

13. Elizabeth Grosz writes, "[Alphonso] Lingis has recognized the link between horror and lust: the transformative, transubstantiating effects of erotic attachments, desire, are echoed in the seeping out beyond boundaries and the dissolution of lines of bodily organization prompted by orgasmic dissolution" (1995: 292).

14. For more on the relationship between disintegration and circulation, bodies and hunger, see Ellmann (1993: especially 91–113).

15. This ambivalent relationship that converges in Katari can be found as well in Diez de Medina's account of the sieges of La Paz. On the one hand, the judge depicts Tupak Katari as a charlatan. On the other, he mentions stories that circulated in which Tupak Katari claimed that Tomás Katari had been resuscitated in him (del Valle de Siles 1980: 48). On Tupak Katari and reincarnation see also Szeminski (1987: 183–185).

16. Albó writes: "[The Aymaras'] most militant sectors like to call themselves 'kataristas,' in memory of, and as testimony to the ideological and historical link with, the hero of 1781. Their principal leader, Jenaro Flores, comes from a community in the region of Sicasica close to Katari's birthplace, and more recently the birthplace of katarismo. There is an evident continuity at least in the memory of this people, a memory awakened in the last few decades" (Albó 1987: 379).

17. On the spatial relationship between the feminine and the modern European city, see Swanson (1995).

18. For instance, in the introduction to the collection of essays that comprise the volume *Unbearable Weight*, Susan Bordo similarly argues that "what remains the constant element throughout historical variation is the *construction* of body as something apart from the true self (whether conceived as soul, mind, spirit, will, creativity, freedom . . .) and as undermining the best efforts of that self. That which is not-body is the highest, the best, the noblest, the closest to God; that which is body is the albatross, the heavy drag on self-realization"

(1993: 5; emphasis in the original). In the context of Bolivia, the symbolic and practical control of *chola* and indigenous female bodies figured as a resurgent problem in dominant discourses on the nation.

19. According to Antonio Paredes Candia, the *chola* prefers to live with her family in a particular kind of one-room space opening directly onto the street called a *tienda redonda*. The *tienda redonda* is generally a storefront house where the *chola* lives, entertains friends, and sells foodstuffs, liquor, or dry goods; it is a multipurpose space that facilitates her desire for an independent lifestyle, economic profit, and tasty food (1992: 236–237).

20. I borrow here from Doris Witt's analysis of the Quaker Oats Company trademark figure Aunt Jemima. Witt notes: "What are we to make of the longevity of the Aunt Jemima trademark and of the ambiguity of the symbolic attributes which Quaker Oats wants to preserve by keeping it? After all, 'warmth' is surely a characteristic of Aunt Jemima as cook; 'good taste,' of Aunt Jemima food products. 'Quality,' 'heritage,' and 'reliability' could refer to either. One might infer from this symbolic slippage that the trademark is intended to signify both cook and food. Like her precursors, the big-breasted mammies of post–Civil War lore, Aunt Jemima *prepares* and *is* food; she/it is the ever-smiling source of sustenance for infants and adults" (1994–1995: 99; emphasis in the original).

21. For Doris Witt, (U.S.) fixation on the black woman's appetite similarly points to an obsession with and fear of black female eating habits: "This concern has played itself out on numerous levels, from gastronomic to sexual to economic. The (foreclosed) question, What does Aunt Jemima eat?, quickly mutates to encompass other aspects of black female consumption, including access to the wealth and power that can satisfy desire" (1994–1995: 100).

22. Writing on gender and desire in the United States, Susan Bordo notes, "Eating is not really a metaphor for the sexual act; rather, the sexual act, when initiated and desired by a woman, is imagined as itself an act of eating, of incorporation and destruction of the object of desire. Thus, women's sexual appetites must be curtailed and controlled, because they threaten to deplete and consume the body and soul of the male" (1993: 117).

23. A parallel could be drawn here with anorexia because, as Morag MacSween's work has shown, the disorder begins as an effort to restrain the feminine body that is comprehended as the locus of insatiable appetites (1993: 248).

24. My discussion of the workers being represented as figures of instability has been influenced by Shuttleworth (1990: see especially p. 55).

25. The use of diet to control workers was not a new practice in the 1960s. Vincent C. Peloso's research indicates that the manipulation of food distribution was a routine procedure strategic to the structuring of colonial and postcolonial relations during the nineteenth century: "By comparison with the highland communities, laborers on the coastal plantation fields and in nearby freeholds ate meagerly. Spanish and then republican law in Peru called for a daily plantation ration of meat and vegetables for each slave, but in reality not even jerked beef was a major item of the landlord's budget. Indeed, until the abolition of black slavery in 1854, the total diet of the plantation work force consisted of *menestras* (vegetables). Plantation owners sometimes supplemented the daily bowl of greens with

chicha de jora and *guarapo* (cane whiskey) on the weekends and holidays. The diet of the indentured Chinese who followed the black slaves into the fields was thought to be even less adequate. Rice was not a significant food on early republican plantations, but by 1850 it was in constant demand to meet the needs of the Chinese field hands. Often rice was the only food distributed to the Asian contractees, who were fed hurriedly in the field at midday. At night, however, once the men were returned to the locked *galpón* (barracks), they were issued mind-numbing rations of opium, coca leaf, and the ubiquitous guarapo" (Peloso 1985: 54).

26. Vincent Peloso notes that this image of the coca-chewing Indian as not needing more food than the sustenance he received from the coca leaf itself prevailed among the urban and rural Peruvian elites throughout the nineteenth century: "It was said repeatedly that an Indian chewing coca leaf could work in the mines for long periods without much more nourishment than that provided by a daily ration of the leaf. Another [image] was the opium-sotted, indentured Chinese worker who likewise demanded little sustenance when he was under the influence of the drug. Yet another was the black cannibal, an image that reduced blacks to an uncivilized condition" (1985: 56).

27. Ellmann argues that "[s]elf-starvation is above all a performance. Like Hamlet's mousetrap, it is staged to trick the conscience of its viewers, forcing them to recognize that they are implicated in the spectacle that they behold" (1993: 17).

28. "Testamento político espiritual" was written in 1978, just two years before Espinal's abduction and brutal murder by the García Meza government. Espinal's essay was also published as "Testamento espiritual: Testimonio personal de Lucho sobre sus 19 días de Huelga de Hambre (La Paz, 31 de diciembre 1977–18 enero 1978)," in Asamblea Permanente de los Derechos Humanos en Bolivia, *Luis Espinal: El grito de un pueblo,* 3rd ed. (Lima: Centro de Estudios y Publicaciones, 1982), pp. 117–126; and as "El testimonio de una experiencia," in Asamblea Permanente de los Derechos Humanos en Bolivia, *Huelga de hambre* (La Paz: APDHB, 1978), pp. 153–169.

29. Indeed, the strikers who occupied the headquarters of the major newspaper, *Presencia,* including priests Luis Espinal and Xavier Albó as well as Barrios de Chungara herself, stayed in a glassed-in room where they could be seen by all who passed by (Barrios de Chungara 1985: 59). Even as the strikers were highly visible, on display, as Espinal mentions, this arrangement enabled them to return the gaze back to the public, thereby provoking a sense of complicity in those who came to observe their actions.

30. In 1987 the rate was stabilized at 10 percent and in 1988 at 21 percent (Toranzo 1989a: 11).

31. For a perceptive analysis of the factors influencing the downfall of the tin mining industry, see Toranzo (1989b: 219–247); and Crabtree, Duffy, and Pearce (1987).

32. The bordering urban areas of La Paz and El Alto evoke the counterpart images from colonial times of La Paz, the Spanish-criollo world, and Chukiyawu, the indigenous-mestizo world.

33. The Oqharikuna program, funded by the Fundación San Gabriel, points to the devastating effects of neoliberal reform in Bolivia on poor families, many of whom have no recourse but to push children, especially girls, out on their own. Young girls must make their way as best they can in spite of increasing violence on the streets. See Programa Oqharikuna (1994).

34. Juan Lechín Oquendo, the executive secretary of the Federación Sindical de Trabajadores Mineros de Bolivia (Union Federation of Bolivian Mine Workers) and representative to the first national meeting of miners' housewives in January 1986, gave testimony to the unprecedented conditions of devastation which the miners and their families were undergoing as a consequence of the NEP: "Yo soy dirigente cuarenta años. Hemos sufrido represiones de todo tipo, masacres, destierros sin número, pero nunca se ha llegado a esta situación. En las épocas duras de la rosca, no se ha llegado a estas condiciones, realmente infrahumanas para un pueblo. Nunca nos hemos tropezado con un gobierno que quiere llevar adelante un plan genocida, un plan de hambre para el pueblo y un debilitamiento al Estado" (Federación Sindical de Trabajadores Mineros de Bolivia 1986: 5–6) [I have been a leader for forty years. We have suffered all kinds of repression, massacres, and unlimited numbers of exiles, but we have never reached these extremes. Even during the hard years of the *rosca* (upper-class oligarchy) we never lived under such inhuman conditions. We have run into a government that wants to carry out a plan of genocide, a plan of starvation against the people, a plan that undermines the state].

35. CEPROMIN's report states that approximately fifty thousand people participated in the march (CEPROMIN n.d.: 4).

36. During the 1940s and 1950s, educators foregrounded the relationship between racialized bodies, development, and consumption. Rural indigenous peoples who employed traditional Andean agricultural practices to grow native crops were perceived as "underdeveloped" and in need of modernization. In his study *Filosofía de la educación boliviana* (1946), educator and president of the Consejo Nacional de Educación Vicente Donoso Torres linked the transformation of Bolivia's indigenous peoples into cultural and biological mestizos with technological development and the deliberate creation of needs so that they might become consumers: "¿Y cómo se hará dicha transformación? Organizando en nuevos núcleos la educación campesina e incrementando los sostenidos por el Consejo Nacional; cambiando sus métodos de vida y de trabajo, creándole necesidades higiénicas, domésticas y culturales para que sea consumidor; enseñándole a mejorar sus cultivos y ganados, la selección de las semillas, la rotación de los terrenos, el empleo de los abonos y de los instrumentos de labranza; a formar cooperativas de producción, de venta y de consumo . . . " (Donoso Torres 1946: 179) ["And how will said transformation take place? By organizing indigenous education into new centers and augmenting those supported by the National Council; by changing (his) lifestyle and work mores, creating in the *campesino* hygienic, domestic, and cultural needs so that he will become a consumer; by teaching him to improve his crops and cattle, the selection of seeds, the rotation of crops, the use of fertilizers and farming implements; by teaching him to form cooperatives for production, sales, and consumption . . . "]. According to Donoso

Torres's plan for educating the indigenous peoples, the expansion of consumerism together with a program of technological development would seemingly result in the creation of acculturated mestizos who could be incorporated into the market. The educator's methodology apparently rests on the creation of desire (read: appetite) in the indigenous peoples so that they become, in effect, consumers. For more on the technological development of the Indian as producer and consumer, see Salmón (1986: especially 106–207). On the complex relations between the indigenous peoples and the market, see Rivera Cusicanqui (1990); Larson and Harris with Tandeter (1995); and Platt (1987).

37. In their study *Paradojas de la modernidad,* Fernando Calderón and Roberto Laserna observe that the increase in imported products and changing urban consumer demands are exacerbating the decline of many indigenous communities: "Pero son probablemente los campesinos de las comunidades más tradicionales los que se encuentran en posición de más franco deterioro. No solamente su nivel de producción es menor, lo cual de por sí constituye una desventaja en el mercado, sino que la calidad y variedad de sus productos satisface cada vez menos la demanda urbana, fuertemente influenciada por la estandardización de los gustos" (Calderón and Laserna 1995: 44) [But probably the *campesinos* from rural communities are the ones who are in the worst position. Not only is their level of production lower, which in itself constitutes a disadvantage in the market, but also the quality and variety of their products increasingly fails to satisfy urban demand, which is greatly influenced by the standardization of taste].

38. My discussion of the smoothing and hypersegmentation of civil society draws from Michael Hardt (1995: especially 37).

39. Useful studies on the social and economic impact of food donations on Bolivia are: Julio Prudencio B. and Mónica Velasco (1987); Julio Prudencio B. and André Franqueville (1995); and Terpstra (1994).

40. In the early to mid 1980s, state-run centers and religion-sponsored organizations such as CARITAS began to impose strict rules on the women who received donated food, increasingly regulating their lives (*Mujer, participación y donación* 1990: 23; see also Jiménez et al. 1989: 12). For example, some centers required attendance, and if a woman missed more than three meetings she was asked to leave the group; in the same way, if a woman arrived late for a meeting, she could be charged a fine. Lack of adequate child care constituted a serious problem for which mothers often had to miss a meeting. The fear that she could lose her food aid typically obliged a woman to leave her children home alone, unsupervised, so that she might attend the meeting and not be penalized (*Mujer, participación y donación* 1990: 37).

41. For example, in 1991 it was announced that a popular mother-infant program supported by food donations would dry up the following year. The thirty mothers' clubs of the Eastern District of La Paz came together to find alternatives to the food donation program that would allow the centers to stay organized. In the past, when food sources dried up the organizations also folded. Given this impending crisis, the Eastern District of La Paz designed a series of food cooperatives that would be run by the women themselves. The formation of these cooperatives has initiated a new credit structure. The women of the center receive

credit as a group and, likewise, are responsible for repaying the debt as a group. To date, the Fundación San Gabriel maintains that the project has been very successful and that the women have more control over the food purchased. Each center must take the responsibility to keep the cooperative stocked and functioning (see *Tiendas de consumo* n.d.).

42. Among the Fundación San Gabriel's many publications are included: *Demanda de participación en la constitución del concejo municipal distrital este* (1991); *Taller de participación en el distrito municipal este de la ciudad de La Paz* (1991); *Partidos políticos: ¿Espacios de participación democrática para la mujer?* (1992); *Elecciones generales 1993: La Paz-Bolivia* (n.d.); and *Propuesta de participación local de la Asociación de Centros de Madres de la Zona Este de la ciudad de La Paz* (1990). See also their newsletter *Participación: Boletín de Prensa del Programa "Promoción y Participación de la Mujer."* Finally, the foundation has also put out a series of educational board games to be played in the mothers' clubs and designed to promote reflection, discussion, and action. Sample titles include "Mujer y participación"; "Aclarando nuestros conceptos"; "La pirámide de la participación"; "Definiendo políticamente al país"; "Construyendo la democracia participativa"; and "La constitución política del Estado."

43. Rivera Cusicanqui's observations draw from F. Aguiló's paper "El lik'ichiri," presented at the III Encuentro de Estudios Bolivianos in Cochabamba (1983).

44. As early as the 1950s, food aid dispensed under the auspices of Public Law 480 became a basic component of U.S. foreign policy. According to agricultural economist Lana L. Hall, "President Eisenhower's sale of surplus commodities to Communist countries signaled that food had definite political security potential" (Hall 1985: 136).

45. For more on the body as a site of struggle, see Bordo (1993), especially p. 184.

46. See Grewal and Kaplan's introduction to *Scattered Hegemonies* for a critique of this simplistic model (1994: 1–33).

47. I would like to thank Abdul Mustafa, who called this transformation to my attention.

AFTERWORD

1. This is the final pronouncement of Wigberto Rivero Pinto and Ives Encinas Cueto's essay "La presencia aimara en la ciudad de La Paz, *Chuquiyawu Marka:* Entre la participación y la sobrevivencia" (1991: 291).

2. Zavaleta Mercado's remarks evoke the continuum studied throughout this book: Indian woman, chola, mestiza, criolla.

3. It is beyond the scope of this study to examine the history and complex ideological premises of *katarismo*. For in-depth discussion of the movement, see Albó (1987); Rivera Cusicanqui (1984), (1987), (1993); Hurtado (1986); and Pacheco (1992).

4. An important work that describes the terms of this struggle in Bolivia is

Territorio y dignidad: Pueblos indígenas y medio ambiente en Bolivia, ed. Kitula Libermann and Armando Godínez (1992).

5. Some of the most frequently cited studies on this subject are Criales Burgos (1994); Albó, Greaves, and Sandoval (1981, 1982, 1983); Calderón (1984).

6. The phrase "'alterNative' institutions" was coined by the Kahnawake Mohawks in the Canadian province of Quebec. Cited in Gerald R. Alfred (1995: 17).

BIBLIOGRAPHY

¿60 años para qué?: Situación de las mujeres pobladoras de El Alto de La Paz. 1987/1988[?]. Ed. Nancy Ventiades Rivero, Etelvina Marconi Ojeda, and Luis Antonio Cabrerizo Barrientos. La Paz: CEBIAE.

Alarcón, Norma. 1990a. "Chicana Feminism: In the Tracks of 'the' Native Woman." *Cultural Studies* 4, no. 3: 248–256.

———. 1990b. "The Theoretical Subject(s) of *This Bridge Called My Back* and Anglo-American Feminism." In *Making Face, Making Soul. Haciendo Caras: Creative and Critical Perspectives by Women of Color*, ed. Gloria Anzaldúa, 356–369. San Francisco: Aunt Lute Foundation Books.

———. 1996. "Conjugating Subjects in the Age of Multiculturalism." In *Mapping Multiculturalism*, ed. Avery F. Gordon and Christopher Newfield, 127–148. Minneapolis and London: University of Minnesota Press.

Albó, Xavier. 1987. "From MNRistas to Kataristas to Katari." In *Resistance, Rebellion, and Consciousness in the Andean Peasant World: 18th to 20th Centuries*, ed. Steve J. Stern, 379–419. Madison: University of Wisconsin Press.

———. 1993. "Our Identity Starting from Pluralism in the Base." Special Issue: "The Postmodernism Debate in Latin America," ed. John Beverley and José Oviedo. *Boundary 2* 20, no. 3: 18–33.

Albó, Xavier, Tomás Greaves, and Godofredo Sandoval. 1981. *Chukiyawu: La cara aymara de La Paz.* Vol. 1, "El paso a la ciudad." La Paz: CIPCA.

———. 1982. *Chukiyawu: La cara aymara de La Paz.* Vol. 2, "Una odisea: Buscar 'Pega.'" La Paz: CIPCA.

———. 1983. *Chukiyawu: La cara aymara de La Paz.* Vol. 3, "Cabalgando entre dos mundos." La Paz: CIPCA.

Albó, Xavier, and Félix Layme. 1992. *Literatura aymara: Antología.* Vol. 1, Prosa. Serie: Cuadernos de Investigación, no. 37. La Paz: CIPCA; HISBOL; JAYMA.

Albó, Xavier, Kitula Libermann, Armando Godínez, and Francisco Pifarré. 1990. *Para comprender las culturas rurales en Bolivia.* 2d ed. Serie Bolivia Pluricultural y Multilingüe. La Paz: Ministerio de Educación y Cultura; CIPCA; UNICEF.

Alfred, Gerald R. 1995. *Heeding the Voices of Our Ancestors: Kahnawake Mohawk Politics and the Rise of Native Nationalism.* Toronto, New York, and Oxford: Oxford University Press.

Alvarez, Sonia E. 1990. *Engendering Democracy in Brazil: Women's Movements in Transition Politics.* Princeton: Princeton University Press.

Antezana, Luis H. 1987. "Sistema y proceso ideológicos en Bolivia (1935–1979)." In *Bolivia, hoy,* ed. René Zavaleta Mercado, 60–84. 2d ed. Mexico: Siglo Veintiuno Editores.

Aranzaes v. de Butrón, Emma. 1980. *Para ti, mujer boliviana.* La Paz: Empresa Editora "Proinsa."

Ardaya, Gloria. 1989. "La mujer en la lucha del pueblo boliviano: Las barzolas y el comité de amas de casa." In *Y hasta cuándo esperaremos. Mandan-dirun-dirun-dán: Mujer y poder en América Latina,* ed. Alberto Koschützke, 183–202. Caracas: Nueva Sociedad.

———. 1992. *Política sin rostro: Mujeres en Bolivia.* Caracas: Nueva Sociedad.

Arguedas, Alcides. 1936. *Pueblo enfermo* (3rd ed.). La Paz: Ediciones "Puerta del Sol."

Armstrong, Nancy. 1987. *Desire and Domestic Fiction: A Political History of the Novel.* New York and Oxford: Oxford University Press.

Arnold, David. 1988. "Touching the Body: Perspectives on the Indian Plague." In *Selected Subaltern Studies,* ed. Ranajit Guha and Gayatri Chakravorty Spivak, 391–426. New York and Oxford: Oxford University Press.

Arnold, Denise Y. 1992. "La casa de adobes y piedras del Inka: Género, memoria, y cosmos en Qaqachaka." In *Hacia un orden andino de las cosas: Tres pistas de los Andes meridionales,* ed. Denise Y. Arnold, Domingo Jiménez, and Juan de Dios Yapita, 31–108. La Paz: HISBOL.

Arze O., Silvia. 1988. "Rasgos de identidad y superposición cultural en los textiles bolivianos actuales." In *Arte popular en Bolivia,* 24–32. La Paz: Instituto Boliviano de Cultura; Instituto Andino de Artes Populares.

Asamblea Permanente de los Derechos Humanos en Bolivia. 1978. *Huelga de hambre.* La Paz: Asamblea Permanente de los Derechos Humanos.

Balibar, Etienne. 1991a. "Racism and Nationalism." In *Race, Nation, Class: Ambiguous Identities,* ed. Etienne Balibar and Immanuel Wallerstein. Trans. of Balibar, Chris Turner, 37–67. London: Verso.

———. 1991b. "The Nation Form: History and Ideology." In *Race, Nation, Class: Ambiguous Identities,* ed. Etienne Balibar and Immanuel Wallerstein. Trans. of Balibar, Chris Turner, 86–106. London: Verso.

Barragán, Rossana. 1990. *Espacio urbano y dinámica étnica: La Paz en el siglo XIX.* La Paz: HISBOL.

———. 1992. "Entre polleras, ñañacas y lliqllas: Los mestizos y cholas en la conformación de la 'tercera república.'" In *Tradición y modernidad en los andes,* ed. Henrique Urbano, 43–73. Cusco: Centro de Estudios Regionales Andinos, "Bartolomé de las Casas."

Barrios de Chungara, Domitila. 1978. *Let Me Speak!: Testimony of Domitila, a*

Woman of the Bolivian Mines. With Moema Viezzer. Trans. Victoria Ortiz. New York and London: Monthly Review Press.

———. 1980. *La mujer y la organización.* 2d ed. Cusco: Centro Las Casas.

———. 1985. *¡Aquí también, Domitila!.* With David Acebey. Mexico: Siglo Veintiuno Editores.

———. 1987. *Si me permiten hablar . . .* With Moema Viezzer. 11th ed. Mexico: Siglo Veintiuno Editores.

Barthes, Roland. 1975. *The Pleasure of the Text,* trans. Richard Miller. New York: The Noonday Press.

Beltrán, Luis Ramiro, ed. 1987. *"Feminiflor": Un hito en el periodismo femenino de Bolivia.* La Paz: CIMCA; Círculo de Mujeres Periodistas; CIDEM.

Best, Sue. 1995. "Sexualizing Space." In *Sexy Bodies: The Strange Carnalities of Feminism,* ed. Elizabeth Grosz and Elspeth Probyn, 181–194. London and New York: Routledge.

Bhabha, Homi K. 1983. "The Other Question . . ." *Screen* 24, no.6: 18–36.

———. 1994. *The Location of Culture.* London and New York: Routledge.

Bocock, Robert. 1993. *Consumption.* Key Ideas Series. London and New York: Routledge.

Bordo, Susan. 1993. *Unbearable Weight: Feminism, Western Culture, and the Body.* Berkeley: University of California Press.

Butler, Judith. 1990. *Gender Trouble: Feminism and the Subversion of Identity.* Routledge: New York and London.

Cajías, Lupe. 1987. "¿Qué escribían ellas? Análisis de contenido." *"Feminiflor": Un hito en el periodismo femenino de Bolivia,* ed. Luis Ramiro Beltrán, 61–70. La Paz: CIMCA, Círculo de Mujeres Periodistas; CIPCA.

Calderón, Fernando. 1984. *Urbanización y etnicidad: El caso de La Paz.* La Paz: CERES.

Calderón, Fernando, and Roberto Laserna. 1995. *Paradojas de la modernidad: Sociedad y cambios en Bolivia.* 2nd ed. La Paz: Fundación Milenio; CERES.

Canavesi de Sahonero, Lic. M. Lissette. 1987. *El traje de la chola paceña.* Colección Descubra Bolivia. La Paz and Cochabamba: Los Amigos del Libro.

Carby, Hazel. 1987. *Reconstructing Womanhood: The Emergence of the Afro-American Woman Novelist.* New York and Oxford: Oxford University Press.

Castillo, Debra A. 1992. *Talking Back: Toward a Latin American Feminist Literary Criticism.* Ithaca: Cornell University Press.

Centro de Promoción Minera (CEPROMIN). 1987. *Testimonio colectivo de la lucha de las mujeres mineras.* Cuaderno de formación no. 8. La Paz: Ediciones CEPROMIN.

———. 1988. *II Ampliado nacional de comités de amas de casa mineras.* La Paz: Ediciones CEPROMIN.

———. 1990. *La conciencia, el comité y el sindicato.* Cuadernos Populares series, "La mujer minera," no. 1. La Paz: CEPROMIN.

———. n.d. *Una marcha histórica "Por la vida y la paz."* La Paz: CEPROMIN.

Choque Canqui, Roberto. 1986a. *La masacre de Jesús de Machaca.* La Paz: Ediciones Chitakolla.

———. 1986b. "Una experiencia histórica de la educación indígena en Bolivia."

In *Educación, escuelas y culturas indígenas de América Latina,* ed. Emanuele Amodio. Vol. 1, 57–64. Ecuador: Ediciones ABYA YALA.

Choque Canqui, Roberto, Vitaliano Soria, et al. 1992. *Educación indígena: ¿Ciudadanía o colonización?* La Paz: Aruwiyiri.

Choque Quispe, María Eugenia. 1995. "Dominación colonial y subordinación de la mujer indígena." *Presencia* (La Paz), July 30, pp. 11–13.

———. 1998. "Colonial Domination and the Subordination of the Indigenous Woman in Bolivia," trans. Christine Taff with Marcia Stephenson. Special Issue: "Contested Spaces in the Caribbean and the Americas," ed. Aparajita Sagar and Marcia Stephenson. *Modern Fiction Studies* 44, no. 1: 10–23.

Choque Quispe, María Eugenia, and Taller de Historia Oral Andina. n.d. *"P'iqi Aptañani:* Formación de liderazgo femenino con capacidad de participación y gestión propia." Proyecto. Chukiyawu-La Paz: n.p.

Chow, Rey. 1991. *Woman and Chinese Modernity: The Politics of Reading between West and East.* Minneapolis: University of Minnesota Press.

Cixous, Hélène, and Catherine Clément. 1986. *The Newly Born Woman,* trans. Betsy Wing. Theory and History of Literature, vol. 24. Minneapolis: University of Minnesota Press.

Claure, Karen. 1989. *Las escuelas indigenales: Otra forma de resistencia comunaria.* La Paz: HISBOL.

Colomina, Beatriz, ed. 1992. *Sexuality and Space.* Princeton Papers on Architecture. Princeton, N.J.: Princeton University School of Architecture.

———. 1994. *Privacy and Publicity: Modern Architecture as Mass Media.* Cambridge, Mass.: MIT Press.

Condarco Morales, Ramiro. 1965. *Zárate, el temible Willka: Historia de la rebelión indígena de 1899.* La Paz: Talleres Gráficos Bolivianos.

Condori, Ana María, with Ineke Dibbits and Elizabeth Peredo. 1988. *Nayan Uñatatawi: Mi despertar.* La Paz: HISBOL; TAHIPAMU.

Condori Chura, Leandro, and Esteban Ticona Alejo. 1992. *El escribano de los caciques apoderados: Kasikinakan Purirarunakan Qillqiripa.* La Paz: HISBOL; THOA.

Consejo Nacional de Educación. 1940. *El estado de la educación indigenal en el país.* La Paz: n.p.

Cornejo S., Alberto. 1949. *El problema social de la vivienda.* Cochabamba: Imprenta Universitaria.

Crabtree, John, Gavan Duffy, and Jenny Pearce. 1987. *The Great Tin Crash: Bolivia and the World Tin Market.* London: Latin America Bureau.

Craik, Jennifer. 1994. *The Face of Fashion: Cultural Studies in Fashion.* London and New York: Routledge.

Crandon-Malamud, Libbet. 1991. *From the Fat of Our Souls: Social Change, Political Process, and Medical Pluralism in Bolivia.* Berkeley: University of California Press.

Crespo-Rodas, Alberto, Mariano Baptista Gumucio, and José de Mesa. 1989. *La ciudad de La Paz: Su historia, su cultura.* La Paz: Alcaldía Municipal; Casa Municipal de la Cultura.

Criales Burgos. Lucila. 1994. *Mujer y conflictos socio-culturales: El caso de las migrantes de Caquiaviri en la ciudad de La Paz.* La Paz: Aruwiyiri.

Davila, Sonia. 1991. "In Another Vein." In *Report on the Americas* (North American Congress on Latin America) 25, no. 1: 10–16.

de la Rosa Torres, Laura Graciela. 1935. *La Guerra del Chaco: Mi visita a las trincheras y zanjas del "Velo,"* edición ilustrada con fotograbados y autógrafos de nuestros combatientes. La Paz: Imp. "Atenea" de Crespi hermanos.

de Lauretis, Teresa. 1984. *Alice Doesn't: Feminism, Semiotics, Cinema.* Bloomington: Indiana University Press.

del Valle de Siles, María Eugenia. 1980. *Testimonios del cerco de La Paz: El campo contra la ciudad, 1781.* La Paz: Biblioteca Popular Boliviana de "Ultima Hora."

———. 1990. *Historia de la rebelión de Tupac Catari, 1781–1782.* La Paz: Don Bosco.

———, ed. 1981. *Diario del alzamiento de indios conjurados contra la ciudad de nuestra señora de La Paz, 1781,* by Francisco Tadeo Diez de Medina. La Paz: Escuela de Artes Gráficas del Colegio "Don Bosco"; Banco Boliviano Americano.

Delgado P., Guillermo. 1985. "Industrial Stagnation and Women's Strategies for Survival at the Siglo XX and Uncía Mines." In *Miners and Mining in the Americas,* ed. W. W. Culver and T. C. Greaves, 162–170. Manchester: Manchester University Press.

———. 1989. "La mina vista desde el guardatojo." Centro de Estudios para la Ecología Humana. Vol. 1, Documento de Trabajo, n.p. Department of Anthropology. Gustavus Adolphus College.

———. 1994. "Ethnic Politics and the Popular Movement." In *Latin America Faces the Twenty-First Century: Reconstructing a Social Justice Agenda,* ed. Susanne Jonas and Edward J. McCaughan, 77–88. Boulder: Westview Press.

Díaz Villamil, Antonio. 1956. *La niña de sus ojos.* 2d ed. La Paz: "Juventud."

Dietz, Mary. 1992. "Context Is All: Feminism and Theories of Citizenship." In *Dimensions of Radical Democracy: Pluralism, Citizenship, Community,* ed. Chantal Mouffe, 63–85. London and New York: Verso.

Diez de Medina, Fernando. 1954. *Literatura boliviana.* Madrid: Aguilar.

Donald, James. 1992. *Sentimental Education: Schooling, Popular Culture and the Regulation of Liberty.* London and New York: Verso.

Donoso Torres, Vicente. 1946. *Filosofía de la educación boliviana.* Buenos Aires: Atlántida.

Douglas, Mary. 1992. Reprint. *Purity and Danger: An Analysis of the Concepts of Pollution and Taboo.* London and New York: Routledge.

Duren, Brian. 1981. "Cixous' Exorbitant Texts." *Sub-Stance* 32: 39–51.

Ellmann, Maud. 1993. *The Hunger Artists: Starving, Writing, and Imprisonment.* Cambridge, Mass.: Harvard University Press.

Emberley, Julia. 1987. "The Fashion Apparatus and the Deconstruction of Postmodern Subjectivity." In *Body Invaders: Panic Sex in America,* ed. Arthur and Marilouise Kroker, 47–60. New York: St. Martin's Press.

Escobar, Arturo. 1995. *Encountering Development: The Making and Unmaking of the Third World.* Princeton, N.J.: Princeton University Press.

Escóbar, Filemón. 1984. *Testimonio de un militante obrero.* La Paz: HISBOL.

Escuela Normal de Señoritas: Reorganización. 1927. Sucre: Imp. Bolívar.

Espinal, Luis. 1991. "Testamento político-espiritual." In *El testamento político-espiritual de Luis Espinal,* ed. Javier Medina, 9–19. Series: Religión y sociedad. La Paz: HISBOL.

Fanon, Frantz. 1967. *Black Skin, White Masks,* trans. Charles Lam Markmann. New York: Grove Press.

Farthing, Linda. 1991. "The New Underground." *Report on the Americas* (North American Congress on Latin America) 25, no. 1: 17–23.

Farthing, Linda, with Carlos Villegas. 1991. "After the Crash." *Report on the Americas* (North American Congress on Latin America) 25, no. 1: 24–29.

Federación Sindical de Trabajadores Mineros de Bolivia. 1986. *Ampliado nacional de amas de casa mineras.* La Paz: CEPROMIN.

Felski, Rita. 1995. *The Gender of Modernity.* Cambridge, Mass.: Harvard University Press.

Fernández Retamar, Roberto. 1989. *Caliban and Other Essays,* trans. Edward Baker. Minneapolis: University of Minnesota Press.

Finot, Enrique. 1917. *Historia de la pedagogía boliviana.* La Paz: n.p.

———. 1955. *Historia de la literatura boliviana.* 2d ed. La Paz: Gisbert y CIA. S.A.

Foucault, Michel. 1979. *Discipline and Punish: The Birth of the Prison,* trans. Alan Sheridan. New York: Vintage.

———. 1980. *Power/Knowledge: Selected Interviews and Other Writings, 1972–1977,* ed. Colin Gordon; trans. Colin Gordon, Leo Marshall, John Mepham, and Kate Soper. New York: Pantheon.

Franco, Jean. 1988. "*Si me permiten hablar:* La lucha por el poder interpretativo." *Casa de las Américas* 29, no. 171: 88–94.

———. 1989. *Plotting Women: Gender and Representation in Mexico.* New York: Columbia University Press.

———. 1992. "Going Public: Reinhabiting the Private." *On Edge: The Crisis of Contemporary Latin American Culture,* ed. George Yúdice, Jean Franco, and Juan Flores, 65–83. Minneapolis: University of Minnesota Press.

Fraser, Nancy. 1989. *Unruly Practices: Power, Discourse and Gender in Contemporary Social Theory.* Minneapolis: University of Minnesota Press.

———. 1990. "Rethinking the Public Sphere: A Contribution to the Critique of Actually Existing Democracy." *Social Text* 8, no. 3; 9, no. 1: 56–80.

Freire, Paulo. 1989. *Pedagogy of the Oppressed,* trans. Myra Bergman Ramos. New York: Continuum Press.

Freud, Sigmund. 1955. "The Uncanny." In *The Standard Edition of the Complete Psychological Works of Sigmund Freud,* trans. James Strachey with Anna Freud, Alix Strachey, and Alan Tyson. Vol. 17, 217–256. London: Hogarth Press and the Institute of Psychoanalysis.

Fundación San Gabriel. 1991a. *Demanda de participación en la constitución del concejo municipal distrital este.* La Paz: Fundación San Gabriel; Asociación de Centros de Madres Distrito Este; Fejuve Este; and Asociación de Padres.

———. 1991b. *Taller de participación en el distrito municipal este de la ciudad de La Paz*. La Paz: Fundación San Gabriel.

———. 1992. *Partidos políticos: ¿Espacios de participación democrática para la mujer?* La Paz: Fundación San Gabriel.

———. 1993. *Elecciones generales 1993: La Paz–Bolivia*. La Paz: Fundación San Gabriel.

Fuss, Diana. 1989. *Essentially Speaking: Feminism, Nature and Difference*. New York and London: Routledge.

———. 1991. "Inside/Out." In *Inside/Out: Lesbian Theories, Gay Theories*, ed. Diana Fuss, 1–10. New York and London: Routledge.

———. 1995. *Identification Papers*. New York and London: Routledge.

Garber, Marjorie. 1993. *Vested Interests: Cross-Dressing and Cultural Anxiety*. Reprinted by arrangement with Routledge, Chapman and Hall. New York: Harper Collins.

Gill, Lesley. 1990. "Painted Faces: Conflict and Ambiguity in Domestic Servant–Employer Relations in La Paz, 1930–1988." *Latin American Research Review* 25, no. 1: 119–136.

———. 1994. *Precarious Dependencies: Gender, Class, and Domestic Service in Bolivia*. New York: Columbia University Press.

Gisbert, Teresa. 1988. *Historia de la vivienda y los asentamientos humanos en Bolivia*. No. 431. México: Instituto Panamericano de Geografía e Historia; Academia Nacional de Ciencias de Bolivia.

———. 1991. *Historia de la vivienda y los conjuntos urbanos en Bolivia*. No. 454. México: Instituto Panamericano de Geografía e Historia; Academia Nacional de Ciencias de Bolivia.

Grewal, Inderpal, and Caren Kaplan. 1994. Introduction. In *Scattered Hegemonies: Postmodernity and Transnational Feminist Practices*, ed. Inderpal Grewal and Caren Kaplan, 1–33. Minneapolis: University of Minnesota Press.

Grosz, Elizabeth. 1995. "Animal Sex: Libido as Desire and Death." In *Sexy Bodies: The Strange Carnalities of Feminism*, ed. Elizabeth Grosz and Elspeth Probyn, 278–299. London and New York: Routledge.

Guía didáctica de educación rural. 1963. No. 2. Preparada por la Dirección General de Educación Rural en cooperación con el SCIDE. La Paz: Ministerio de Asuntos Campesinos.

Guillén Pinto, Alfredo. 1919. *La educación del indio: (Contribución a la pedagogía nacional)*. La Paz: González y Medina.

Gumucio Dagrón, Alfonso. 1983. *Bolivia, radios mineros; Nicaragua, cine obrero sandinista: Aporte de la experiencia a la teoría de la comunicación alternativa*. La Paz: CIMCA.

Gumucio Dagrón, Alfonso, and Lupe Cajías. 1989. *Las radios mineras de Bolivia*. La Paz: CIMCA, UNESCO.

Guzmán, Augusto. 1982. *Biografías de la literatura boliviana, 1520–1925*. Cochabamba and La Paz: Los Amigos del Libro.

Hall, Lana L. 1985. "United States Food Aid and the Agricultural Development of Brazil and Colombia, 1954–73." In *Food, Politics, and Society in Latin*

America, ed. John C. Super and Thomas C. Wright, 133–149. Lincoln: University of Nebraska Press.

Hardt, Michael. 1995. "The Withering of Civil Society." *Social Text* 14, no.4: 27–44.

Harlow, Barbara. 1992. *Barred: Women, Writing, and Political Detention.* Hanover and London: Wesleyan University Press/University Press of New England.

Harris, Olivia. 1995. "Ethnic Identity and Market Relations: Indians and Mestizos in the Andes." In *Ethnicity, Markets, and Migration in the Andes: At the Crossroads of History and Anthropology,* ed. Brooke Larson and Olivia Harris, with Enrique Tandeter, 351–390. Durham: Duke University Press.

Harris, Olivia, and Javier Albó. 1976. *Monteras y guardatojos: Campesinos y mineros en el norte de Potosí.* La Paz: CIPCA.

Heng, Geraldine, and Janadas Devan. 1992. "State Fatherhood: The Politics of Nationalism, Sexuality, and Race in Singapore." In *Nationalisms and Sexualities,* ed. Andrew Parker, Mary Russo, Doris Sommer, and Patricia Yaeger, 343–364. New York and London: Routledge.

Hill Collins, Patricia. 1990. *Black Feminist Thought: Knowledge, Consciousness, and the Politics of Empowerment.* Boston: Unwin Hyman.

hooks, bell. 1989. *Talking Back: Thinking Feminist, Thinking Black.* Boston: South End Press.

———. 1990. *Yearning: Race, Gender, and Cultural Politics.* Boston: South End Press.

Hurtado, Javier. 1986. *El katarismo.* La Paz: HISBOL.

Ichaso Vásquez, Raquel. 1927. *La enseñanza nacional femenina.* La Paz: Imp. Intendencia de Guerra.

ILDIS (Instituto Latinoamericano de Investigaciones Sociales). 1992. *Diversidad étnica y cultural,* ed. Carlos F. Toranzo Roca. La Paz: ILDIS.

Ingraham, Catherine. 1988. "The Faults of Architecture: Troping the Proper." *Assemblage* 7: 7–13.

Instituto Nacional de Estadística. 1980. *La situación de la vivienda según el censo nacional de población y vivienda de 1976.* Departamento de Estadísticas Sociales. La Paz: Instituto Nacional de Estadística.

Irigaray, Luce. 1985. *This Sex Which Is Not One,* trans. Catherine Porter. Ithaca: Cornell University Press.

Jiménez, Maritza, Griselda Sillerico, and Jimena Freitas. 1989. *Sobrevivencia y conciencia política: Sistematización de una experiencia de educación popular en la zona este de la ciudad de La Paz.* La Paz: Fundación San Gabriel.

Keith, Michael, and Steve Pile. 1993. "Introduction Part One: The Politics of Place," and "Introduction Part Two: The Place of Politics." In *Place and the Politics of Identity,* ed. Michael Keith and Steve Pile, 1–40. London and New York: Routledge.

Kolbowski, Silvia, Laurie Hawkinson, and Henry Smith-Miller. 1994. "Homelette: An (in)Habitable Proposal." *Assemblage* 24: 60–67.

Larson, Brooke. 1995. "Andean Communities, Political Cultures, and Markets: The Changing Contours of a Field." In *Ethnicity, Markets, and Migration in* the Andes: At the Crossroads of History and Anthropology, ed. Brooke Larson and Olivia Harris, with Enrique Tandeter, 5–53. Durham: Duke University Press.

Larson, Brooke, and Olivia Harris, with Enrique Tandeter, eds. 1995. *Ethnicity, Markets, and Migration in the Andes: At the Crossroads of History and Anthropology.* Durham and London: Duke University Press.

Lazarte Rojas, Jorge. 1988. "Movimiento sindical y transformaciones del sistema político boliviano." Paper presented at the International Seminar on "Movimientos Sociales y Estructuras Políticas: la Participación Popular." Documento de Trabajo, no. 28. La Paz: FLACSO Programa Bolivia.

Lehm A., Zulema, and Silvia Rivera Cusicanqui. 1988. *Los artesanos libertarios y la ética del trabajo.* La Paz: "Gramma."

León, Rosario. 1990. "Bartolina Sisa: The Peasant Women's Organization in Bolivia." In *Women and Social Change in Latin America,* ed. Elizabeth Jelin, 135–150. London and Atlantic Highlands, N.J.: Zed Books Ltd.

Levy, Anita. 1991. *Other Women: The Writing of Class, Race, and Gender, 1832–1898.* Princeton, N.J.: Princeton University Press.

Libermann, Kitula, and Armando Godínez. 1992. *Territorio y dignidad: Pueblos indígenas y medio ambiente en Bolivia.* Caracas: ILDIS; Editorial Nueva Sociedad.

Lind, Amy Conger. 1992. "Power, Gender, and Development: Popular Women's Organizations and the Politics of Needs in Ecuador." In *The Making of Social Movements in Latin America: Identity, Strategy, and Democracy,* ed. Arturo Escobar and Sonia E. Alvarez, 134–149. Boulder: Westview Press.

MacSween, Morag. 1993. *Anorexic Bodies: A Feminist and Sociological Perspective on Anorexia Nervosa.* London: Routledge.

Mamani Capchiri, Humberto. 1992. "La educación india en la visión de la sociedad criolla: 1920–1943." In *Educación indígena: ¿ciudadanía o colonización?,* ed. Roberto Choque, Vitaliano Soria, et al., 79–98. La Paz: Aruwiyiri.

Mamani Condori, Carlos. 1991. *Taraqu, 1866–1935: Masacre, guerra, y "renovación" en la biografía de Eduardo L. Nina Qhispi.* La Paz: Aruwiyiri.

———. 1992. *Los aymaras frente a la historia: Dos ensayos metodológicos.* Serie: Cuadernos de debate, no. 2. Chukiyawu-La Paz: Aruwiyiri.

Mansilla T., Jorge. 1978. *Huelga de hambre: Bolivia, mujeres mineras, victoria popular.* Lima: n.p.

Martin, Biddy, and Chandra Talpade Mohanty. 1986. "Feminist Politics: What's Home Got to Do with It?" In *Feminist Studies/Critical Studies,* ed. Teresa de Lauretis, 191–212. Bloomington: Indiana University Press.

Martínez P., Juan Luis. 1991. *Algunas experiencias de educación popular en Bolivia: (Estado de arte).* La Paz: CEBIAE.

Massey, Doreen. 1994. *Space, Place, and Gender.* Minneapolis: University of Minnesota Press.

Masiello, Francine. 1990. "Women, State, and Family in Latin American Literature of the 1920s." In *Women, Culture, and Politics in Latin America: Seminar on Feminism and Culture in Latin America,* 27–47. Berkeley: University of California Press.

Mayorga, Fernando. 1993. *Discurso y política en Bolivia*. La Paz: CERES; ILDIS.

McClintock, Anne. 1995. *Imperial Leather: Race, Gender, and Sexuality in the Colonial Contest*. New York and London: Routledge.

McIntosh, Jane. 1981. "Bolivia—the Struggle Continues: An Interview with Domitila Barrios de Chungara." *Race and Class* 22: 301–310.

McLaren, Peter. 1995. *Critical Pedagogy and Predatory Culture: Oppositional Politics in a Postmodern Era*. London and New York: Routledge.

Medina, Javier, ed. 1991. *El testamento político-espiritual de Luis Espinal*. Serie: Religión y sociedad. La Paz: HISBOL.

Medinaceli, Carlos. 1955. *La Chaskañawi*. 2d ed. La Paz: "Juventud."

Medinaceli, Ximena. 1989. *Alterando la rutina: Mujeres en las ciudades de Bolivia, 1920–1930*. La Paz: CIDEM.

Meléndez, Mariselle. 1995. "La vestimenta como retórica del poder y símbolo de producción cultural en la América colonial: De Colón a *El lazarillo de ciegos caminantes*." *Revista de Estudios Hispánicos* 29: 411–439.

Memoria: III encuentro de mujeres receptoras de alimentos donados. 1990. La Paz: UNICEF; Fundación San Gabriel; CIDEM.

Mercer, Kobena. 1994. *Welcome to the Jungle: New Positions in Black Cultural Studies*. Routledge: New York and London.

Ministerio de Instrucción Pública y Agricultura. 1928. *La reforma de nuestras escuelas rurales*. Dirección General de Instrucción. Folleto núm. 30. La Paz: Ministerio de Instrucción Pública y Agricultura.

Mitchell, Don. 1993. "Public Housing in Single-Industry Towns: Changing Landscapes of Paternalism." In *Place/Culture/Representation*, ed. James Duncan and David Ley, 110–127. London and New York: Routledge.

Montes, María Rosa. 1987. "Catholic Radios under Attack." *Index on Censorship* 16, no. 2: 16–17.

Mujer/Fempress. 1990. Special issue "La mujer y el humor," no. 2.

Mujer, participación y donación de alimentos. 1990. Cuaderno de Capacitación Popular no. 7. Serie: Instrumental. La Paz: Instituto Nacional de Estudios Sociales y Capacitación.

North American Congress on Latin America (NACLA). 1991. "The NACLA Report. Bolivia: The Poverty of Progress." *Report on the Americas* 25, no. 1: 9.

Nash, June. 1979. *We Eat the Mines and the Mines Eat Us: Dependency and Exploitation in Bolivian Tin Mines*. New York: Columbia University Press.

Nast, Heidi J., and Mabel O. Wilson. 1994. "Lawful Transgressions: This Is the House That Jackie Built . . ." *Assemblage* 24: 48–55.

Ng, Roxana. 1993. "Racism, Sexism, and Nation Building in Canada." In *Race, Identity and Representation in Education*, ed. Cameron McCarthy and Warren Crichlow, 50–59. New York: Routledge.

Oliver, Kelly. 1992. "Nourishing the Speaking Subject: A Psychoanalytic Approach to Abominable Food and Women." In *Cooking, Eating, Thinking: Transformative Philosophies of Food*, ed. Deane W. Curtin and Lisa M. Heldke, 68–84. Bloomington: Indiana University Press.

Pacheco, Diego. 1992. *El indianismo y los indios contemporáneos en Bolivia*. La Paz: HISBOL; MUSEF.

Paredes, Julieta, and María Galindo. 1992. *¿Y si fuésemos una, espejo de la otra?: Por un feminismo no racista.* La Paz: Ediciones Gráficas.

Paredes Candia, Antonio. 1992. *La chola boliviana.* La Paz: Ediciones ISLA.

Paredes de Salazar, Elssa. 1976. *Presencia de nuestro pueblo.* La Paz: "Universo."

Payne, Johnny. 1995. "Migrant Flesh: Head-Choppers, Eye Pluckers and Foreigners." *Chasqui* 24, no. 2: 64–81.

Peloso, Vincent C. 1985. "Succulence and Sustenance: Region, Class, and Diet in Nineteenth-Century Peru." In *Food, Politics, and Society in Latin America,* ed. John C. Super and Thomas C. Wright, 46–64. Lincoln and London: University of Nebraska Press, 1985.

Pérez, Elizardo. 1962. *Warisata: La escuela-ayllu.* La Paz: Burillo.

Platt, Tristan. 1982. *Estado boliviano y ayllu andino: Tierra y tributo en el norte de Potosí.* Lima: Instituto de Estudios Peruanos.

———. 1984. "Liberalism and Ethnocide in the Southern Andes." *History Workshop* no. 17: 3–18.

———. 1987. "The Andean Experience of Bolivian Liberalism, 1825–1900: Roots of Rebellion in 19th-Century Chayanta (Potosí)." In *Resistance, Rebellion, and Consciousness in the Andean Peasant World: 18th to 20th Centuries,* ed. Steve J. Stern, 280–323. Madison: University of Wisconsin Press.

Polleras libertarias: Federación obrera femenina, 1927–1964. 1986. La Paz: TAHIPAMU.

Por la vida y por la paz: Testimonio de la marcha minera. 1986. La Paz: CEBIAE; CEDLA.

Portocarrero Maisch, Gonzalo, Isidro Valentín, and Soraya Irigoyen. 1991. *Sacaojos: Crisis social y fantasmas coloniales.* Lima: Tarea.

Preiswerk, Matías. 1988. *La radio Pío XII.* La Paz: CEBIAE; CTP.

Programa Oqharikuna. 1994. *Niñas y adolescentes en la calle.* n.p.

Prudencio B., Julio, and André Franqueville. 1995. *La incidencia de la ayuda alimentaria en Bolivia.* La Paz: UNITAS.

Prudencio B., Julio, and Mónica Velasco, with the collaboration of Alberto Rivera and Gonzalo Flores. 1987. *Mujeres y alimentos donados.* La Paz: CERES; Programa Mundial de Alimentos.

Reyeros, Rafael. 1949. *El pongueaje: La servidumbre personal de los indios bolivianos.* La Paz: "Universo."

Rivera Cusicanqui, Silvia. 1984. *"Oprimidos pero no vencidos": Luchas del campesinado aymara y qhechwa de Bolivia, 1900–1980.* La Paz: HISBOL; CSUTCB.

———. 1987. "Luchas campesinas contemporáneas en Bolivia: El movimiento 'katarista,' 1970–1980." In *Bolivia, hoy,* ed. René Zavaleta Mercado, 129–168. 2d ed. México: Siglo Veintiuno Editores.

———. 1990. "Liberal Democracy and Ayllu Democracy in Bolivia: The Case of Northern Potosí." *The Journal of Development Studies* 26, no. 4: 97–121.

———. 1993. "La raíz: colonizadores y colonizados." In *Violencias encubiertas en Bolivia,* ed. Silvia Rivera C. y Raúl Barrios. Vol. 1: Cultura y política, 25–139. Coordinación general Xavier Albó y Raúl Barrios. La Paz: CIPCA; Aruwiyiri.

Rivera Cusicanqui, Silvia, compiler, with the Andean Oral History Workshop (THOA). 1990. "Indigenous Women and Community Resistance: History and Memory." In *Women and Social Change in Latin America*, ed. Elizabeth Jelin; trans. J. Ann Zammit and Marilyn Thomson, 151–183. London and Atlantic Highlands, N.J.: UNRISD; Zed Books.

Rivero Pinto, Wigberto, and Ives Encinas Cueto. 1991. "La presencia aimara en la ciudad de La Paz, *Chuquiyawu Marka*: Entre la participación y la sobrevivencia." *América Indígena* 51, no. 2–3: 273–292.

Rodríguez, Ileana. 1994. *House/Garden/Nation: Space, Gender, and Ethnicity in Post-Colonial Latin American Literatures by Women*, trans. Robert Carr and Ileana Rodríguez. Durham and London: Duke University Press.

Rollins, Judith. 1985. *Between Women: Domestics and Their Employers*. Philadelphia: Temple University Press.

Rosaldo, Renato. 1989. *Culture and Truth: The Remaking of Social Analysis*. Boston: Beacon Press.

Rose, Gillian. 1993. *Feminism and Geography: The Limits of Geographical Knowledge*. Minneapolis: University of Minnesota Press.

Ross, Kristin. 1994. "Starting Afresh: Hygiene and Modernization in Postwar France." *October* 67: 23–57.

Rossells, Beatriz. 1988. *La mujer: Una ilusión. Ideologías e imágenes de la mujer en Bolivia en el siglo XIX*. La Paz: CIDEM.

Rowe, William, and Vivian Schelling. 1991. *Memory and Modernity: Popular Culture in Latin America*. London: Verso.

Sagar, Aparajita. n.d. "Indian Modernity and Early Muslim Writing in English: 1913–1953." Unpublished manuscript.

Saignes, Thierry, ed. 1993. *Borrachera y memoria: La experiencia de lo sagrado en los Andes*. La Paz: HISBOL/IFEA.

Salazar Mostajo, Carlos. 1986. *La Taika: Teoría y práctica de la escuela-ayllu*. La Paz: Universidad Mayor de San Andrés.

Salmón, Josefa. 1986. El discurso indigenista en Bolivia, 1900–1956. Ph.D. diss., University of Maryland.

Sandoval, Chela. 1991. "U.S. Third World Feminism: The Theory and Method of Oppositional Consciousness in the Postmodern World." *Genders* 10: 1–24.

Sandoval Z., Godofredo. 1993. *Las ong's y los caminos del desarrollo. (Aproximación a su estudio)*. La Paz: CEP.

Sanjinés C., Javier. 1991. "From Domitila to 'los relocalizados': An Essay on Marginality in Bolivia." In *Translating Latin America: Culture as Text*. Translation Perspectives VI, ed. William Luis and Julio Rodríguez-Luis, 185–196. Binghamton: Center for Research in Translation, State University of New York.

———. 1992a. *Literatura contemporánea y grotesco social en Bolivia*. La Paz: Fundación BHN; ILDIS.

———. 1992b. "Testimonial Discourse and New Popular Trends in Bolivia." *Mediations* 17, no. 1: 50–59.

———. 1992c. "Entre la cruz y la tribuna del pueblo: 'Relocalización' y nuevos movimientos populares en Bolivia." In *Hermeneuticas de lo popular*, ed.

Hernán Vidal, 341–377. Series: Literature and Human Rights, no. 9. Minneapolis: Institute for the Study of Ideologies and Literature.

Sanjinés, Jorge. 1971. *El coraje del pueblo*. Bolivia: Grupo Ukamau. Film.

Santos Escóbar, Roberto. 1992. *Fechas históricas indígenas: Luchas anticoloniales de aymaras, qhischwas y tupiguaranís en Bolivia*. Serie: Cuadernos de Formación, núm. 4. La Paz: Aruwiyiri.

Saravia Valle, Jorge. 1986. *Planificación de aldeas rurales*. La Paz: "Juventud."

Sawchuk, Kim. 1987. "A Tale of Inscription: Fashion Statements." In *Body Invaders: Panic Sex in America*, ed. Arthur and Marilouise Kroker, 61–77. New York: St. Martin's Press.

Shiva, Vandana. 1992. "Development, Ecology and Women." In *Cooking, Eating, Thinking: Transformative Philosophies of Food*, ed. Deane W. Curtin and Lisa M. Heldke, 336–346. Bloomington and Indianapolis: Indiana University Press.

Shuttleworth, Sally. 1990. "Female Circulation: Medical Discourse and Popular Advertising in the Mid-Victorian Era." In *Body/Politics: Women and The Discourses of Science*, ed. Mary Jacobus, Evelyn Fox Keller, and Sally Shuttleworth, 47–68. New York: Routledge.

Silverman, Kaja. 1983. *The Subject of Semiotics*. Oxford: Oxford University Press.

———. 1988. *The Acoustic Mirror: The Female Voice in Psychoanalysis and Cinema*. Bloomington: Indiana University Press.

———. 1994. "Fragments of a Fashionable Discourse." In *On Fashion*, ed. Shari Benstock and Suzanne Ferriss, 183–196. New Brunswick, N.J.: Rutgers University Press. Originally published in 1986 in *Studies in Entertainment*, ed. Tania Modleski. Bloomington: Indiana University Press.

———. 1996. *The Threshold of the Visible World*. New York and London: Routledge.

Singley, Paulette, and Deborah Fausch. 1994. Introduction. In *Architecture: In Fashion*, ed. Deborah Fausch, Paulette Singley, Rodolphe El Khoury, and Zvi Efrat, 6–36. Princeton, N.J.: Princeton Architectural Press.

Slaughter, Jane. 1989. "Tin Miner's Radio on the Ropes." *Progressive* 53, no. 2: 11.

Sommer, Doris. 1990. "Irresistible Romance: The Foundational Fictions of Latin America." In *Nation and Narration*, ed. Homi K. Bhabha, 71–98. London and New York: Routledge.

———. 1991. *Foundational Fictions: The National Romances of Latin America*. Berkeley: University of California Press.

Soria Choque, Vitaliano. 1992. "Los caciques-apoderados y la lucha por la escuela, 1900–1952." In *Educación indígena: ¿ciudadanía o colonización?*, ed. Roberto Choque, Vitaliano Soria, et al., 41–78. La Paz: Aruwiyiri.

Stallybrass, Peter. 1986. "Patriarchal Territories: The Body Enclosed." In *Rewriting the Renaissance: The Discourses of Sexual Difference in Early Modern Europe*, ed. Margaret W. Ferguson, Maureen Quilligan, and Nancy J. Vickers, 123–142. Chicago and London: University of Chicago Press.

Stern, Steve J. 1987. "The Age of Andean Insurrection, 1742–1782: A Reappraisal." In *Resistance, Rebellion, and Consciousness in the Andean Peasant*

World: 18th to 20th Centuries, ed. Steve J. Stern, 34–93. Madison: University of Wisconsin Press.

———. 1995. "The Variety and Ambiguity of Native Andean Intervention in European Colonial Markets." In *Ethnicity, Markets, and Migration in the Andes: At the Crossroads of History and Anthropology,* ed. Brooke Larson and Olivia Harris with Enrique Tandeter, 73–100. Durham and London: Duke University Press.

Ströbele-Gregor, Juliana. 1996. "Culture and Political Practice of the Aymara and Quechua in Bolivia: Autonomous Forms of Modernity in the Andes." *Latin American Perspectives* 23, no. 2 (Issue 89): 72–90.

Super, John C. 1985. "The Formation of Nutritional Regimes in Colonial Latin America." In *Food, Politics, and Society in Latin America,* ed. John C. Super and Thomas C. Wright, 1–23. Lincoln and London: University of Nebraska Press.

Swanson, Gillian. 1995. "'Drunk with the Glitter': Consuming Spaces and Sexual Geographies." In *Postmodern Cities and Spaces,* ed. Sophie Watson and Katherine Gibson, 80–98. Oxford, Eng,. and Cambridge, Mass.: Blackwell.

Szeminski, Jan. 1987. "Why Kill the Spaniard? New Perspectives on Andean Insurrectionary Ideology in the 18th Century." In *Resistance, Rebellion, and Consciousness in the Andean Peasant World: 18th to 20th Centuries,* ed. Steve J. Stern, 166–192. Madison: University of Wisconsin Press.

Taller de Historia Oral Andina (THOA). 1986. *Mujer y resistencia comunaria: Historia y memoria.* La Paz: HISBOL.

———. 1988. *El indio Santos Marka T'ula: Cacique principal de los ayllus de Qallapa y apoderado general de las comunidades originarias de la república* (3rd ed.). La Paz: Ediciones del THOA.

———. 1990. *La mujer andina en la historia.* Series: Cuadernos de Formación, no. 2. La Paz-Chukiyawu: Ediciones del THOA.

Tamayo, Franz. 1944. *Creación de la pedagogía nacional* (2nd ed.). La Paz: Editoriales de "El Diario."

Taussig, Michael T. 1980. *The Devil and Commodity Fetishism in South America.* Chapel Hill: University of North Carolina Press.

Terán de Pohl, Lola Mercedes. 1950. *Anticomunismo.* La Paz: Don Bosco.

Terpstra, Tony. 1994. *Donaciones alimentarias y seguridad alimentaria: Memoria taller.* La Paz: CIDEM.

Tiendas de consumo. n.d. La Paz: Fundación San Gabriel.

Toranzo, Carlos F. 1989a. Introduction. In *Bolivia hacia el 2000: Desafíos y opciones,* ed. Carlos F. Toranzo et al., 9–19. Caracas: Nueva Sociedad.

———. 1989b. "Desproletarización e 'informalización' de la sociedad boliviana." In *Bolivia hacia el 2000: Desafíos y opciones,* ed. Carlos F. Toranzo et al., 219–247. Caracas: Nueva Sociedad.

Tritten, Susan. 1986. "Los cholos y la búsqueda de una nueva sociedad." *Revista Iberoamericana* 52, no. 134: 219–224.

Vega, Magalí C. de, and Teresa Flores Bedregal. 1987. "Con el periodismo en las venas: Testimonio de la jefe de Redacción Betshabé Salmon." In *"Feminiflor":*

Un hito en el periodismo femenino de Bolivia, ed. Luis Ramiro Beltrán, 83–100. La Paz: CIMCA; Círculo de Mujeres Periodistas; CIDEM.

Vidler, Anthony. 1992. *The Architectural Uncanny: Essays in the Modern Unhomely*. Cambridge, Mass.: MIT Press.

Viezzer, Moema. 1977. "El 'Comité de Amas de Casa del Siglo XX,' una experiencia política boliviana." *Nueva Antropología* (México) 2: 29–45.

———. 1980. *Un granito de arena más: Elementos teórico-metodológicos implícitos en* Si me permiten hablar. Panamá: Centro de Comunicación Popular.

Vigarello, Georges. 1988. *Concepts of Cleanliness: Changing Attitudes in France since the Middle Ages*, trans. Jean Birrell. Cambridge and Paris: Cambridge University Press; Editions de la Maison des Sciences de l'Homme.

Villanueva y Saavedra, Etelvina. 1970. *Acción socialista de la mujer en Bolivia*. La Paz: Burillo.

Voces de libertad. 1989. Video. Director, Raquel Romero. Executive Production: CIDEM; THOA.

Wachtel, Nathan. 1994. *Gods and Vampires: Return to Chipaya*, trans. Carol Volk. Chicago: University of Chicago Press.

Wadsworth, Ana Cecilia, and Ineke Dibbits. 1989. *Agitadoras de buen gusto: Historia del Sindicato de Culinarias, 1935–1958*. La Paz: TAHIPAMU; HISBOL.

Waldby, Catherine. 1995. "Destruction: Boundary Erotics and Refigurations of the Heterosexual Male Body." In *Sexy Bodies: The Strange Carnalities of Feminism*, ed. Elizabeth Grosz and Elspeth Probyn, 266–277. London and New York: Routledge.

Welter, Barbara. 1966. "The Cult of True Womanhood: 1820–1860." *American Quarterly* 18: 151–74.

Wigley, Mark. 1992. "Untitled: The Housing of Gender." In *Sexuality and Space*, ed. Beatriz Colomina, 327–389. Princeton Papers on Architecture. Princeton, N.J.: Princeton University School of Architecture.

———. 1993. *The Architecture of Deconstruction: Derrida's Haunt*. Cambridge, Mass., and London: MIT Press.

———. 1994a. "White Out: Fashioning the Modern." In *Architecture: In Fashion*, ed. Deborah Fausch, Paulette Singley, Rodolphe El Khoury, and Zvi Efrat, 148–268. Princeton, N.J.: Princeton Architectural Press.

———. 1994b. "White Out: Fashioning the Modern [Part 2]." *Assemblage* 22: 6–49.

Witt, Doris. 1994–95. "What (N)ever Happened to Aunt Jemima: Eating Disorders, Fetal Rights, and Black Female Appetite in Contemporary American Culture." *Discourse* 17, no. 2: 98–112.

Young, Grace Esther. 1987. "The Myth of Being 'Like a Daughter.'" *Latin American Perspectives*. Issue 54 14.3: 365–380.

Yúdice, George. 1988. "Marginality and the Ethics of Survival." In *Universal Abandon?: The Politics of Postmodernism*, ed. Andrew Ross, 214–236. Minneapolis: University of Minnesota Press.

Yúdice, George, Jean Franco, and Juan Flores, eds. 1992. *On Edge: The Crisis of Contemporary Latin American Culture*. Minneapolis: University of Minnesota Press.

Zamudio, Adela. 1913. *Intimas.* La Paz: Velarde.

Zavaleta Mercado, René. 1986. *Lo nacional-popular en Bolivia* (1st ed.). Mexico City: Siglo Veintiuno Editores.

———. 1987a. "Forma clase y forma multitud en el proletariado minero en Bolivia." In *Bolivia, hoy* (2nd ed.), ed. René Zavaleta Mercado, 219–240. Mexico City: Siglo Veintiuno Editores.

———. 1987b. *El poder dual.* Cochabamba: Los Amigos del Libro.

———. 1990. *La formación de la conciencia nacional.* Cochabamba: Los Amigos del Libro.

INDEX

abject, the: crucifixion of relocated miners as, 194; depicted by the *chola*, 175–176; and miners' housing, 91; and the siege of La Paz, 163

Alarcón, Norma, 109, 206, 207–208n.5

Albó, Xavier, 88, 171–172, 226n.16, 228n.29; and Kitula Libermann, Armando Godínez, and Francisco Pifarré, 214n.13

El Alto: as evocation of colonial relations, 228n.32; migration to, 189

Alvarez, Sonia, 12

Antezana, Luis H., 36, 211–212n.16

anxiety, upper-class: and the *chola's* dietary practices, 175; toward the indigenous Other, 7, 113, 129, 172

Apasa, Julián. *See* Tupak Katari

appetite: creation of, 196; female, as threat, 175; insatiability of, 201; and racial homogenization, 158; regulation of, 172–181

appetitive relations: between North and South, 201–202

Aranzaes v. de Butrón, Emma, 186

architecture: associated with hygiene, 129–134; as expression of the proper, 63–65, 86, 231n.8; gen-

der construction and, 64, 130–134; and modernity, 63–76; as textile/text, 76–77, 79–81

Ardaya, Gloria, 28, 96, 100–101, 108–109

Arguedas, Alcides, *Pueblo enfermo* (1909): 19–20, 211n.13

Arnold, David, 218n.1

Arnold, Denise Y., 77–82, 215n.26

Arze O., Silvia, 77

authority, criollo: and the criolla, 149–150; the *pollera* as target of, 154–156

authority, maternal: over indigenous peoples, 50–53

ayllu, the: abrogation of, 74; defined, 208n.9; and indigenous history, 73–74; loss of ties with, 8; and NGOs, 199–200; and the state, 205–206

ayllu-schools: and hygiene, 120–128; as instrument of indigenous resistance, 117–118, 128

Aymaras, the: compared to Caribs, 165–166; and the siege of La Paz, 159–172. *See also* resistance, indigenous

Balibar, Etienne, 29, 136, 219–220n.8

Housewives Committees, miners':
and the mobilization of women,
96, 182–183; national meeting
of (1986), 191; organization of,
102–103; transforming gender
and political roles, 92, 105–110
housing: in mining centers, 87–92; as
social control, 60, 67, 89
hunger: and cannibalism, 160, 166;
collective experience of, 178–181;
dialectic of, 188, 200–202; effect
of neoliberal reform, 229n.34;
memory of, 172, 179; politics of,
158–172, 182, 186, 191; regulation of, 172–181; as resistance,
180–181, 183. See also appetite;
desire
hunger strike: and the miners' housewives, 6–7, 96–97, 183–187, 201
hygiene: as body management, 6,
136; and class struggle, 127–128;
and housing, 129–134; identificatory processes of, 122–126,
128; impact on racial acculturation,
111–114, 120–134; introduction
of, into curriculum, 120–121; link
with modernization, 125–126;
and modernity, 5–6; opposed to
fashion, 136–137, 139–140; as
paradox, 7; racial politics of, 141–
146; as science, 220n.15; and skirt
lengths, 138
Hygiene Police: and cholas, 142–146

Ichaso Vásquez, Raquel, 18, 21, 41,
135, 222n.22, 224n.36
identification: hygienic practices as
strategic to, 122–126, 128; and
racial difference, 52–53
identity: consolidation of, 225nn.6,8;
pollera as symbol of, 32–33; race-
based organization of, 129–134,
163, 219n.4; relationship between
modernity and, 2–3, 156–157,
219n.4; slippage of, 151; and space,
212n.2; as structured through the

home, 59–110; transformation
of, 92
identity, chola: association of, with
clothing, 143, 147–148; formation of, 33–34
identity, criollo: disintegration of,
161, 165–166; disrupted by the
chola, 71–72
identity, indigenous: affected by
colonialism, 73–74; as depicted
through textiles, 76–77; and
memory, 78; transformation of,
135
identity politics: male-female, 9
ILDIS (Instituto Latinoamericano
de Investigaciones Sociales), 204
imitation: and hygienic practices,
121–122; as resistance, 128; as
strategy of power and knowledge,
122
Indian: abuse of, under pongueaje,
15–17; and acculturation, 113;
characterized as child, 50, 51;
defined, 2–3; education of, 114–
134, 229–230n.36; elimination of
term, 54; as gendered and racialized category, 13; spatial representation of, 116
Ingraham, Catherine, 83, 213n.8
Irigaray, Luce, 102

Jaimes Freyre, Ricardo, 137
Jesús de Machaca: 1921 massacre,
116
Jiménez, Maritza, Griselda Sillerico,
and Jimena Freitas, 196

Katari, 168–170, 226n.12. See also
Tupak Katari
katarismo, 204, 226n.16
kataristas, 171
khoyas locas, 217n.35
Kolbowski, Silvia, Laurie Hawkinson,
and Henry Smith-Miller, 90
Kristeva, Julia, 175